leabarlanna puiblíóe áċa cliaċ.

## Dublin Public Libraries

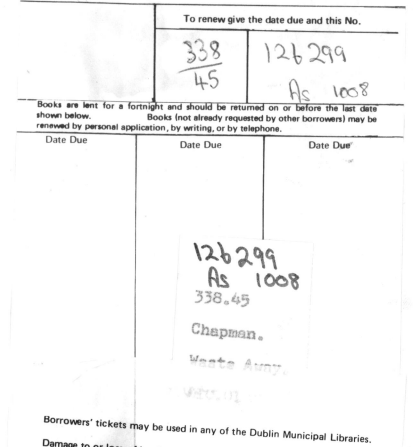

| To renew give the date due and this No. | |
|---|---|
| $\frac{338}{45}$ | 126299 As 1008 |

Books are lent for a fortnight and should be returned on or before the last date shown below.         Books (not already requested by other borrowers) may be renewed by personal application, by writing, or by telephone.

| Date Due | Date Due | Date Due |
|---|---|---|
| | | |

126299
As 1008
338.45

Chapman.

Waste Away.

# WASTE AWAY

By the same author

YOUR DISOBEDIENT SERVANT

# WASTE AWAY

## Leslie Chapman

1982

CHATTO & WINDUS

LONDON

Published by
Chatto & Windus Ltd
40 William IV Street
London WC2N 4DF

Clarke, Irwin & Co. Ltd
Toronto

BRITISH LIBRARY CATALOGUING IN
PUBLICATION DATA
Chapman, Leslie
Waste away.
1. Civil service – Great Britain
I. Title
354.41'001    JN425

ISBN 0 7011 2629 9

Phototypeset by
Western Printing Services Ltd
Bristol
Printed in Great Britain by
Redwood Burn Ltd
Trowbridge, Wiltshire

# Contents

# Acknowledgements

In addition to acknowledgements made where appropriate in the text, I have to thank the following:

For extracts quoted in Chapter 1 and elsewhere: *Daily Mail*; *Daily Telegraph*; *Financial Times*; *Guardian*; Manpower; *The Observer*; Reader's Digest Association; *Sunday Telegraph*; *The Sunday Times*; *The Times*.

For data used in Chapter 2 and elsewhere, and for help of other kinds: Central Statistical Office; the Department of the Environment; the Board of Inland Revenue; the Chartered Institute of Public Finance and Accounts; the National Association of Chambers of Commerce; the National Federation of Building Trades Employers; the National Federation of Self-Employed and Small Businesses; the Guildhall Library, London; the London Business Library; the London School of Economics Library; the Institute of Economic Affairs; Aims of Industry; Berkshire County Council (especially the Chairman, Mr Lewis Moss, and the Chief Executive, Mr R. Gash); Ivor Duxbury (late of the Transport & General Workers' Union); Mr Cecil Margolis of Harrogate (believed to be the last elected representative of the Whig Party in the UK); the Freedom of Information Campaign; the London *Evening Standard*; the Information Services of the *Daily Telegraph* and the *Financial Times*; *Construction News* (and especially the Editor-in-Chief, John Allen); Her Majesty's Stationery Office; Penguin Books; the BBC; Granada Television; and a host of groups and individuals from the public services who prefer, very wisely in some cases, to remain anonymous, including 328 past and present employees of London Transport.

Finally, I am grateful to those who gave permission, where this was needed, to quote their letters.

# Introduction

When I wrote *Your Disobedient Servant* (1978) my purpose was
threefold: first, to draw attention to the waste of scarce resources
which was found in a typical group of public sector activities, the
main focus of my study being the Civil Service; second, to identify the
weaknesses of the system which allowed this waste to occur and,
usually, to go unnoticed; and, third, to suggest a range of remedies
which, between them, would have a reasonable chance of helping to
reduce the frightening proportions of waste, overmanning, inefficiency and mismanagement.

In a limited sense these purposes were achieved. The book received
a good deal of attention from politicians, press and public. Politicians
appeared to be convinced that the problems were real, that the
proposed solutions were practicable and that they should be incorpor-
ated into Government policy. Letters from readers of all kinds,
including Heads of Governments, came (and still come) from many
parts of the world. A number of public authorities asked for opportunities to discuss their problems, although to date only Berkshire
County Council (see Chapter 11) has felt sufficiently confident to
permit publication of the results.

Unfortunately, movement and talk cannot be equated with progress, and so far, as this book sadly chronicles, very little has been
achieved in terms of reducing wasteful spending. Whatever the
reasons may be, neither elected representatives nor officials seem for
the most part capable of effective action.

Nevertheless, there are welcome signs that taxpayers, ratepayers
and the captive consumers of the products of state industries are
becoming exasperated by this impotence. They are demonstrating
this, and their general disenchantment with the two main political
parties, in the only way that politicians understand – by voting them
out wherever polling provides an opportunity. Even groups hell-bent
on pushing public spending still higher are being forced to admit the
need to reconsider their policies.

I hope that *Waste Away* will help this process by providing further
hard evidence that the waste *is* there, *is* very large, and *is* curable by

quite modest contributions of common sense and determination from those who are already being well paid to provide both. Public exasperation with the lack of action is fully justified and, if expressed forcefully enough, will lead to improvements. The last chapter is intended to help convert exasperation into effective methods for making progress despite all the artificial obstacles placed in the way of would-be cost-cutters.

PUBLISHER'S NOTE

Readers of Mr Chapman's first book, *Your Disobedient Servant*, will know that he declined to accept payment of any kind for it. In the case of *Waste Away* he will again make no personal gain: royalties will be paid to a charitable organisation whose purpose is to help with the problem of waste in the public sector.

# I

# 'A Damned Scandal'

In 1978 a property dealer went bankrupt, with assets of about £10,000 and total liabilities of over £100,000,000. Despite the spectacular margin by which this bankruptcy beat previous records, it was kept firmly in perspective by the unshakeable aplomb of the British Civil Service. In the London Bankruptcy Court the Official Receiver said: 'This bankruptcy has been described as the world's biggest, but really it is a very ordinary bankruptcy with noughts at the end.'

Waste in public spending is rather like this: it is mostly very ordinary waste but with a lot of noughts at the end. Some of this waste hits the headlines, but most of it does not. Much the biggest part is made up of small things which go unnoticed day in, day out, often for years, sometimes for generations. The kinds of human failing which cause these things to happen and persist – laziness, greed, limited competence, a desire for a quiet life, a reluctance to see jobs and promotion prospects diminish – are weaknesses we all suffer from. The difference is that in public sector spending there are almost no natural safeguards, especially in the way of disagreeable consequences, to stop waste from happening.

Occasionally, despite all the obstacles, some examples of wasteful spending come to the surface. Even more occasionally they become public knowledge. In that sense most of the examples of waste which follow are not typical, because typically they would never have been heard of. In every other sense, however, they are typical, as are the examples of hardship caused by spending cuts which are interspersed with them, as well as some of the responses to both. Together they serve as indicators of the recurring patterns and characteristics of public sector spending with which this book is concerned.

In Islington a firm was paid £730 by the Council to weed two square metres of shrubbery. £63 was paid to another firm for five minutes grass cutting.

A cost investigator found that productivity was unusually low in a storage building attached to a site handling dangerous substances. It transpired that all staff were required, as a safety measure, to go to a special compound if they wished to smoke. The time involved in walking at approved intervals to the compound, smoking the permitted amount and walking back again, took nearly two-thirds of working-time. The investigator noted that the store was heated by coke-fired slow combustion stoves.

Three gas-lamp lighters and a mate are still (1981) employed by Liverpool Council although the last gas lamp was extinguished eight years ago. The cost to the ratepayers and taxpayers has so far been over £250,000. The matter attracted attention only because the union was demanding that a foreman be appointed to look after the four men.

Three hundred and sixty people attended a buffet party, paid for by the ratepayers and taxpayers, to celebrate the selection of a new Mayor of Slough. The cost of food was £4.50 per head. Drinks were supplied at public expense from a bar. Eight councillors from the three main political parties claimed and received a £7 allowance for attending the thirty-minute meeting before the reception.

The Equal Opportunities Commission spends nearly £3-million per annum on schemes which include printing and displaying posters encouraging girls to become truck drivers (although there are plenty of unemployed truck drivers already).

Dustmen at Harrow (London) were ordered to slow down because they were completing their work too quickly. A spokesman for NUPE said: 'Running is frowned upon although it is true that some of our men take longer strides at more frequent intervals than others. We discourage it.'

Twelve free places on a two-week educational sunshine cruise were allocated, not to deprived children but to senior county council members, officials and their wives. Working teachers paid £600 for their wives to attend. One of the authority's teachers said: 'There are two words to describe the way free places have been allocated on this trip: opportunism and greed.'

David Brodie was paid £250 plus £110 insurance to sculpt a dead elm tree, with a chain saw, by Lambeth Borough Council, with ratepayers' money.

Special treatment for privileged individuals in VIP lounges at British airports costs taxpayers and ratepayers £2,000 per day.

Barbara Castle, leader of the Labour Party group in the European Parliament, called for a boycott of a trip to West Africa unless expense allowances and staffs were reduced. Although everything was being paid for from public funds, except possibly one meal a day, £38-a-day expenses were being allowed. And although all the arrangements for the tour were completed in advance, the 61 Euro MPs were being accompanied by 74 staff. Mrs Castle said the arrangements and the cost were 'a damned scandal'.

These events are a regular feature of Euro-Parliamentary life. Two weeks before, 36 MPs accompanied by 67 EEC staff had spent £250,000 on a trip to Colombia.

In the same week that Mrs Castle pronounced on Euro-Parliamentary expenses, Mr Prentice, Minister for Social Security, said he could give no assurance about continued facilities for handicapped and disabled. 'None of us in the Government is hard-hearted,' he said, 'it all depends on the national economy.'

Four hundred children in the 3rd, 4th and 5th years at Newbold Grange school in Rugby use two standard biology textbooks. The school has (1981) 30 copies of each.

Daventry comprehensive school has no physics or chemistry textbooks at all for its 178 3rd-year pupils, and only 40 geography books.

Activities subsidised by councils using ratepayers' and taxpayers' money include judo, tennis, gymnastics, yoga, bridge, glass-engraving, wine-tasting, tap-dancing, science fiction, fire-eating, vegetarians-against-Nazism, athletes-for-Moscow and the Ad Hoc Committee against the police.

In Lewes, 17 old people were made very unhappy by the decision of the East Sussex County Council to close their home. Most were blind but, having spent years at the Mabel Lister Home, they were familiar with its layout, devoted to its matron and to each other. Last October (1980) they were dispersed to other homes so that the council could save an annual £53,000 – just £3,000 more than last year's cost of buying 17 new cars for its 125-vehicle pool.

A seven-storey office block owned by the Property Services Agency, worth £2,500,000, may be demolished because remedial work on faults costing over £1-million 'would not be economic'.

British Airways leads the field in at least one respect. Their losses for 1980 were the biggest of all the 110 members of the International Air

Transport Association. By the end of 1981/82 the position will be worse, with total losses for the two years estimated at £250 million, equal to £200 a minute.

Manchester has two mayoral Rolls-Royces. According to the writer of a letter to the *Daily Telegraph* (21 March 1981), the Chief Executive of the City Council does not know how many other vehicles are in use, 'but it is probably around 2,000'.

The council has a work force of 42,000 or 1 in 11 of the City's population.

The Civic Centre and Sports Centre in Bognor costs ratepayers of Arun District council approximately £300,000 per annum.

A new swimming-pool will cost £1,600,000 to build and £136,000 a year to run.

Large new hospitals are standing empty because of lack of money to run them, and shortages of trained staff. One example is the University Hospital, Nottingham (1,000 beds) which cost £83 million to build and is costing £250,000 per annum to heat and maintain in its empty state. At Plymouth, the new 1,700-bed Derriford Hospital (cost £20 million) will have in use, when it is opened, only five out of twelve wards and three out of seven operating theatres.

Local Authority officials from all over Britain, discussing government spending cuts, elected to hold their conference (paid for by ratepayers and taxpayers) in London – at the Café Royal, in the heart of London's expensive West End.

In Southampton, Hampshire County Council shut down a day nursery for 20 under-fives to save £20,000 a year – but is spending £33,000 on bone china, cut glass, antique furniture and improvements for a VIP dining-room at its Winchester headquarters.

In Leicestershire, 200 physically handicapped people lost their holidays because the council cut the subsidy by 65 per cent to save £4,700. The same council then approved increases in their own chairman's allowances and hospitality fund to a figure nearly four times greater than that saved by the cut for the disabled.

In Glasgow, Strathclyde Regional Council put up its charges to old age pensioners for meals on wheels and lunch clubs by 20 per cent to raise an extra annual £50,000. A month later it celebrated the completion of a new £1.8 million headquarters with a £3,000 banquet. Guests

were shown the office suites of its elected head and its chief executives
– shag-pile carpeted private office, bathroom, kitchen and dining-
room.

Brixton's sports centre, planned at a cost of £3.8 million, was by early
1979 estimated to be going to cost at least £9.5 million. Even unions
were shocked. Pickets (TGWU) carried banners complaining of bad
management and waste of ratepayers' money.

   Facilities being provided by ratepayers and taxpayers include two
swimming-pools, two sauna suites, a rifle range, a bowling-alley,
eight squash courts, a climbing-wall, gymnasium, a ski slope, a
restaurant, a bar, two cafés and a discothèque.

Executives of British Gas attended a conference in Canada and were
allowed to take their wives. The estimated cost to gas consumers was
£150,000 – estimated because British Gas refused to say exactly how
much public money had been spent.

Thames Water Board made losses of over £200,000 on farming in one
year. The same authority used five chauffeur-driven London-based
cars to pick up executives daily from Reading and take them back to
London to work.

Queen Elizabeth Comprehensive School at Crediton was found to
have a telephone in every classroom, leading to telephone bills of
£6,700 in a year.

A tax official was sent 12 miles by chauffeur-driven car to collect the
signature on a cheque for a small amount.

The cost of paying council workers could be reduced from £25 million
per annum to less than £3 million per anum if payment were made by
cheque or bank credit instead of in cash.

Three years ago, a team of management consultants who investigated
the bonus scheme operating in the London Borough of Hammer-
smith's building department concluded that it was costing ratepayers
an unnecessary £221,000 a year. Unless changed, the scheme this
year (1981) will waste a sum approaching the £270,000 which the
council wants to squeeze from its social services budget by closing a
children's home and raising charges for day centres and meals on
wheels. The same survey showed that output per man was about
two-thirds normal.

By the time a coachload of officials and councillors had twice visited a scenic spot in Maltby, South Yorkshire, to site a £30 park bench, the cost in travel, meals and other expenses was estimated at £700.

In a single month, Liverpool officials spent £4,000 on car-hire: in some cases cars were kept waiting for up to four hours.

In the London Borough of Lambeth, housing officers spent £1 million in a year on accommodating families in bed-and-breakfast hotels – while 4,000 of the council's 32,000 homes stood empty.

Dorset County Council Education Committee decided in July 1980 to end school meals for all pupils at primary schools.

In February 1981 Lincolnshire County Council decided to end school meals in primary schools for most children. The Education Committee Chairman blamed NUPE for the situation, on the grounds that the union was pricing its members out of jobs.

A financial crisis of 'near Domesday proportions' was forecast in June 1980 by the leader of Manchester's Labour-controlled city council. He foresaw the spectre of a rate of almost £2.50 in the £ 'just to maintain essential services'. At the same time it was announced that staff employed by the Council had increased by over 1,000, the biggest net increase for any local authority in the UK.

It was estimated in 1980 that more than £400 million was needed for urgent repairs to hospitals. The work involved included the removal of known health hazards, the replacement of completely unsatisfactory heating and other services, and alterations required to meet minimum statutory fire and safety regulations.

In 1981, it was estimated that 600,000 patients were on hospital waiting-lists. Some had waited eight years for an operation, according to the Department of Health and Social Security.

In 1981, several universities were facing bankruptcy, and 3,000 dons (one in every eight) were expected to be made redundant.

Thirty-nine members of the European Parliament planned to hold a private political group conference (a 'study meeting') at a luxury beach hotel in the Caribbean in 1981. A similar conference was to be held by the Progressive Democrats in nearby Guadeloupe. Because they are French overseas territories they are technically part of the EEC.

Harrogate District Council has 60 councillors. Their general services committee approved the purchase of 215 pocket diaries for them and some other unknown recipients at a cost of £990 to the ratepayers.

Lothian Council has increased its work-force by 14 per cent in the three years since Labour gained control.

Three-course meals for pensioners are served at 10p. The charge is the same for meals on wheels. Home help is charged out at 50p an hour.

The ratio of education department staff to pupils is one to five. Non-teaching staff outnumber teachers by 10,300 to 10,050.

The rates have rocketed upwards during the same period. One city centre store paid £200,000 in rates in 1978: for 1981 the rate demand was £500,000.

A Monopolies and Mergers Commission report on a Water Board urged reduction in the number of members, and reductions in over-generous car allowances to staff. The number of directors could be cut by 75 per cent. Car allowance rates varied from £1.64 to £2.59 per mile for low-mileage users, and 44p to 70p for higher mileage users.

Manual workers numbers had dropped by 3.3 per cent; non-manual staffs have gone up by 16.5 per cent. Bonus schemes payments had increased sharply, but productivity had not gone up.

Maldon District Council saved nearly one-third of its £200,000 p.a. refuse-collection budget by replacing direct-labour with private contractors. When nearby Rochford Council announced that it was considering making a similar switch, their dustmen immediately offered a new productivity deal which saved £100,000 p.a.

Conservative philosophy questions the need for a large Department of Industry, which it regards as interventiontist and useless. In the year 1980/81 the salary bill for the Department rose by 26 per cent over the preceding year.

A porter drunk on duty in a hospital was suspended, on full pay, pending an enquiry. The union immediately called out all ancillary staff in sympathy.

Lambeth Borough Council produces consumer comics for children, and distributed an annual 160,000 leaflets on such topics as caring for house plants and how to restore stripped pine furniture.

Humberside Council saved £50,000 by getting private contractors to clean school windows.

Subsidies to Harrogate theatre from rates and taxes are nearly £3,400 per week.

In Manchester, waste in the council's building department was costing at least £340,000 per annum and some estimates put the figure far higher.

In 1979, Scarborough cut concessionary fares for OAPs as part of an economy drive. In the same week, a new Daimler costing £17,000 was bought for the mayor out of taxpayers' and ratepayers' money.

Councils regularly approve capital projects on the basis of a total cost subsequently found to be far too low. Ratepayers have no choice but to go on paying up. A prime example is the conference centre that Harrogate District Council hopes to open at the end of 1981. Originally estimated at £6 million, costs have since risen to £15 million – say £46 million by the time interest charges have been paid off over 20 years.

The London Borough of Haringey set up 70 employees in a subsidised co-operative to carry out building work: should the men make a profit, 20 per cent would go to the council; should they make a loss, the council would foot the bill. In four years, this arrangement has swollen council spending by £100,000.

The same London borough decided that it should supervise the borough's youngsters in out-of-school-hours play. The council now has three 'play officers' and a fluctuating cast of assistant 'play leaders'. Their budget with transport costs and outings is £275,000 a year.

In the London Borough of Brent ratepayers recently refused to let the mayor keep his new Daimler. With air-conditioning, stereo, colour television and cocktail cabinet, this had cost £38,500. The vehicle was put up for sale.

Liverpool City Council proposed sending 30,000 employees to London to join a national demonstration against job cuts. On this occasion ratepayers rebelled and saved themselves at least £250,000.

Gordon Wilkinson is paid £3,250 of ratepayers' money a year to paint murals for Lambeth Borough Council.

A Bromley (London) ratepayer objected to a request that he authorise the Council to draw unspecified amounts direct from his bank account. In reply, the Borough Treasurer explained: 'I find it much easier to tell the Banks what I need rather than to ask the ratepayer to authorise me to do so.'

Councillors are no better at reducing staff perks than their own. While withdrawing free bus passes for old people, many authorities continue to lend employees money to buy cars at interest rates as low as 12 per cent – leaving ratepayers to make up the 6 per cent shortfall.

As talks of cuts in a wide range of services were going on, the London Borough of Southwark announced the upgrading of 500 posts at a cost of £600,000 over the next three years. The official explanation was that this had been done in order to prevent staff defecting to even higher-paying councils.

The London Borough of Lambeth has a £3,000 a year poet-in-residence and a £3,000 a year artist-in-residence. (For two days a week, they advise electors how to write poetry and paint pictures.)

Local authorities are beginning to be infected with the love for buying up stately homes that already is a characteristic of nationalised industries and government departments (especially the Defence Department). One example is the 80-room Edwardian mansion of Burton Manor, set amid 30 acres of beautifully kept gardens and parkland in Wirral. Here citizens can study bee-keeping, science fiction, the Renaissance, and folk-dancing. Local ratepayers have to find an annual subsidy of £100,000.

Losses and practices officially described as 'scandalous' cost the GLC direct-labour building department over £1.5 million. The losses had been going on for years. They still are.

It cost taxpayers over £73,000, or about £35 per civil servant, to provide potted plants at the Welsh Office in Cardiff, and it will go on costing £20,000 per annum minimum to maintain them.

The Commission for Racial Equality spends over £7 million per annum for projects such as the Zimbabwe Students' Centre and 'free' leaflets on 'Afro Hair and Skin Care'. In this context 'free' means, as it always does, that it is paid for by the taxpayer, not by those for whom the leaflets are intended.

A cleaner employed by the London Borough of Haringey is being paid £6.54 a week for watering and feeding the borough's horses. The council has not had any horses for 16 years.

The leader of the Conservative opposition, Mr Douglas Smith, said

that extracting the information from the personnel department had
not been easy.

The council's Labour leader said that the payments would continue. He said that there would have been no trouble if this small sum
had been called a special allowance.

Cambridgeshire County Council wanted to save £100,000 per annum
by using a new labour-saving cleaning-polish. The cleaners' trade
union refused to agree to the new technique because its members
would lose £5 a week. 'Enough is enough', said the union spokesman.

Free school meals are given daily to 457,000 adults. Of these, 205,000
are teachers, very many more than could be said to be 'on dinner
duty'. Ratepayers and taxpayers are paying £56,439,500 per annum
for these meals.

Cuts in the Special Temporary Employment Scheme (September
1979) were expected to cause the closure of employment centres for
the mentally handicapped. Both the handicapped and their instruc-
tors were expected in consequence to become unemployed. A number
of the handicapped would need to be admitted to psychiatric hospitals at an annual cost of £7,000 per patient.

In June 1980, schools were said to be facing a crisis over the supply of
books. Children in the North-West of England were having to write
on scraps of paper because schools could not afford exercise books.
Thirteen 'A' level students in a sixth-form college at Salford had to
share three textbooks. By 1984 the number of books available to
children in the UK was expected to be cut by 50 per cent.

In an answer to Mr Harry Greenway (Conservative, North Ealing),
Mr Carlisle, Secretary of State for Education, said that he expected
his Department to cut its staff by 'the equivalent of 65 posts' during
1980. Mr Greenway pointed out that school pupil numbers were
expected to fall by 1 million in the next four years. No decision
on further cuts in Department of Education numbers has been
made.

Councillor John Darling, chairman of Hampshire social services
committee, said (1981) that the council could no longer provide a
service for everyone needing assistance.

A representative of the Printing and Publishing Training Board
inspected the 'Training Programme' of a news agency. He criticised

the agency for 'failing to notify, in writing, the location of the toilet' to a trainee investigative journalist.

The Manpower Services Commission spent £611,200,000 in 1979/80 helping the unemployed. Nearly half that total was for administrative costs. Presumably it could argue that its own lavish staffing had at least brought the unemployed figure down, even if the usefully employed figure was unchanged.

A Midlands Council has paid £3,500 to a firm of consultants for advice on how to arrange office furniture to produce the best effects.

One hundred thousand council houses were standing empty in England and Wales, partly because of inexcusably long delays in reletting, and partly because many councils cleared whole blocks of flats when doing modernisation work, instead of dealing with one flat or one floor at a time.

Among projects undertaken by the Road Research Laboratory at Crowthorne at the taxpayers' expense: measurement of pavement deflections in tropical and sub-tropical climates; performance of sections of the Nairobi to Mombasa road in Kenya; effect of simple road improvement measures on vehicle operating costs in the Eastern Caribbean; a survey of recreational traffic in the Yorkshire Dales; a survey of transport on pleasure trips from Newport, Gwent; micro-simulation of organised car-sharing; a survey of long-distance journeys made by Manchester residents in 1974 (and published five years later); road-surface irregularity and vehicle ride, part 3 (riding comfort in coaches and heavy goods vehicles).

Wolverhampton Council are putting £900 of ratepayers' money towards the cost (£1,800) of a painting of a packet of 20 cigarettes. The remaining £900 will be supplied by the Department of Education and Science at taxpayers' expense. This is the department which explains why there is insufficient money for textbooks.

The Health Service enforces staffing patterns and structures rigidly and without regard for real-life conditions. A typical example is the Barking and Havering Area Health Authority which is a two-district authority covering a small geographical area. It did not need and did not want the kind of works organisation suitable for bigger authorities – but it was forced to have them at a cost of over £30,000 p.a. for salaries alone. According to an independent survey, there are

hundreds of examples of wasteful staffing of this kind all through the
NHS support services.

The Conservative-controlled Basildon District Council in Essex is to
pay £100 a week of ratepayers' and taxpayers' money to a toe-nail-
cutting administrator. Seventy unpaid volunteers have been happily
running, on their own, a toe-nail-cutting service for old people. The
Council has decided that they must be professionally administered.

A blunder by a junior Luton council official over a loan to a company
run by a Luton football club director cost the ratepayers and taxpayers £65,000. No explanation was given of the circumstances in
which 'a junior official' was in a position to make such an error.
    Commenting on the case, Councillor Eric Haldane, Labour leader
on the Council, said that blunders were numerous and expensive. He
went on: 'We have to start with the premise that what an officer tells
us is wrong, and if he is right we are pleasantly surprised.'
    He told the Council that when councillors had probed on land
deals, they had been given wrong information or had been fobbed off.

An independent enquiry sponsored by the CBI concluded that it
would be possible to reduce overmanning in 'non front line' jobs in
the public sector by about 10 per cent. This would produce savings of
about £3,500 million.
    Other items in the report were:
  i) 37 local authorities each had had 100 council homes empty for
more than one year; 12 had had over 500 empty; 7 (including four
London boroughs, all Labour-controlled) had had over 1,000 each.
Manchester had had over 2,000 empty.
  ii) Employees of the GLC dealt with 2.2 planning applications per
year per head of professional staff employed in development control.
Merseyside dealt with 14; North Yorkshire 21.4; Clwyd 28.3; East
Sussex 26.7; West Sussex 8.3; Kent 75.4; Powys 110.
  iv) One district general hospital employs three times as many catering staff per 100 beds, and twice as many porters, as another.
  v) NHS staff numbers in 1978 varied from 1,418 for every 100,000 in
East Anglia to 1,838 in South-East Thames. The latter employed 17
per cent more nurses, 23 per cent more administrative and clerical
staff, and 37 per cent more ancillaries.

Three hundred Gas Board workers are to receive 'free' four-course
lunches for two years when they move into a new office block in the
centre of Leeds. The change entitles them to the free meals as a

compensation for disturbance even though they are moving only a few yards. A Gas Board spokesman explained that there was a standing arrangement with NALGO that if workers are asked to make any move they get free lunches for two years.

The cost to the taxpayer and gas consumers is estimated to be at least £100,000.

There was no firm evidence that the £5,000 million of Government investment over the last ten years has directly provided more jobs and factories in depressed areas, decided the PAC (Committee of Public Accounts, 5th Report, 1981).

The prize for the newspaper with the most telling anecdote in this series, coupled with the commentary which most accurately and forcefully sums up so many of the problems implied by this chapter, belongs to the *Sunday Express*. On 3 August 1980, John Junor reported as follows:

'It was a splendid idea of the Tory-controlled Edinburgh Council to present Jack Nicklaus with a silver putter.

'But ever since the decision was taken, Scotland has been rocked by the story of how the putter came to be placed in Mr Nicklaus's hand.

'Not one but four council officials, headed by the Lord Provost, flew the Atlantic to the Ohio Open in May to present it. Not only at ratepayers' expense. Not only first class. But – just to show that expense didn't matter – by Concorde.

'Isn't it enough to make you weep – especially when just eight weeks later Mr Nicklaus was coming to Edinburgh anyway to play in the British Open at Muirfield and was to be guest of honour at a civic reception?

'*When their snouts are in the trough, isn't it extraordinary how difficult it is from a rear view to tell a Socialist pig from a Tory pig?*'

The anecdotal material and comment printed above, all taken, as reported, from newspapers, magazines and other published sources, can be assessed in two ways. It can be dismissed as probably inaccurate in part, almost certainly a reflection of a hostile, politically biased media, and quite certainly insignificant when set against the scale and range of public sector activities.

The alternative assessment is that, trivial though the examples may be, they are symptomatic of a deep-seated malaise. Given the difficulties in the way of ascertaining the facts, it is significant that so much, rather than so little, has evaded the restrictions and become public knowledge.

The most effective way of resolving this difference is to consider what happens when for some reason it does become possible to penetrate the smokescreen, and to find out, in detail, what really happens. If in these circumstances very little is found which supports claims of widespread waste, then the material in this chapter, and much more like it, can be shrugged off. On the other hand, if effective probings into public expenditure show that large-scale economies *can* be made, there is a prima facie case for treating the position more seriously. Then the defence that these examples which have provoked public criticism are just the 'one rotten apple in a large barrel' is demolished. Without leaping to any conclusions about the other apples, there would at least be justification for taking a good look at many more of them.

Later chapters in this book give accounts of just such inquiries and the results.

# 2

# 'The State Takes Too Much'

Before proceeding to these detailed investigations and their implications, it is necessary to look briefly at the general background,
economic and political, against which criticisms of public spending
must be considered. Recent years have seen marked changes in the
overall economic picture, and in the position of the public sector
within it. The attitudes of both the public and the politicians have
changed and hardened.

At all times, it seems, incompetence, waste and mismanagement of
the affairs of the public sector have been taken by many to be amongst
the indisputable and unalterable facts of life. Nearly everyone outside
the public sector believed this, and a great many within it believed it
of other parts of the sector, if not of their own.

Part of the general passive acceptance stemmed from the long-
standing nature of these unchallenged beliefs, and part from the
feeling that it was no great matter in any case. In recent years,
however, there have been indications of growing restiveness with this
state of affairs, and an increased reluctance to accept it as inevitable.
The irritation of choleric individual taxpayers with the outrageous
activities of the Inland Revenue has provided the material for several
generations of jokes. It is being replaced by widespread misgivings of
a different order about the long-term effects of high taxation of all
kinds on the nation's economic health and possibly even on its
survival as a major power. In recent years, too, local authority rates
and the way those authorities spend their money have become issues
of urgent national concern. Indeed one side effect of the general
recession has been, in the case of the commercial ratepayers, to cause
rates to replace taxation as the principal worry. No profits and no tax
to pay is a situation which can perhaps be weathered: no profits and
rapidly increasing rates to pay is altogether more worrying.

The effects of recession, pressure on incomes and profits, and
increasing public expenditure have caused taxpayers and ratepayers
of all kinds, private citizens or large business organisations, to
become far more critical. More and more often they are moved to
expressions of exasperation and anger by the crippling effects of local

and central government demands on their diminishing resources. Bitter criticism is commonplace; talk of direct action – rate strikes, legal action against councils – is becoming so. Increasingly the statements of a sizeable proportion of elected representatives reflect this change of attitudes and temper. A declaration by the Secretary of State for the Environment that he will seek statutory powers to restrain high-spending councils was countered by the Leader of the GLC asserting that he would refuse to comply and would face the prospect of imprisonment. A number of Labour Party leaders appeared to be supporting him. Nor do rebellious reactions find an outlet only in words and lawful action. The black economy of undeclared money-earning activities ('moonlighting') was estimated by the Public Accounts Committee in July 1981 to amount to £16,000 million per annum, involving a loss to national revenue of about £4,000 million. Other estimates based on sources of information not readily available to the gentlemen of the Select Committees of the House of Commons, but none the less credible for that, put the figures rather higher. There was good reason to believe that the lowest realistic estimate of revenue losses was £7,000 million, and the highest £28,000 million.

The opportunities for the evasion of payment of rates are much more limited. Nevertheless failures to pay rates, and prosecutions for failure, have risen to unprecedented levels.

It is not difficult to explain why emotions should be rising. Before the Second World War, when the activities of central and local government made much less impact on the ordinary citizen than they do now, the shortcomings of the Civil Service could be treated with mainly good-humoured tolerance and dismissed with a resigned and indulgent chuckle. Much the same was true of local government spending. The scene today is much changed.

Although many of the figures bandied about in this connection are misleading, because they are distorted by inflation and other factors, there are some basic ones which cannot be disputed and whose relevance cannot be ignored.

In 1910 the equivalent of less than 6 pence in the £ of the nation's wealth was disposed of by the public sector. In 1980 the corresponding figure was around 60p in the £. Public sector expenditure is paid for by the public, and this increase was therefore accompanied by corresponding increases in the numbers paying tax. In 1909/10 the number of taxpayers was 426,338; in 1910/11, 435,851; in 1911/12, 452,496. This was an average 0.96 per cent of the population.

By 1938, taxpayers numbered 3,800,000 or about 8 per cent of the population.

In 1980/81, the estimated number of taxpayers was 21,300,000, equal to about 38.1 per cent of the population.

These figures need to be weighed against changes in the population. At about the time covered by the figures of taxpayers given above for the three years 1909–12, the population of the U K (including Ireland) was 45,521,615 (1911 census figure). In 1938, it was approximately 47,494,000 (mid-year 1938, based on the 1931 census). In 1981 the figure was 55,672,133 (based on the 1981 census).

Thus in about three-quarters of a century the population has increased by about one fifth. The public sector take from the community has increased tenfold, if expressed as a proportion of national income.* And the number of people paying tax has increased by about forty times.

The feeling that somehow public expenditure had gone out of control and was pushing upwards at ever faster rates gradually ceased to be the view of an eccentric minority, and is supported by the facts. In the half century from 1701–51 national expenditure rose from £3,400,000 to £6,425,000, i.e. less than 100 per cent increase (in actual not real money terms) in 50 years. In the period 1821 to 1871 it rose from £58,400,000 to £67,800,000, i.e. a rise of about 9 per cent in 50 years. From 1931 (when it was lower than it had been in 1921) to the end of 1938 it rose from £814,200,000 to £909 million, i.e. just over 10 per cent in 7 years, although the latter years were being pushed higher by rearmament.

It was not until the 1950s that the pace quickened, with a roughly 50 per cent increase in 10 years. In the 1970s, *after allowing for inflation*, the increase was fourfold.

Comparisons based on costs can be misleading for a number of reasons, including the effects of inflation and changes in methods and bases of calculations. An alternative method which avoids at least some of these disadvantages is to compare numbers of people involved.

During the 1970s the population changed very little, and at one time (1975–78) was actually dwindling slightly. By 1980 it had just overtaken, by a margin of about half a million, the 1970 figure.

* The effects of inflation make comparison in money terms largely meaningless. For what it is worth, however, central and local government spending combined has increased nearly 300 times.

Against this, the manpower employed by the public sector has in-creased, during the same period, by just under 20 per cent.

The detailed figures for local authority manpower are consistent with the belief that no matter who is in power, or what state the national economy is in, the public sector goes on growing inexorably.

Between 1952 and 1979 (see Appendix 1) the total number of full-and part-time staff employed by local authorities in Great Britain *increased every year* except i) in 1974 when large blocks of staff were transferred to other public authorities, and ii) in 1977, when there was an apparent small drop, but this coincided with changes in some counting methods.

The numbers of staff employed by central government show simi-lar signs of growth during recent years, although these figures are distorted at intervals by the effect of wars. Avoiding, as far as possible, these major hiccups, produces the following:

| | | |
|---|---|---|
| 1902 | 50,000 | |
| 1910 | 55,000 | |
| 1914 | 70,000 | |
| 1924 | 115,000 | |
| 1934 | 117,000 | |
| 1939 | 347,000* | *(163,000 plus 184,000 industrial staff) |
| 1949 | 784,000 | (includes large wartime staffs) |
| 1959 | 646,000 | |
| 1969 | 684,000 | |
| 1979 | 733,176 | |

* For 1939 and onwards, totals include industrial staff which were not noted for earlier years.

Detailed figures are given in Appendix 2.

One of the recurring themes which any examination of public sector spending seems to bring out is that generally total numbers of staff, especially administrative staff, increase without any evidence that effective output had increased. In 1965 there were 456,000 teachers and lecturers, and 398,000 non-teaching staff. In 1980 there were 693,000 teachers and lecturers, and 717,000 non-teaching staff. It is unlikely that many members of the public would claim a corres-ponding rise in educational standards. On the contrary, such evidence as is available seems to point the other way.

Similar increases in staff and costs took place in the National Health Service. In September 1981 the Public Accounts Committee published the results of enquiries into a number of NHS activities and policies. The facts on which their criticisms were based were the results of detailed investigations by Exchequer and Audit Department. That department invariably checks its findings with the authorities concerned before making a report. The Public Accounts Committee itself is made up of MPs of all parties, and in 1981 its chairman was Mr Joel Barnett, a former Labour Government Chief Secretary to the Treasury. The findings cannot therefore be easily dismissed as inaccurate or politically biased.

The Committee said that in the period 1948 to 1979 the total number employed by the health services had more than doubled to 930,000 (this mirrored the increase in local authority staffs, see p. 177).

Between 1971 and 1979 staff numbers had increased by 174,000, a rise of 22 per cent in England and Wales, and 29 per cent in Scotland. (Here again there is a close correlation with the local authority figures.)

Hospital medical staff in England and Wales had gone up by 31.5 per cent, nursing staff by 24.6 per cent and ambulance staff by 12.2 per cent. In the same period administrative and clerical staff went up by 45.4 per cent. These increases occurred during a period of nearly nil growth in the population.

The PAC described the performance of both the Department of Health and Social Security and the NHS regional authorities as 'quite unsatisfactory'. For a PAC report this is strong language.

Figures for the NHS calculated on different bases suggest that between 1961 and 1978 the total number employed rose from 575,000 to 1,175,000, during which period the number of hospital beds fell from 478,000 to 396,000. Here again numbers of non-medical staff rose sharply. These figures are borne out by the 1981 CBI survey which calculated that between 1971 and 1980 the total NHS staff (on a full-time equivalent basis) rose by 25 per cent. In the same period administrative and clerical staff rose by 50 per cent. Both figures need to be considered against an increase of .003 per cent* in the population on the one hand and deteriorating services on the other.

Increases in staff numbers, and in costs, however, are not the sole source of public dissatisfaction. Rising rate and tax demands reflected vast extensions in the responsibilities of local and central government, many of which had admittedly been created by the demands of minorities, but which had not been actively opposed by the general

* Based on total population figures for the UK including the Isle of Man and the Channel Islands.

public until the bills began to reach alarming totals. But there was more to it than costs.

Government expenditure at the turn of the century was concerned mostly with defence, foreign affairs and other matters which the man in the street had usually neither knowledge of nor interest in. Just occasionally incompetence in handling the affairs of the Army and Navy would cause a furore, usually in the first stages of a war, but generally such matters were far away and soon forgotten. As for foreign affairs, so much was kept wrapped in mystery, and so much was opinion rather than fact, that if mistakes were made they could not as a rule be proven.

This is not true of public sector activities nowadays. Their impact affects the ordinary life of citizens in a myriad ways: 'the structures and processes of government now loom so large in British conscious-ness (because) the decisions of government both central and local have become more consequential and more pervasive in people's lives. . . . Any incompetence, any harshness, any unfairness in gov-ernment bears down upon individuals as never before.'*

Nor is it only a matter of scale and range of activities. There has been since the last war a falling off in the standards of the public services. It is unlikely, for example, that it would be possible to discover in pre-war public authorities examples of waste, overman-ning and other forms of inefficiency and poor service such as are now commonplace. The L C C of the 1930s was a very different organis-ation from the G L C of 1980, and the London boroughs within it.

Much the same is true of the publicly owned enterprises. A large part of the B B C's continuing financial problems would disappear if today's management were as efficient and cost-conscious as its coun-terpart in the 1930s. And there is no guesswork whatsoever in the assertion that the way London Transport was run in 1930 was very different from the situation found fifty years later – which will be the subject of examination in later chapters.

For members of the public doing business with a public authority, especially the publicly owned utilities, there was the constant irri-tation of dealing with staff who appeared to be exempt from any pressure likely to improve standards of efficiency and courtesy. Se-cure in employment by the possession of an inviolable monopoly; protected by unions from the consequences of almost any trans-gression; answerable to no one save a management which shared the

* *British Government and its Discontents*, by Geoffrey Smith and Nelson W. Polsby (Harper & Row, 1981).

same staff unions as well as other interests, it was little wonder that a complaining member of the public usually received short shrift. Beneath a very thin veneer, the publicly owned organisations were in a position to tell their customers that they could take it or leave it – high prices, bad service, studied indifference and all. Not surprisingly the effects began to be felt in many ways.

Interruptions in supply are now one of the accepted hazards of late twentieth-century life. Few households nowadays would go without emergency lighting and in many cases emergency cooking equipment. The telephone service, despite the progress made by the supporting technology, is atrocious. Despite rapidly mounting expenditure on education, growing parental misgivings, shared by employers, about falling standards of education have proved to be only too well-founded, as have similar criticisms of standards in the NHS. And while this may be, as British Rail expensively insists, the Age of the Train, for many passengers what registers is the age of the trains, the dirt, and the unreliability. In 38 journeys I undertook in 1979 *not one* was completed both ways without a failure of some kind – in timing, heating or services. Usually, there was more than one failure. In 1981, surveys of users of the main publicly owned services showed that by a margin of four to one, people regarded those services as unsatisfactory – and this was unconnected with prices.

In terms of prices, the nationalised industries had also performed badly. Between 1960 and mid-1976 their prices to the captive customer increased by 25 per cent relative to the general level of retail price increases.*

In the five years 1973–78, *after making full allowances for inflation*, the changes in real costs were:†

|  | % up | % down |
| --- | --- | --- |
| Coal | 58 | |
| National & Scottish Buses | 24 | |
| Post | 19 | |
| British Leyland | 21 | |
| British Steel Corporation | 22 | |
| Rail | 14 | |
| Electricity | 23 | |
| Telecommunications | | 14 |
| Gas | 6 | |

* Taken from *The Nationalised Industries*, by Richard Pryke (Martin Robertson, Oxford).
† *Public Enterprise in Crisis*, by John Redwood (Blackwell, 1980).

No doubt there will be those who argue that the past always tends to be seen, in these circumstances, through rosy spectacles and that in reality not much, if anything, has changed. It is not a defence which I believe can be sustained. It is rare to find a long-serving manager of any grade who will not, given the chance, launch into an explanation of the difference between how things were done then (i.e. anything from 20 – 40 years ago) and now. These wry reminiscences are not based on good-old-days generalisations. They are accompanied by a wealth of detailed examples and explanations which show how great are the changes which have occurred, and how disastrous the effects of those changes for the organisation concerned. Interestingly, too, much the same disapproval of today's way of going on is to be found amongst long-serving employees who have remained in lowly grades. Indeed, the comments of this group are often more pungent – and not infrequently more to the point – than those coming from managers. Managers generally, perhaps inevitably, seem to be in danger of learning to come to terms with low levels of efficiency, with over-staffing, and with indifferent performance by both individuals and organisations. This is true to some extent in the private sector but is far more noticeable in the public sector, for reasons which will be discussed later.

To that sorely tried character, the average citizen, the main charac-teristics of public spending are that i) it seems to keep going up and up; ii) a lot gets spent in many ways which range from being not really essential through those which are hardly desirable to those which look remarkably like criminal negligence, non-temporary insanity, or a mixture of the two; iii) at the same time services which by general consent are at least highly desirable, and are possibly essential, have to be ended for lack of money; and iv) nothing changes except for the worse.

A great many people and organisations who are aware of these contradictions, and of the threat they offer to their way of life, are beginning to say so frequently, loudly and clearly. At national level most Conservative politicians demand cuts in public spending, and most if not all MPs of all parties are opposed to wasteful expenditure. A large number of influential national organisations keep up the pressure on government, and the members of these organisations keep the pressure on their national headquarters. None of this was new in 1979. Concern about spending in the public sector, though lacking the urgency of the late '70s, had regularly caused local and national political parties to promise action in the past, although their efforts were at best half-hearted and inept and rarely met with even limited success.

In the spring of 1979 it seemed that in the United Kingdom all the elements existed for action by government in almost ideal conditions. The issues were in the open. The burdensome spending was there, and so were the allegations of waste. The ever-growing staffs in central and local government were there to be seen, and their existence (and their growth) could not be disputed. Public opinion was aroused and well-informed as never before. The opposition party at national level had espoused with renewed enthusiasm a cause always near to its heart, and was clearly proposing to seek a mandate to 'grasp the nettle of public spending', as their leaders became increasingly prone to say in speeches to the faithful. As never before the need, the opportunity, the political and the public will were there. The way in which the opportunity was used, and the net result of the exercise of so much pressure on public spending levels, is highly instructive.

# 3
# 'Public Spending
# is Going through the Roof'

The Conservative manifesto which was published in April 1979, immediately before the General Election, was obviously intended to wring the last drop of electoral advantage from the public mood then prevailing. The Conservatives were fully entitled to do this, and, in so far as was consistent with the party's philosophies, to identify, propose solutions for, and make political capital out of the problems which were causing widespread concern. Equally the nation was entitled to expect that the promises made in the manifesto were not merely restatements of long-standing policies or desirable very long-term objectives. The manifesto pledges constituted the programme of government action which could be expected from a party which, if successful at the polls, would be in office within a few months, at most.

The reduction of public expenditure generally, and of waste and overmanning in particular, figured prominently in the proposed action programme. The manifesto rightly drew attention to the importance of such reductions if the nation's economic health was to be restored. Proper monetary discipline, including a reduction in the size of the Government's borrowing requirement, was vital. The enlargement of the role of the State, and the consequential diminution in the role of the individual, both closely linked with increasing public spending, had crippled the enterprise and effort which was so badly needed, not least by those to whom the social services were important. There can be no doubt that all this made good sense not only to the Conservative Party, but to many others amongst the floating voters whose support had to be ensured. On the subject of waste, especially, the Conservatives rightly believed that they would be tapping a rich vein of discontent about the public sector by the following unequivocal pronouncements:

'The reduction of waste, bureaucracy and over-government will also yield substantial savings. For example we shall look for economies in the cost (about £1.2 billion) of running our tax and social security systems. By comparison with private industry local direct labour schemes waste an estimated £400 million a year. Other examples of waste abound . . .'

and

'The State takes too much of the nation's income; its share must be steadily reduced. When it spends and borrows too much, taxes, interest rates, prices and unemployment rise . . .'

The sacrifices of ordinary people, it was argued, would be all the greater if the Government did not economise.

For a community which had just emerged from a winter where those employed in the public services had been causing as much inconvenience as they could for those same 'ordinary people' – and simultaneously demanding and getting more and more money for doing so – the idea of limiting the future scope and the future cost of these activities had an irresistible appeal. It was high time, in the view of a large majority outside the public sector (and a not inconsiderable minority within it), as the opinion polls of the time showed, that a good deal of the fat was trimmed off. The Conservatives seemed to have the will and the ideas needed. 'Big Income Tax cuts fundamental to Tory strategy' stated the headline in the *Times* report on the manifesto. So they were. And big cuts in public spending and borrowing were equally fundamental to the policy of justifiable tax cuts.

In the event, it was only a matter of weeks before the Conservatives were forming their Government, and there was therefore no room for claims that circumstances had changed. The manifesto was in consequence something of a firm contract between the successful party and the electorate, who had in turn a much stronger claim than usual to look for delivery in full.

The presentation of the third Conservative budget and the end of their first two years* in office, provides a convenient time for assessing the extent to which the manifesto promises have been kept. Most are outside the scope of this book, although the rate of government spending has a considerable influence on inflation, government borrowing, unemployment and all kinds of taxation, as the Conservatives themselves were at pains to point out. Certainly the pattern of the results of their first two years was consistent with the theory of a close connection and interaction between these factors.

By March 1981 public spending had *not* been cut. It rose from £60.6

* written in June 1981.

billion in 1978 to £70.4 billion in 1979/80, to £85.99 billion in 1980/81. The forecast for 1981/82 is £106 billion.

Taxation reductions – big ones, not just minor adjustments, were fundamental, remember – have not been made.

In the first budget, in June 1979, the standard rate of tax was reduced by 3 pence from 33p to 30p. It was generally conceded to be a step in the right direction, and an earnest of the way in which the new government could be expected to get on with the job of implementing the promised manifesto programme. True, as some Labour and Liberal Opposition spokesmen pointed out, the overall effect of the extra cash incentive provided by this small cut was hardly likely to bring about the much heralded change of attitude towards hard work and the rewards thereof. In the general atmosphere of goodwill towards the Government, such criticism was brushed off as carping and sour grapes. The important thing was that, despite all the difficulties, the Government was keeping its promise and a start had to be made towards those big cuts in taxation levels. Only 3 pence in the £ this year, but it might be a different story next year and the year after. It was!

The further cuts did not materialise in 1980. In 1981 the budget, while leaving income tax rates unchanged, effectively increased taxation by not updating personal and other allowances in line with inflation – a device which dismayed even staunch Government supporters. Equally dispiriting were the increases in the taxes on drink, tobacco and, above all, an extra 20 pence on petrol and Derv.* These were the last straws which, less than two years after the General Election, had helped to cause popular support for the Government to slump alarmingly, Conservative MPs to vote against it, or abstain from supporting the Budget proposals, and a widening of the rift in the Cabinet. The continuing fall in the rate of inflation was the one item of moderately good news – moderate because the Budget increases would push up the rate again, and it was in any case already higher than it had been when the Conservatives took office.

The failure of the Government to make even a modest start on achieving the objectives which it had itself specified as being of such fundamental importance if its strategies were to succeed was apparent not only in terms of the amount of increases in gross public expenditure. It was the nature of many of the increases. In opposition, the Conservatives had loudly proclaimed that State handouts to firms like British Leyland should be halved. By the spring of 1981,

* Subsequently rescinded.

two years after the Conservatives took office, they had not been halved, nor even kept at the level for which they had criticised the Labour Government.*

Similarly, in opposition, the Conservatives had been highly critical of the performance of the nationalised industries. Billions of pounds had been poured into them in the form of open subsidies, and billions more in the form of concealed subsidies. Most of the industries had a monopoly or near monopoly of essential goods and services, so that consumers had no choice but to buy their products. Other subsidies were disguised as consumer assistance. In many cases they were in a position to dictate terms not only to their customers but also to their suppliers. Yet despite this, and despite the fact that the nationalised industries were increasing costs at a rate higher than average cost-of-living figures, standards of performance were falling.

A comprehensive indictment of the general performance of the nationalised industries, and more especially since the Conservative Government took office, was given by Mr Michael Shanks, Chairman of the National Consumer Council, early in June 1981. The record of these industries, said Mr Shanks, had been appalling. In the year ending March 1981 the prices of their goods and services had been increased by 24.1 per cent compared with the all retail price index increase of 12.6 per cent. Coal, rail, gas and electricity were specifically mentioned as examples of 'steadily worsening' services from the publicly owned industries.

These higher prices were being imposed despite the fact that the Conservative Government was putting in further billions to cover investment by the public sector – billions taken from the sorely pressed private sector.

This heavy subsidising of the public sector industries amounted to a complete disavowal of all that the Government had held to be central to their strategy for curing the nation's economic and other ills, but there were many Conservative supporters who believed that it was new Ministers and not old beliefs that were wrong. On the other hand, the only alternative to a confession that the Govern-

---

* A tacit admission that the Government had recognised that it was not likely to be effective in the field of expenditure reductions was first made by Michael Heseltine in a little-noticed letter to the Association of British Chambers of Commerce as early as November 1979. In this he referred not to the major reductions in expenditure but to 'proposals to *stabilise* the volume of Government *expenditure*' and *reduce* Government and local government *intervention* in business affairs. (My added emphasis.)

ment's strategy had been based on a comprehensive miscalculation was that there had been an equally comprehensive failure of political will where it most mattered.

The local authority picture was similarly gloomy. In May 1979, local government employed 2,093,901 full-time staff. Michael Heseltine, Secretary of State for the Environment, appealed for a ban on recruiting, and the figure fell marginally for a month of two. By the end of 1979 the total figure was back to the May level, or higher. There was a small drop by the end of 1980, the most optimistic estimate being 45,000. However there were doubts about even this modest decline (less than 2 per cent) as some authorities may have changed the rules for counting.

At the end of March 1981, Mr Heseltine confirmed a decrease of 1.9 per cent between December 1979 and December 1980. There was little further change in the first three months of 1981.

In financial terms the consequences for both domestic and business ratepayers were serious indeed. In addition to the rising costs which the majority of councils were facing, there was the result of the new system for assessing rate support grants by the Government which had the effect of benefiting the rural areas at the expense of the cities.

According to a comprehensive survey of all Local Authorities in the United Kingdom carried out by the *Sunday Times*, the net results of Conservative promises and boasts (pre-election) and Government pleas, threats, advice and inducements (post-election) were as follows:

| Rate increases % | England and Wales | Scotland |
|---|---|---|
| above 50 | 5 | 3 |
| 40–50 | 10 | 9 |
| 30–40 | 13 | 21 |
| 20–30 | 62 | 13 |
| 10–20 | 208 | 8 |
| under 10 | 92 | 3 |
| Decreases (0.9–5.5) | 8 | Nil |

The recession had already destroyed the profitability of many of even the biggest and best known companies. In the same edition of the *Sunday Times* which carried the analysis of local authority rate demands there was a report of the trading results of Guest Keen and

Nettlefold. A profit of £126 million before tax for the year before had turned into a total deficit of £103 million for the current year. Generally tax was payable, however, only when profits were being made. Not so with rates, which take no account of trading results. Big firms began to consider whether they could afford to stay in the highly rated urban areas. Small concerns did not have the luxury of choice: many of them were driven out of business altogether. In 1980 bankruptcies rose by over 50 per cent to a record high level.

Domestic ratepayers in these areas suffered about as badly. Nicholas Freeman, leader of the council for Kensington and Chelsea, where the increase was 52.5 per cent, asserted: 'There are thousands of ordinary homes in the borough now faced with rate bills of £1,500.'

The position is even worse than these figures suggest. High as it is, the public sector expenditure figure would have been higher still but for slashes in capital expenditure which are 'savings' only in a very limited and short-term sense. Edward du Cann, MP, correctly diagnosed the character of economies of this kind as cuts in the muscle, not from the fat in the economy.

The following shows the changes in volume of Public Expenditure for the years 1978/9 to 1980/81.*

|  | Final Labour Plans (%) (Jan 1979) | Initial Conservative Plans (%) (Nov 1979) | Estimated outcome (%) (March 1981) |
|---|---|---|---|
| Defence | +7.7 | +7.4 | +8.0 |
| Law & Order etc. | +4.2 | +7.3 | +9.1 |
| Social Security | +4.9 | +5.9 | +6.1 |
| Education etc. | +1.8 | −3.4 | −2.9 |
| Health etc. | +3.5 | +1.5 | +1.0 |
| Industry, Employment etc. | −1.4 | −12.2 | +10.5 |
| Nationalised Industries Lending | −27.3 | +29.9 | +152.5 |
| Debt Interest | +9.1 | +9.6 | +50.4 |

The Government can hardly plead bad luck and circumstances outside its control, world-wide depression in particular, as the

* Taken from *The Times*, 'Why public spending has gone through the roof', by Gavyn Davies and David Piachaud, 8 July 1981.

reason for increased spending on Defence, or on Law and Order. Both were envisaged in its pre-election promises and strategy. Similarly, although very little if anything was made of it before the election, post-election speeches by Ministers appeared to claim that higher unemployment – temporary, of course! – was the inevitable and on the whole desirable consequence of the creation of the slimmer, more competitive British industrial sector which was so badly needed. Higher social security expenditure should therefore have been expected and taken into account.

The figure which stands out, of course, is the increase in 'lending' to the nationalised industries. On that item the real increase was greater than this comparison suggests. In Labour's last complete year of office (1978) the expenditure figure was £745m. In 1979, with Conservatives in control for most of the year, it was £1,709m, and, in 1980, £1,942m.

Like the Conservatives' spending record in other parts of the public sector, it amounts to an astonishing reversal of its advertised intentions and an abandonment of policies which had been claimed to be essential to national survival.

As *The Times* remarked thoughtfully, it was a strange achievement for a government and a party whose manifesto proclaimed 'The State takes too much of the nation's income; its share must be steadily reduced'.

The same article, referring to Conservative pressure for further spending cuts, points out that more cuts would merely add to unemployment and worsen the situation. Although this chapter is not strictly the logical place to examine this objection to cuts, the objection itself is canvassed so frequently and accepted so widely that I believe it worthwhile to look at it in detail sooner rather than later. Without such an appraisal, spending cuts can be discredited before they have even begun.

Reductions in spending made in the manner so far adopted by the Government (and in justice, it must be added, all other Governments) certainly do attract just such objections. The overwhelming need by all governments, and therefore the common characteristic of how they all choose to make reductions, seems to be a high-speed response in the periodic published expenditure figures. Only two kinds of spending, whether public or otherwise, are capable of producing what appears to be such a speedy response. First, capital expenditure; and second, expenditure which for some reason is not irrevocably committed long in advance.

Capital programmes are tempting targets. Is the programme for roads (or bridges, or fuel conservation – see Chapter 11) £1,000 million? Fine. A cut of 50 per cent produces, by a stroke of a Chancellor's pen, a saving of £500 million. Already we are, if not painlessly, at least successfully, on the way to the desired target. The headlines write themselves.

Unfortunately it does not work like that. Most of the expenditure in a capital programme *cannot* be shut off at short notice. Some is owed for work completed; much more is committed in one way or another for work in progress. That work, and other work not yet started, can, in theory be slowed down considerably although in the process some very hard-to-defend decisions will have to be taken. But that will be *work* stopping or slowing down – *not spending*. The cost of closing down operations, compensation and the rest will probably *increase* spending for a time. And the price paid in other ways is heavy indeed.

This leaves uncommitted expenditure as the only available sacrifice ready to hand. The two most noticeable characteristics of this type of expenditure in the public sector are first, that it amounts to a fairly small proportion of the total; and secondly, the fact of its being uncommitted has nothing whatever to do with its importance in relation to other kinds of expenditure. The biggest component of local authority spending, and of central government administrative costs, is made up of payments directly or indirectly connected with salaries and wages. It is impossible – not difficult, not undesirable, but impossible – to make big staff cuts quickly, and those few that can be made quickly often cannot be made cheaply. In the context of substantial reductions in spending, if they cannot be made cheaply there is no point in making them quickly.

The immediate consequences of this is that low priority expenditure of all kinds which cannot be changed rapidly and still save money has to go on, while the purchase of school textbooks can be halved and the food for meals on wheels can be stopped altogether. This explains why wages and salaries have to go on being paid to unneeded staffs, at the expense of badly needed services, a circumstance which appears to puzzle government and exasperate ratepayers.

In this connection one of the facts that Conservative Ministers seem quite unable to understand, or give credence to if they do understand it, arises from this problem with staff costs. They always come back to the old argument that natural staff wastage in the public services is 6 per cent or 7 per cent or whatever the going rate is, a figure that comfortably accommodates the sort of reductions thay have in

mind. But natural wastage can only be used to the limit of wastage
which occurs where you want to make cuts. If you have a department
employing teachers, bricklayers and lorry drivers, you will get natural wastage in all three categories. If you are in a position to reduce
bricklayers and lorry drivers by 50 per cent you can use all the natural
wastage that comes along. If, however, your teacher numbers are
right, you have to replace natural wastage – and you cannot use the
surplus bricklayers and lorry drivers. Local authorities who employ a
bewildering mixture of non-interchangeable skills are hit much harder by this than central government where, for example, there are
large numbers of clerical and other grades which are interchangeable.

It is this apparent inability by Government to understand that
sensible short notice cuts are not practicable which has led in the
main to the clash between the Secretary of State for the Environment
and local authorities, many of whom are not being wilfully defiant.
And it has caused, too, such cuts as are made to be, very often,
unnecessarily painful.

The alternative to this unrewarding (for everyone, Government,
authorities and public alike) way of proceeding is to look at public
spending in a more orderly and rational way. It is what this book is
primarily about – conducting patient, skilled, based-on-reality examinations of how and where our money goes. It cannot be done
overnight. Finding the facts takes time; persuading all those involved,
management, trade unions and others, takes time; implementing the
decisions takes even more time. In one corner of one Government
Department I spent five years doing the kind of investigation which
was warranted. When you come to Chapter 11 you will find that a
local authority took three years to get to the point of beginning to
implement economies, although it was anxious to save money.

Suppose, however, that the Government, when they were elected,
had appointed someone with powers to investigate and report of
a kind which the size of the problem within the Civil Service
calls for. They would probably have needed about 1,500–2,000 staff
for this purpose. In the first year the savings would have been enough,
and some more besides, to pay costs. In the second year, the savings
would have been measured still in only a few hundreds of millions –
not to be dismissed, but not enough to make any impact on the
national budget. In the third year the figure might have gone over the
£1 billion mark, but the really massive cuts would probably not show
until the fourth, fifth or later years. True, it would be costing jobs
then, but is not the government strategy based on the reasonable

assumption that taking the public sector load off the private sector's back is going to make the latter more competitive, and thereby able to provide more jobs?

The one big disadvantage about proceeding in this way is that it is much slower to produce results than politicians like. It is a disadvantage that has its own compensations. Whatever else it does or does not do, it does not produce large-scale unemployment overnight.

The stock answer to the argument for cost investigations of this kind is that the size of the areas of waste and unnecessary spending is grossly exaggerated, and value-for-money enquiries just will not produce these massive savings. Only the radical surgery of the Government's measures to date can do that, and cost investigation does not offer a credible alternative.

The available figures suggest differently. EEC figures show that the number of UK public servants, including local government staffs but excluding revenue earning staffs (postmen, for example), is 5.3 million, serving a population of approximately 56 million. Using the same definition West Germany (population 61.3 million) employs just under 3.6 million and France (population 53.4 million) just over 3 million.* The UK Inland Revenue employs just under 79,000 staff which is roughly the same as the total for Federal tax officers in the United States with a population four times as big. When you see in later chapters the percentage savings achieved or at least shown to be possible by careful investigation, these figures become doubly significant.

If Government cannot take effective action at a time like this, when is it ever going to cut out waste? In the early 1970s I discussed with a senior Army officer the possibilities of concentrating one military complex into a smaller area. There was no defence objection to what we were proposing. The savings in running costs – security, maintenance of all kinds, and reduced handling distances – would have paid off the capital costs within two years. About four thousand acres of good land would have been set free, and the sale of it would have covered the capital costs again.

The scheme – which we used as a pilot one (there were many others available) – never got past the discussion stage. At that time, although it seems hardly credible now, we were in the middle of a building boom. Spare building and construction capacity was just not

* I would not want to make too much of it but many of the economies resulting from the investigations I am familiar with averaged around 30 percent; 30 per cent off the UK 5.3 million produces a figure just below West Germany's 3.6 million.

available. Ordinary building materials were being imported from
France (plasterboard), Belgium (bricks), and half a dozen other
countries, at uneconomic prices. Labour, whether skilled or unskilled, was even harder to come by. 'Anyone warm to the touch', said a
major contractor to me in the process of explaining delays in his
contract, '. . . can walk onto any of our sites and get a basic £150 a
week. Of course if they are completely cold', he added gloomily,
'. . . we can't compete with the Civil Service.'

It was considered wrong at that time to divert scarce resources
from factory building, houses and other urgently needed projects, for
a non-essential purpose such as rationalising an otherwise acceptable
lay-out.

It was probably the right decision. But what has happened since?
In the middle 1970s there was no money to spare, especially for
defence purposes. In the late 1970s and early '80s there was no money
to spare for anything, and certainly not for projects of this kind, which
would begin to save money only in three to four years time. And if the
Government's hopes are realised, their economic strategies pay off in
the end, and the economy takes off? Then look back to the beginning
of this paragraph and the early 1970s, and the recurring pattern will
be plain to see.

A year or so ago one of those authorities which can always explain
to the private sector how they should be conducting their business –
the Bank of England, the Treasury, or a body of that kind – made
some pronouncements about cutting overheads. The current recession, it was said, provided a golden opportunity for firms large and
small to look at their overheads, slim them down, and be that much
better placed to weather the bad times and take advantage of the good
ones when they came. As it happens, it was good advice. It is advice
which no one more than the Government needs to act upon.

The title of the *Sunday Times* article referred to above was 'The Year
the Rates Exploded'. This accurately epitomised the net results of all
the promises of reductions in local authority spending, but could have
been applied with equal accuracy to the Government's record in
other fields. Conservative-controlled councils had done little better
than the Labour ones in the fight to keep down costs. Conservative
Ministers in charge of Departments had performed similarly.

The Labour Government's plans for expenditure by the public
sector had involved an increase of just over 5.5 per cent between
1978/79 and 1980/81. These proposals were greeted with derision
and fury by the Conservative Opposition as no more than a worsen-

ing continuation of policies that had already been a disastrous failure; and one which would impose an intolerable extra burden on an already overburdened private sector, and upon the general body of taxpayers. The essence of the Conservative alternative strategy was to *reduce* public spending far below these figures, and to convert the proposed increases into reductions. As we have already noted, this was *fundamental*, not just rather important, to the successful prosecution of the rest of the Government's plans.

In the event, the first two years of the application of these policies has seen public spending rise by over 7 per cent in real terms. Expressed in a proportion of gross national domestic product, the growth in the two years of Conservative government has been twice as big as that achieved in the whole five years of Labour government. Why and how does this happen? It cannot be other than bitterly disappointing for the Government, no matter how brave a public face they put on. Demands for decreases in public spending from Conservative Party back benchers and a wide range of organisations outside the party are matched and reinforced by inescapable economic pressures. Yet nothing happens. Well-evidenced cases for the practicability of massive cuts are produced by reputable and responsible businessmen. The CBI's working party (September 1981), for example, identified possible economies of £3–4 billion p.a. *without affecting the level of services*.

The disappointing fate of the Government's well-publicised intentions for a drive on Civil Service costs and staffing provides a useful first lesson for politicians and public.

# 4
# 'Whitehall Wins Again'

In 1977 Sir Keith Joseph was generally regarded as being second only to Mrs Thatcher in status in the Conservative Party. In addition to being a very senior ex-Minister, he exerted considerable influence as the head of the party's Centre for Policy Studies. This organisation was, as its title suggests, concerned to examine major political issues and problems, and to see what solutions could be found by the application of reason and logic (as opposed in some cases to those suggested by short-term political expediency).

Joseph was ideally suited to this task. He has a first-rate brain which makes a pleasure out of discussing with him even the dullest aspects of public administration. He also has – even rarer in a politician – great integrity.

In April 1977 he wrote to me* saying that he had seen articles in the *Sunday Times* which had given an account of my Civil Service experience. He asked for a meeting, which was duly arranged, and in June Sir Keith wrote again* making it clear that he really did intend to follow up that first discussion. Further meetings followed, some of them attended by David Howell and Kenneth Baker, and I prepared memoranda, detailed timetables and plans for a campaign against waste in central government departments. The publication of *Your Disobedient Servant* and its reception gave a further fillip to the discussions.* By August 1978, with all questions answered and all loose ends neatly tied, the proposals for changes in the functions and powers of the C and AG† and the scrutiny of central government spending appeared to have been firmly slotted in to Conservative policy.*

The election manifesto of April 1979 pursued vigorously this same theme, as we have already noted. Even more encouraging, one of the

---

* Appendix 3

† Comptroller and Auditor General, head of Exchequer and Audit Department which is the department responsible for auditing central government spending (see Chapter 12).

first acts of the newly elected administration was to appoint Sir Derek Rayner, a managing director of Marks and Spencer, to direct the scrutinising of Whitehall expenditure and methods.

Rayner was a good choice for the job. The Government could expect the appointment to be popular, for the M & S success story in the United Kingdom High Streets was known to, and rightly applauded by, most households in the land and in particular by the professional, managerial and blue-collar groups whose loyalty and imagination the Conservatives needed to win and retain in the years to come. Besides, Rayner was not a complete newcomer to the Whitehall scene. He had been one of the 'businessman advisers' appointed by Edward Heath to inject some private sector realism and businesslike attitudes into central government thinking back in 1970. That enterprise had quietly foundered, as all its predecessors had done, and Rayner himself had resigned, having concluded that he was getting nowhere in his particular field. He could be expected therefore to contribute not only private sector managerial know-how with a proven track record but an awareness of the devious ways of the higher Civil Service.

As the details of the Rayner project became public knowledge, a less encouraging picture took shape. The gargantuan task of putting right all that was wrong in the Civil Service, an organisation made up of 700,000 staff spending £70–80,000 million a year in a myriad different activities, was to be tackled by Rayner himself on a strictly part-time basis. He was to have a staff of two senior civil servants and two or three secretaries. The work of investigation would be carried out by one or two officials in the departments concerned, in consultation with Rayner. The most important weakness was that Rayner had no right of entry into departments. He could investigate by invitation only, and even then in areas selected by the departments themselves. With all its weaknesses, the Exchequer and Audit Department had never been asked to work within such crippling constraints.

Rayner invited me to meet him in May 1979 and we spent an hour or two going through *Your Disobedient Servant* which Rayner had by him, carefully annotated. Towards the end of the discussion he asked me whether I would be interested in helping with his project. He had, he said, already discussed this possibility with Mrs Thatcher who was hopeful that I could undertake 'a sharp-edged job'. I explained my doubts about the way in which I understood the project was being tackled, and ended by saying that I was not the least bit interested in joining some sort of discussion group-cum-steering committee which would, and could, do nothing but talk about economies rather than achieving something. Rayner heard me out patiently and courteously but at the end reminded me of the 'sharp-edged' phrase he had used. It was agreed that he would get in touch with me again after his next talk with Mrs Thatcher, and after he had made a trip to Canada on Marks and Spencer's business.

Whatever the intentions were at that meeting, when the offer came towards the end of the next month it was not for a job of any kind, much less a sharp-edged one. The suggestion was limited to my giving one address to one group of officials at the beginning of the first round of investigations. I declined the offer with thanks, and the letters we exchanged are reproduced in full in Appendix 4.

At the end of the first year, Rayner's team had completed the investigative work for some 29 projects and were well on with the process of consultation and implementation. Also in hand were 38 'scrutiny programmes' intended to succeed the Programme Analysis and Review activities started by the Heath Government in 1970.

It sounded good, and at first glance appeared to vindicate Rayner's view that a small, able and dedicated team (which, in the Cabinet Office, he had) was all that was needed – as he had proved to be the case in Marks and Spencer. But whereas in Marks and Spencer the managerial climate was right and Rayner was leading willing horses to the cost-effective well (and unwillingness, if any, was easily dealt with), the Civil Service set up was very different. The projects which proved acceptable were for the most part penny-ante items. In the two key departments involved with Civil Service costs and management, the Treasury and the Civil Service Department, the areas for investigation were the Treasury Registry (i.e. the filing) system and the arrangements for charging for courses at the Civil Service College. Both were no doubt useful in their way. Neither had even the remotest prospect of making the major impacts on costs and staffing which the Conservatives claimed they were going to make. On the other hand, some of the others could fairly be represented as dipstick enterprises which, if successful, could lead to greater things. Rayner admitted at the end of the first year that he had had to call on his strong backing from the Prime Minister in order to achieve even these limited successes but insisted that the cash savings so far secured were not the measure of his group's achievements. He had taken a few tactical sighting shots as a preparation for fundamental changes, dealing with causes rather than effects. First, ministers would have to take more interest in the efficient running of their departments. This would involve a change of attitudes and philosophies, and also fundamental changes in the machinery of government. Rayner had discovered the truth of what a number of people had been saying for years – that 'the Government's internal accounting procedures are a shambles'.*

The second major change involved the future of the Civil Service Department and consequently the future overall responsibility for the management of the Civil Service. The department had been set up, with high hopes and much publicity, as one of the most important end-products of the 1960s Fulton Committee. As a 'managing' department it had never even began to function, nor is there much evidence that it ever seriously tried to do so. Responsibility for the conduct of their own affairs was claimed by spending departments and the claims were not disputed by the Civil Service Department. On the contrary that department took the lead in reasserting and reaffirming those claims. At the same time, the Treasury which, before Fulton, was a force to be reckoned with throughout the Service – and a force which all in all kept a tight grip on the public purse and the taxpayers' interests – found itself impotent in important areas. The spending departments quickly discovered that the brakes were off.

New ministers, whatever their political flavour, could soon be taught that ministerial effectiveness, loyalty and ability were to be measured by their success in 'fighting for their corner' – which, freely translated, amounts to ensuring that whoever else faces the consequences of expenditure cuts, it is not their department.

This interpretation of a minister's function is an essential part of the machinery for keeping up public spending levels, and I do not think that generally its importance is understood.

Spending ministers in governments elected with a mandate to cut public spending should not have to devote their energies to fighting recalcitrant high-spending civil servants. A book† published in 1974 contained a completely accurate analysis of the role of Ministers in this connection, and it is no less valid today:

'Spending ministers do not acquire the name for nothing. They deal, not merely with money, but with the things money can buy. In a

---

* Interview with P. Kellner, *Sunday Times*, 24 August 1980. For more about the blocking of reform of the Civil Service by civil servants, see also *The Civil Servants* by P. Kellner and Lord Crowther-Hunt, and *Managing the Civil Service* by John Garrett, MP.

† *The Private Government of Public Money,*, by Hugh Helco and Aaron Wildavsky (Macmillan).

way, they are merchants of human happiness, providing one believes
that the money is well spent and does not dwell overly long on those
who pay the taxes to support it. . . .

'Inside his department, the spending minister who is uninterested
in increased spending is likely to be viewed, if not with distaste, at
least with despair. The minister himself, after an initial period during
which he may revise his predecessor's policies, easily identifies with
his department. Ministerial responsibility means that the department's successes and failures are also his own. The normal way to
gain respect and advance himself is to enhance some of the great
purposes of his department. And great purposes usually cost
money. 'This rule of ministerial advocacy knows no party bound-
aries.'*

That was put to the test in 1970. Few governments can have started
out more devoted to government economy than the Conservatives,
with their business-minded reforms in education: charges for school
meals and an ending of free school milk. But a year later the econo-
mising Minister of Education, like other Conservative spending
ministers, could be found in the usual political operation of commending herself to a client audience by citing increased spending. 'I
have,' she said, 'done everything possible to show my confidence in
the future of higher education. In my monthly battles with the
Treasury, I managed to get another £76 million for student grants
and last week announced the biggest ever development programme
for further education and polytechnics.'†

It was against this background that the critical battles were fought
in public before the Expenditure Committee of the House of Commons, and in private before the Prime Minister at No. 10 Downing
Street. Although Rayner was involved only in the efficiency with
which the Civil Service carried out policies, not with the policies
themselves, there is an overlap. True, great purposes usually cost
money. They also usually require staff.

On the question of ministers taking more interest in the running of
their departments, there seems to be good reason for thinking that
with some notable exceptions (Sir Keith Joseph at the Department of
Trade and Industry; Michael Heseltine at the Department of the
Environment) most Conservative ministers felt that management of

* And, as already noted, this is true for local authority spending.
† Speech of Mrs Margaret Thatcher, at the Royal Festival Hall, reported in the *Daily
Telegraph*, 23 November 1971.

their departments was not very far removed from doing a clerk's job, and far beneath their dignity as policy-framing intellectuals and statesmen. There is, however, an understandable (given the way public affairs are conducted) absence of direct evidence on this point, and in any case it was very much a subsidiary issue compared with the main one – what was to be done about the Civil Service Department, and the whole overall direction and management of the Civil Service? Were the individual spending departments to go on as they had been doing, with or without more cost-conscious ministers? Or was the problem to be really taken in hand, and the Service given the tough, effective management which so many – including Rayner – deemed essential and which the spending departments so patently feared and for such obvious reasons?

Given the Conservative Party's loudly and frequently proclaimed views on the incompetence and waste in the Civil Service, it would have appeared that the answer was a foregone conclusion. Leaving departments and their ministers to look after their own affairs without central control and direction (as some would see it) or without intolerable interference (as the spenders saw it) had totally failed. This was not merely the assessment of a minority of reformers and cranks. It was a central and vital theme of Conservative Party pre-election publicity, subsequently confirmed on innumerable occasions. Whatever the cure for this grave disability, therefore, it could hardly be to leave things unchanged, and muddle along on the same basis that had produced the unacceptable results identified so clearly by the Conservatives.

The advocates of more effective control of the Civil Service were not to be found only at home. Professor Friedman, the Nobel prize-winning economist who had had a considerable influence on Conservative Party thinking on public expenditure issues (and on the Prime Minister's thinking in particular), made two points in a speech towards the end of 1980.

First, he believed that the Government's economic programme and strategy were the only answers to Britain's problems – but their success depended on the Government's ability to control the Civil Service.

Secondly, on the performance of the Civil Service he said (and subsequently expanded on his statement): 'The Civil Service and the Bank of England have been unbelievably incompetent. I am almost inclined to use stronger terms. . . .'

The final verdict after all the hearings and arguments, private and

public, is best summed up in two sentences from the first page of
'The Future of the Civil Service Department – Government Obser-
vations on the First Report from the Treasury and Civil Service
Committee':*

'On the key machinery-of-government issue . . . the Prime Minister announced to the House on 29 January 1981 her conclusion that
the Treasury and the Civil Service Department should not be
merged. The Prime Minister agrees with the Committee that the
right course at the present time is to strengthen and improve the
existing organisation rather than to change the machinery of government.'

In other words, no change. The remainder of this paper is distinguished only by bringing together more platitudes and more meaningless high-flown verbiage than is usual in such circumstances. The
following examples illustrate the point:

'The Government welcome the Committee's support for their continuing commitment to the proper and economical management of
the Civil Service' (para 8). Their support for such a worthy cause was
hardly likely to be unwelcome, was it?
'The Government consider that . . . the primary responsibility for
achieving good management . . . rests with the Minister and his
senior staff' (para 11). And it was the Government itself, of course,
and no one more than the Prime Minister, who had said that this
system had failed.
'The Committee . . . criticised the Civil Service Department's
effectiveness in controlling manpower numbers – and efficiency'
(para 13). And so had almost everyone else. The Government's
answer was to leave things unchanged.
'The Government intend to press forward vigorously with measures to improve financial control and management in Departments'
(para 27). Was there ever a Government which would have claimed
something different? In the first two years of 'vigorous pressing
forward' since coming to office and of 'best leaving matters in the
hands of Ministers and their senior staffs', the cost of running central
government (not what is spent, but the cost of spending it) had
risen from £6,800 million to £8,300 million, an increase of 22 per
cent.

* Cmd 8170 Session 1980/81 HC 54, February 1981.

A more informative account of events, which I know to be accurate, was contained in a report in *The Times*:*

'Since last speaking to *The Times* in August, Sir Derek has acquired a battle scar which he makes no attempt to disguise. If he had had his way his team would no longer be at the Cabinet Office but down the road in a new ministry devoted to achieving greater efficiency and economy created by the disbandment of the Civil Service Department and the integration of its functions with the Treasury.

'Sir Derek Rayner said: "I did lose. I have not been persuaded I am wrong. . ."

'He will not talk about it but it is clear from several sources that there was much bureaucratic blood on the carpet in No. 10 after a now almost legendary meeting . . . As a result the Civil Service Department still lives . . .

'Sir Derek said: "The Civil Service has got the talent needed to bring about changes. As individuals they have responded extremely well to what they have been asked to do."

'Why as individuals and not as Departments? Sir Derek laughs and declines to reply.'

We hear daily about the owners of businesses struggling, and in a good many cases failing, to keep their firms going; of the near three million unemployed; and of the hundreds of thousands who are having services cut. I suppose we must hope that all these groups will see the joke, and laugh with Sir Derek at the prospect of defeat for plans to cut back public spending and waste. If M&S were to conduct their business like that, and to start turning in some record losses, would it be a laughing matter in the boardroom? Perhaps the explanation is that he laughed that he might not weep.

In the summer of 1981 it became known that a senior civil servant would be taking over the day-to-day running of what had been known as the Rayner operation. Sir Derek himself would be spending less time on it. Not that he would be retiring without success. On 23 February 1981 Mr Hayhoe, Civil Service Minister of State, announced in a Commons answer that the Rayner cost-cutting reviews had produced savings of about £29 million per annum.† On an £8,300 million budget for central government administration this will produce a situation where the taxpayer has to pay 99.7 pence instead of 100

* 'Whitehall brief: Much bureaucratic blood spilt at No. 10' by Peter Hennessy, 3 March 1981.
† Plus once-for-all capital savings of about £23 million.

pence, and in terms of total government spending about 99.96 pence instead of 100 pence. Heady stuff, these Conservative government cuts!

*The Times* report was wrong on only one point. It was not bureaucratic blood which was metaphorically spilled at No. 10. Nor was it the Prime Minister's or Rayner's. It was the taxpayers'.

# 5

# London Transport: In Private

9th May 1978

Leslie Chapman, Esq., c/o Chatto & Windus Ltd.
40 William IV Street WC 2

Must see you urgently about matter of great importance.
Please contact me at County Hall, London S.E.1

> Horace Cutler
> Leader GLC

So ran the telegram which began my acquaintanceship with Horace Cutler,* and subsequently with London Transport Executive. It was sufficiently intriguing to cause me to agree to a meeting a couple of days later, where I duly met Cutler and two of his principal aides from the Conservative majority party then holding the reins, at least in theory, at County Hall.

Cutler was astonishingly forthcoming for a politician. He said that he had read *Your Disobedient Servant* carefully (he had, too!) and wanted to know if I could help with the problems of the GLC. He was, he said, 'sitting on top of a £2-billion-a-year heap, and not really knowing what to do next'. I explained that in no circumstances could I take on a full-time or nearly full-time job, and London was not a place where I cared to spend more time than was necessary. After another telephone call or two, and an exchange of letters I agreed with no great enthusiasm to take a part-time job as a member of London Transport Executive.

'The Executive' corresponds to the main board of directors in a private sector company, and all the members of it, full-time and part-time are, under the terms of the Transport (London) Act 1969, appointed by the GLC.

Cutler and his colleagues said frankly that London Transport was their biggest headache. Hundreds of millions of pounds of ratepayers' money were being pumped into it annually. This would have been bad anyway but the service was poor and getting worse; and neither

---

* Became Sir Horace Cutler in 1979.

the GLC nor LTE seemed to be able to do anything about it. It was, said Cutler crossly, 'a bloody albatross round our necks and if we lose [the election in 1981] it will be because of London Transport'. The burning questions were, how much of the problem was inevitable (as London Transport claimed) and how much stemmed from misman-agement (as the County Hall Tories believed, but had been unable to prove)? Were the millions being soaked up by London Transport being well or ill spent? What, if anything, could be done to bring about fundamental changes?

My appointment to the Executive took effect from 1st January 1979, and initially was for two years. I declined the salary which went with the appointment, and after the first few months ceased to claim out-of-pocket expenses. I had a preliminary meeting with Ralph Bennett, the chairman, in November 1978 (at which I arrived late owing to a breakdown of London Transport Underground at Liver-pool Street!), and at which I politely but firmly declined to devote all my time and energies to a thorough investigation of the building maintenance side of London Transport's operations. Bennett said he was disappointed and surprised by my decision. It was, he said hopefully, just my special field of interest and there was, he was sure, great scope for improvement. I explained that I thought my brief as a part-time member would be unduly restricted if I confined myself to one aspect of London Transport rather than being free to roam over wider fields. Bennett looked like a man whose worst fears were being realised even earlier than he had expected, and we parted saying, with a noticeable lack of conviction on both sides, how much we looked forward to working together.

The first board meeting was an interesting experience. The mem-bers were at pains, in an unobtrusive way, to let it be known that while modestly disclaiming the whole of the credit for the situation, they were conscious that they were directing the affairs of the biggest and the best urban passenger transport undertaking in the world. True, there were problems, and no one knew this better than they did. However, the problems were generally exaggerated; the difficulties facing London Transport were equally generally underestimated; but despite this, pretty well all the major problems were licked; anyone disagreeing with these broad propositions was either mistaken or deliberately destructive or both. Politicians and the press were in-variably to be found in the third category. There was very little rancour in these board assessments of their critics. The attitude was one of rather resigned, world-weary acceptance that this lack of

understanding by the public and its representatives was inevitable.*
The mark of the man of stature in this unrewarding situation was the
ability to accept the criticism without flinching. As far as I could see,
one possible alternative, i.e. reducing the causes of criticism, was not
seriously entertained by anyone.

Two items struck a jarring note in these proceedings. One was a
brief discussion on the shortcomings of the Leyland Fleetline bus,
generally acknowledged to be an expensive disaster in every way, and
which was being taken out of service and quietly disposed of as fast as
possible, and as far away as possible. The other was a report that,
over Christmas, between 30 and 40 bus engines had been written off
because anti-freeze had not been put into the radiators. These items
seemed curious errors for a group claiming to be the biggest and best
in the world. A transport organisation that had at one end of the scale
specified and bought the wrong basic vehicle, and at the other end
failed in the kind of maintenance adequately managed by elderly
spinsters, might still be the biggest. The claim to be best seemed more
debatable.

The Board lunch, taken in the Executive dining-room and served
by waiters in special London Transport waiters' livery,† was impress-
ive in its way. A full range of apéritifs was followed by a five-course
meal which began with smoked salmon. Appropriate wines were
followed at the end by liqueurs and brandy. Bennett drank sparingly,
I noticed, and was obviously a little put out when, in addition to the
member who was normally inclined to be overcome by the spirit of
these occasions, a second member overbalanced backwards on to the
floor.

The afternoon tour of the premises was also instructive. At
3.30 p.m. ladies with baskets and arms full of parcels returning from
lunch-time shopping expeditions were still a commonplace sight in
the corridors. No one seemed to be very busy, except those in the staff
lending library which duplicated for London Transport Headquarters staff, at considerable public expense, the facilities, including an
admirable record library, provided normally by local authorities.‡ I

* This attitude was not adopted specially for that meeting. A year later PA International were to describe the Board as 'shell-shocked' by criticism.
† The waiters also served coffee and tea, morning and afternoon, in the offices of senior
staff. Having it served by secretaries was not acceptable.
‡ This library service did at least provide one classic example of the way in which 'do
good type spending' on anything remotely connected with welfare and education can
be justified – provided always of course that someone else is paying. Reflecting on

gathered that the Chairman made full use of the latter service. The
general impression was like that given by so many public sector
activities – that is, of soggy, sloppy management insulated from
outside pressures, complacently and effortlessly blocking the occasional half-hearted and unavoidably ill-informed attempt to call them
to account. The business was being run, it seemed, primarily for the
benefit of the staff. When, naively, at 5.30 I was surprised to find a
large limousine waiting to drive me to Paddington it was explained
that it had been there since 2 o'clock, so that it would be ready the
moment I wanted to leave.

In the next few months I continued to collect facts, impressions and
opinions. A steady stream of material reached me from members of
London Transport staff and the public, some of them by way of
newspapers and the G L C. At the beginning of May I felt that I had
enough evidence to justify telling the Chairman that I wanted action
taken on costs. We met privately, and I agreed to hold off for the time
being, pending the publication of a major policy paper which he
(Bennett) had nearly finished. At the end of May 1979, the Chairman
issued the paper which amounted to the traditional standard appraisal of the short- and medium-term problems facing London Transport
and the probable solutions and responses. I believed that this paper
accurately summarised and epitomised more than the recorded wisdom of the Board on these issues. In the process it also reflected much
of what was wrong, in my view, in London Transport management
attitudes. It seemed a convenient opportunity to bring matters to a
head, and since the Board collectively had a well-justified reputation,
even amongst its own members, for postponing awkward issues, I
decided to make my answering paper sufficiently abrasive to cause
procrastination to be more difficult than taking action.

After some delay (at the Chairman's request) I put this paper to the
L T Executive in July 1979. It caused the first open breach between
the Board and myself, and I reproduce it here almost in full:

---

whether the L T library could be regarded as essential, a study group reported as
follows:
'*Need for Activity*
So far as general reading and the record library are concerned we cannot regard these
as essential although general reading can be regarded as desirable in that it encourages
members of the staff to read more widely and to increase their knowledge thereby
aiding their personal development.'
L T Organisation Steering Group,
Report of the Study Group on Welfare and Ancillary Services.

## LONDON TRANSPORT'S FAILURE TO CARRY OUT
## ITS FUNCTIONS SATISFACTORILY

1. This paper is intended to put forward a different assessment of the situation facing LTE from that contained in the Chairman's paper 'The LTE's compliance with its statutory duties in the short and medium term'. . . .

[Paragraphs 2 and 3 review past performance, and are here omitted.]

4. After half a century* which has seen (probably) more technological progress and social changes than the preceding one or two thousand years, the LTE response has been to provide:

a) bigger (170 hp instead of 95 hp) double decker vehicles trundling along fixed routes etc. at average speeds lower than in the 1930s. . . .

b) trains running at speeds not significantly different from those of the 1920/30s . . . on the same tracks . . .

5. In the 1930s the LPTB was considered to be an efficient and thoroughly up-to-date organisation providing a good service at reasonable cost. Vehicles, rolling stock, buildings and stations were modern and well-kept. All-in-all it provided a model for other cities. Fifty years later LTE's public image is one of providing an expensive and inefficient service with scruffy vehicles and rolling stock and dirty stations.

6. The financial situation is one of potential disaster. If LT were a commercial concern the facts which now face us would be regarded as foreshadowing possible bankruptcy in the near future. The September rise will mean that fares will go up by 19% in 1979 which is far higher than the general rise in the level of prices. It also means that if the books balance after that increase, LT's total costs which have already increased 12-fold since 1948 (compared with a general increase of 7-fold) will by September have increased 14.4-fold.

7. The Chairman's appraisal does not reflect the gravity of the financial situation. It looks to a combination of further increases in fares and a bigger hand-out from the ratepayers to keep us afloat. It mentions the possibility (para 6.6) of financial benefits flowing from re-organisation and changes in methods, though not in the short term and only if LT staff give their ready co-operation.

8. I vigorously dispute both the proposition that savings cannot be made in the short term, or that they can be undertaken only if the work force agrees. Obviously there will have to be, and should be, consultation with trade unions and staff associations, and I believe

* i.e. since the 1930s.

that if matters are handled properly, co-operation will be given. But if LT can show beyond reasonable doubt, and after careful evaluation of the facts, that present methods and practices are uneconomic, they have not so much a duty as an absolute obligation to correct the situation as quickly as possible with or without trade union co-operation. In fact, in my view the biggest obstacle to cutting costs, especially administrative and overhead costs, and to curing over-manning and under-employment, lies in the failure of the Executive to carry out its duties or deal with the simplest of staff and cost-cutting problems (see paragraph 9 below).

9.  On 13 March 1979 a study group under Mr J. B. L. Hoban (Civil Engineer (Works)) produced a report which drew attention to, and gave detailed evidence of, widespread waste, involving a big list of uneconomic practices, wasteful use of manpower and general poor value-for-money type activities. Instead of action being taken im-mediately to implement the recommendations of this competent and courageous report, LT's response was that:

a)  The re-organisation was not a cost-cutting and staff-cutting opera-tion.

b)  The wasteful and uneconomic practices were not typical of LT's operations as a whole.

c)  At least one of the people involved was disparaged for making a report which made public facts unpalatable to LTE, and it seems that the career prospects of the most senior member have been damaged.

[Paragraphs 10 and 11 recorded continuing failure to take action on the Hoban report, and a decision by the Executive to keep design work on an in-house basis despite costing far more than outside consultants.]

12.  The Executive is not at present discharging even its minimum function in securing value for money, and I do not believe that this situation can be accepted any longer. I accept that cutting out waste, especially waste of manpower, is not something that can be done overnight. The Executive seems to think that this is a good reason for not taking action, whereas in fact, if anything, it makes it more necessary to make a start quickly.

13.  I therefore propose that, regardless of any other action envisaged or in hand, a cost-cutting and staff-cutting unit should be set up and

be in operation within four weeks with the sole function of bringing
forward proposals for reducing costs. This unit should be responsible
to a member of the Executive, and regular reports on progress (or the
causes of progress being halted or slowed) should be made available,
without editing, to the Executive. The aim of this unit should be to
make a first sweep of LT's activities within two years. It should then
immediately begin a second squeeze. Some of the things it should look
at immediately – the list obviously cannot be anything but an off-the-
cuff random selection from what is available – are: [There follows a
list of items for investigation, workshops, high living, etc., much as
specified in my later letter to Dr Taylor (see pages 62–9).]
All of which, i.e. cars, dining-suites, etc., are the trappings and
perquisites of a successful and profitable organisation, which we are
not.

14.   At the same time (and *not* after this unit has completed its works,
or the reorganisation has been completed, or any of the other unspecified future occasions which figure so largely in our policy-making
timetable) LT should try to decide what it sees as its long-term
future. We seem as an organisation to believe that plans which can be
implemented only in the long term can always be thought about and
planned for in the long term also. In fact we should be planning as a
matter of urgency for things which cannot possibly be implemented
for 20–30 years.

15.1 There are two practicable extremes of basic future strategy open
to us.

15.2 The first is to go on running the system pretty much as it is now,
and as we inherited it. We can do some inexpensive cosmetics on
rolling-stocks, vehicles, stations; tinker with timetables and fare
structures; keep trying to provide a better bus service; and so on. The
aim would be to spend as little as possible in terms of capital, labour
and running costs as is compatible with keeping the system going.
This should provide the cheapest possible transport in the short and
medium term provided that economy measures are ruthlessly
applied. This approach could reasonably be described as accepting
the limitations forced upon us (it is not our fault that there is so much
traffic in London and that bus drivers dislike unsocial hours, etc.,
etc.) and is a down-to-earth, eminently workable policy. More un-
kindly, it might be described as the roll-on-your-back, flap-your-
paws-in-the-air, and whimper-for-help approach to management.

Amongst other advantages this policy could claim to have very substantial precedents all through the public sector and until recently was attracting a growing number of supporters in the private sector.

15.3 The second advantage is that, except for the application of economy measures, this approach would involve almost no change in LT's current policies and as far as the travelling public is concerned, no change in the end product.

15.4 Against this background the cost-cutting activities would have to have regard for how little management and other overhead expenses could be justified. We would in fact be conducting a glorified oil-can operation. After all, there can be very few problems arising from operating trains that have not been met and solved a hundred times in the last half century. And much of the basic financial policy would be made for us. Wages would be determined as they are now by what the Union can persuade an outside authority to give them (or by an acceptable guess from management on what such an award might be). Thereafter it would just be a matter of how big a social fare contract contribution could be negotiated with GLC and government (or putting it another way, how much taxpayers and ratepayers should pay for themselves through the wholesale subsidy method rather than through the retail ticket buying method). Whatever gap was left would be closed by raising fares and from time to time getting rid of uneconomic services.

15.5 None of this would involve much in the way of management. The Executive would be quite adequately manned by a Chairman and two Managing Directors, one for bus and one for rail (all three substantially scaled down in salary) and two unpaid part-time members. Generally, I would think it possible to reduce administrative and overhead staffs and costs by about 75–80 per cent. I accept that this figure is speculative and subjective. So are the views of anyone disputing it.

16.1 The other approach is for LT to rise to the challenges presented by traffic, inner city decay, high wages and other labour problems and to seize the opportunities presented by technological advances, the energy situation (likely to be a major factor in transport matters, but not even mentioned in the Chairman's paper);* and LT's strategic position based on a statute-protected near monopoly of public transport in one of the world's biggest cities.

* This was inaccurate. It was mentioned.

16.2 The qualities most noticeable in LT management grades at
levels just below the Executive are – apart from there being too many
of them at rates of pay which are generous for what is done – that they
are all very conscientious and very much concerned with the well-
being of LT. They are also, in a good many cases, unimaginative,
complacently convinced that they already know all the answers about
transport and openly determined to fight to the death for the status
quo – because they see this as being, in practice, the best way to serve
LT.

[Two further paragraphs deal with the need to ensure fresh thinking, and for the Executive to come to grips with its management
responsibilities.]

13 July 1979                                              Leslie Chapman

The Executive as a whole professed itself to be greatly surprised
and disappointed by this paper, although two of the part-time members, Roger Graef of Granada TV and Michael Robbins, an ex-LT
full-time official, expressed a measure of agreement. One or two of the
full-time members, I thought, would also have liked to have been
more supportive than circumstances, including a realistic estimate of
the consequences for their careers, allowed. The rest followed Bennett's line that this was an unfair attack – I had 'gone for the jugular'
was the curious phrase much in use at this meeting. There was little
effort to deal with facts, although Robbins tried several times to bring
the discussion back to them. The discussion centred mainly on selec-
tive issues of loyalty – loyalty to the Board, to the organisation, to the
Chairman, but never loyalty to taxpayers, ratepayers and the travelling public. There was much invoking of team-game ethics and
terminology of all kinds, of which cricket and rowing were the most
popular. In a spirit more of regret than of anger the Executive seemed
to take the line that criticism of the Board by a part-time member
was fresh evidence of the general decline in standards of conduct
and morality of which street muggings and vandalism on the Under-
ground were merely two further, and, I gathered, rather less unpleasant, symptoms. I declined a suggestion that I withdraw the
paper, leaving the full-time members to keep in mind some of the
specific items, and generously forgiving and forgetting the rest. In the
end it was agreed that the Deputy Chairman, aided as necessary by
other full-time members, should prepare a considered reply, and
present it at the next Board meeting.

The Board was not presented with an answering paper to my

criticisms at its next meeting, nor at the next, nor ever. I could
understand the problem, because all the facts being brought to light
substantiated the fundamental criticisms.

Although I did not know about it until long afterwards, an independent market research report had shown that opinions of LTE
were generally unfavourable, and service quality was thought to be
deteriorating; that LTE was compared unfavourably with other
well-known organisations in the public and private sectors; and that
although there was widespread recognition of the problems faced,
management attracted much of the blame for service shortcomings
and was seen as being remote from customers. Bus services were the
main focus of resentment and irritation, and there was a feeling that
they provided a second-class service for second-class people. In particular, services were considered irregular and unreliable; one-man
buses were seen to be particularly bad; and buses were often found
dirty and appeared uncared for.

Further internal investigations showed that despite technological
advances (using 1970 as a 100 base line) vehicle miles per LT bus
employee were going down (104 in 1973, 96 in 1977) and the same
was true of LT rail – down from 104 in 1973 to 93 in 1977. The
comparison was even worse when made with other public transport
undertakings. While London Transport fell from 100 in 1970 to 96 in
1977, municipal bus operators in the same period had gone up from
100 to 116. And on the railways, while London Transport fell from
100 (in 1970) to 93 in 1977, the much-maligned British Rail had
climbed from 100 to 111.

Claims by London Transport that their foreign counterparts looked
better merely because they had bigger subsidies were also suspect.
An analysis of passenger journeys per employee showed:

| LT | RATP (Paris) | Sao Paulo | New York | Montreal | Toronto |
|------|------|------|------|------|------|
| 33.1 | 53.9 | 86.8 | 36.8 | 60.5 | 40.9 |

It was concluded, realistically if gloomily, that London Transport's performance had worsened, or compared unfavourably with
others, or both, in every respect, and there was therefore a strong case
for a genuine and thorough search for productivity improvements.

These facts and many others were assembled for a paper dated 28

September 1979. It seems likely, though, that some of them were available in one form or another at the time when the Board received Bennett's paper in May and mine in July 1979. In consequence, those who were smarting most may have felt that, just as they were likely to be vulnerable to outside critics if the facts from these external enquiries became public, they were being simultaneously attacked from within.

With the Board not prepared – at least not yet – to change direction, but unable to answer the criticisms, a period of uneasy calm ensued during the late summer and early autumn of 1979. The time was not wasted, as far as I was concerned. One of the objections to my July paper had been that I had not produced enough detailed evidence to justify some of my generalised criticisms. Rather to my surprise, Bennett had agreed to let me have the assistance of a member of London Transport to ensure that I had the facts I needed.

The man allocated to me was Angus Greig, Head of the Management Services Group in London Transport. Both his past experience in this work and his personal qualities, which included an enquiring mind, a genuine abhorrence of waste and inefficiency, and personal integrity, made him ideal for the job. He played absolutely fair with LT as his employers, and with me. If I asked questions, he did his best to ensure that I was given accurate answers, but he did not go outside his brief in order to feed me with damaging material. Facts were neither withheld nor volunteered. The public services ought to value men of this kind. What usually happens to them is indicated later (see especially pp. 101–102).

In October 1979, the need to consider the 1980/81 budget and the financial implications of our then current policies forced the stagnant issues into the open again. For the first time, faced with an increasingly hostile paymaster in the shape of the GLC, and increasing public criticisms, the Board discussed seriously and without much rancour the prospect of setting up and operating an effective cost-cutting unit. Yet once again, no decisions were reached and the discussion petered out inconclusively. I gave notice that if this went on I would be obliged to consider raising these fundamental issues with the GLC. Two days later, on 11 October, Bennett asked for a private meeting with me to discuss the unit. We had what is usually referred to as a frank exchange of views, and the meeting ended with a considerable amount of progress seeming to have been made. Although Bennett was punctilious in saying that he had others to consult before announcing his final decision, every aspect of the unit's staffing, functions and methods of working was discussed and, I thought, agreed, save for the near-formality of these further consultations. I arranged to work full-time without a salary for two to three months while the unit got under way, and thereafter as much as was necessary.

I did not know, at the time of this discussion, that late on the day of the Board meeting John Cameron* had followed up the morning's debate by putting a memorandum to Bennett referring to 'the hopeless muddle we make of our manpower planning' and 'our very patchy and indeterminate way of pursuing economies'. He went on: 'each year we face the same problems and each year they "go away" because we as an Executive soon allow other problems to overtake them. . . . Leslie Chapman was in my view so right today. . . . Doubt . . . remains now . . . which will, if allowed to remain, mean that once again we muddle through and do nothing. . . .' Cameron's memorandum went on to say that he had been saying this for years, and that I was wrong in thinking that these issues had not been raised. What I had objected to, however, was not lack of talks and ideas, but lack of action. The whole thrust of his argument, a courageous one in the circumstances, was on similar lines.

No doubt Bennett's conciliatory and friendly attitude on 11 October reflected his feeling that cost-cutting investigations were becoming unavoidable, if only to keep the peace and to show the willingness of the Board to try everything and anything. He was, however, doing no more than reflecting the profound and unshakeable beliefs of LT management when deriding the possibility of large-scale economies. On 6 September, the Railway Board had recorded: 'There were a number of areas where some reduction in costs could be achieved but this could not be done without affecting the level and standard of service operated, and the revenue received.'

On the other hand there must have been some well-concealed doubts about the wisdom of exposing London Transport's spending to an effective scrutiny from an outsider such as myself because between 11 October, when I thought I had reached agreement with Bennett, and the setting up of the new Central Productivity Unit on 22 October, there had been another change of mind. Although the Unit's stated objectives remained unchanged, investigations were to be directed and conducted solely by full-time LT staff. There was no

* Full-time Executive member for personnel and similar matters.

objection to the Unit hearing what I thought about methods of working, but no commitment of any kind to act on my suggestions. The first three levels of management were to be the responsibility of men who were already fully occupied, and I decided that the time for debate and argument within London Transport was over.

# 6

# London Transport: In Public

My criticisms of London Transport's policies including the proposed operations of the Productivity Unit, were set out in a letter to the Chairman dated 14th November which is reproduced in full except where it reiterates material already covered. At the same time I gave notice that I intended to take my objections outside London Transport. Sadly, and not by any means inevitably, the public phase of London Transport's internal troubles had begun.

14 November 1979

Dear Chairman

When we met for a lengthy and private discussion on 11 October I went over once again, at your request, the reasons why I disagree with current LTE policies. Although I feel sure that the issues were explored more than adequately at that meeting (as indeed they had been many times before) I think that in view of the action I now propose to take I ought to put on record that part of our discussion which was not covered by my agreement to keep some subjects confidential.

Briefly the position as I see it is;

1. LTE as an organisation is 'facing . . . acute financial difficulties' (LTE General Notice No. 2059). The difficulties are likely to increase rather than otherwise.

2. Independent market research shows that:
[There follows much the same evidence as I have reported on p. 54.]

3. Although these assessments amount to a fairly comprehensive indictment of the organisation as a whole, and of management in particular, it represents, in my experience, no more than a restrained version of the feelings of all the individual users and groups with whom I have had contacts.

4. I am convinced that a substantial part of our problems could be solved or reduced by better use of our resources, and most especially by cutting out waste and the misapplication of money and manpower

to purposes which are not even desirable, still less essential. I believe that this waste is not marginal or negligible but probably one of the principal factors in our present and forecast financial difficulties. The more I see of the results of the enquiries which I have been making, the more I am satisfied that the position is even worse than I had at first thought, and that economies in the range £25 million to £50 million per annum (without reducing levels of service) are possible. And I would further guess that the higher figure is more likely to be accurate than the lower.

5. The responsibility for the existence of this state of affairs rests with management at all levels throughout LTE, but particularly at Executive, Chief Officer and one or two levels below that. As I have told you and the Executive on a number of occasions, I find LTE managers generally to be too numerous already, and growing steadily; complacent to a degree astonishing in any circumstances, but particularly so in the light of para 2 above, the substance of which is widely known; and thirdly, with a few notable exceptions, this complacency is complemented by a very moderate level of competence.

6. I recognise that much of what I have said in the foregoing paragraph will be sharply disputed. Nevertheless when LTE has been subjected to the kind of searching investigation which it needs I am confident that these criticisms will be regarded as an accurate assessment by most people outside LTE.

7. I do not believe that the reorganisation will cure these problems despite the confidence which the Executive has had in this proposition. The reorganisation benefits will be mainly long term and may even add to our difficulties in the short term. The difficulties we face cannot wait five or ten years while these benefits work their way through the system.

8. Because of the urgency of the need for economies, the disgraceful (as I see it) nature of some of the waste, and the continuing failure of existing management (including the Executive) to deal with this, I have been advocating, almost from the time I joined LTE, that we set up a powerful central cost-cutting unit with full powers to investigate and report to the Executive. I believe that this body should not be restricted in any way in its recommendations but that all decisions should be taken by the appropriate management with recourse to the Executive as necessary. It is also essential that the unit should be directed and operated by full-time staff relieved of all other duties;

that the directing staff shall not have been associated with or responsible for, policies which must now be challenged; that the investigating staff shall be independent of management in the organisations
being looked at; be protected from recriminations and fears for the
consequence of frank reporting; and be leavened by the addition of
staff from outside LTE.

9. It will come as no surprise to you that I believe that the investigations will cover a wide range of LTE activities including many
hallowed by long-standing tradition. Local authorities and other
bodies are being forced by Government policies and pressures on
rates to cut back and increase charges for services to old people; to
charge for transport and meals for schoolchildren; and shut down
premises for the sick and handicapped. Against this background it
seems to me to be not so much wrong as positively grotesque that in
LTE senior staff are, in part at the expense of the ratepayers, being
provided free with luxury cars for both official and private purposes;
that in addition to the usual subsidised meals in a canteen senior and
higher paid staff have even more heavily subsidised meals in a dining
club reserved for them; and that the Executive members and Chief
Officers should be having the benefit of lavish catering which is yet
more heavily subsidised. I do not think that it would affect my
position if the sums of money involved in what I would regard as
indefensible spending were small. But in fact I believe that in total
they are very substantial.

Even more substantial, however, are the savings which we can and
should make from cutting out overstaffing, non-essential activities,
and services which, though essential, are at present carried out
in-house but which can be bought from contractors far more cheaply.
You will know that evidence on this last point has already been
produced in a survey carried out by LT staff (The Building Department and Building Maintenance Review dated 13 March 1979); that
the report though accepted has not been implemented; and that the
staff who produced it have been taxed by more senior people with
acting as quislings. Yet this report provides evidence over and over
again of gross waste of money and manpower and makes completely
practicable proposals for remedial action.

10. I reiterated these views at our meeting on 11 October. Amongst
the additional things I said in answer to your inquiries were:
a) although I did not want to become a full-time member of the
Executive I was prepared to work on a nearly full-time basis for a

period of months, without salary, to get the cost-cutting unit started;
b) I thought I could help in obtaining staff on loan from other
authorities at minimum costs.

11. I told you at the meeting (which followed yet another unproductive discussion at the Executive meeting on 9 October) that I could
not reconcile the continuing failure of the Executive to take action on
economy measures with my responsibilities as I saw them, and that
unless a control unit along these lines was set up without further
delay, I proposed to raise these matters with the GLC. At your
request I agreed to defer action for a week or two.

12. Since then I have received a copy of John Cameron's minute to
you dated 9 October. Amongst other things he makes the following
points:
    [There follow extracts from the Cameron minute already covered
on p. 56.]

13. On 23 October you issued a note giving details of a new central
productivity unit reporting to John Cameron. Messrs Ingleton and
Hardie, personnel directors in the two businesses, are to be head and
deputy head of the unit.

14. I do not believe that a unit staffed in this way matches the
importance, the urgency or the nature of the problems which have to
be tackled for the following reasons:
    [There follows a statement of my objections to the staffing and
direction of the unit already covered on p. 56–7.]

15. In the circumstances I feel that the unit as now proposed will not
achieve its stated aims and, however well-intentioned, will merely
give the appearance rather than the reality of an effective comprehensive cost-cutting drive.
    I am therefore giving you notice that I feel released from my
promise to defer taking these matters outside LTE. I shall now do so
in whatever ways seem to me to be appropriate to serve the public
interest.
    Yours sincerely,
    Leslie Chapman

Bennett sent a copy of my letter to Sir Horace Cutler and the
Director-General of the GLC and asked that a further copy be sent to
the Leader of the Labour Opposition. At the same time he placed a
ban on staff giving me information of any kind about London Trans-

port matters. In the meanwhile, the GLC had, acting without knowledge of their impending involvement in my criticisms, rejected the
Executive budget proposals for 1980/81. A letter from Cutler to
Bennett dated 14 November, which was leaked to the press even
before it reached LT, gives an idea of the tensions than building up:

## LONDON TRANSPORT BUDGET 1980

By now you will have seen Gordon Taylor's letter rejecting the
Budget submission for next year. I thought that I should express my
view, too.

You will recall your visit here a year ago. You asked for two things –
certain relaxations of financial stringency and a year's sabbatical to
get things done. You have had both.

Since then the promised improvements have not materialised; and
the Budget submissions hold out no hope for the future.

The problem boils down to management, its lack and its quality. At
any given resource-level it should be perfectly possible to provide the
appropriate service, yet time and again there are excuses.

I have to tell you that this attitude, which never commended itself
to me or my colleagues, is now totally unacceptable. If the present
personnel are unable to manage then we must find some who can.

On 22 November I wrote as I had said I would to the GLC,
addressing myself to Dr Gordon Taylor, Chairman of the Transport
Committee. In view of the storm this letter caused, both in the press
and within LT, I reproduce it in full:

22 November 1979
Dear Dr Taylor,

1. You may recall that at the informal meeting which you had with
the Executive on 1 October 1979, I categorically disagreed with the
Chairman's statement that the options facing the GLC and LTE
were, in effect, to reduce services, raise fares still further or provide
bigger grants from the rates. I said that a fourth and realistic option
was open to us, which was that waste, extravagance, over-manning
and other uneconomic practices should be identified and ended as
quickly as possible. I went on to say that to do this would require a
specially formed central cost-cutting group, who would not only find
the opportunities and the means for making large-scale economies
but would in the process bring about a much needed *change in management attitudes in LT*.

2. You may also recall that no one on the Executive spoke in favour

of these views and it was left to you to bring the discussion back to the realities of the economies which are available (para 2 Notes of the meeting.)

3. The exchange that day between the remainder of the Executive and me was, I told you then, merely a restatement of a fundamental policy difference which began to emerge very soon after I took up my appointment on 1 January this year. By 12 May I felt obliged to write to the Chairman, expressing my concern about the waste situation generally; of the lack of management inclination to do anything about it; and of pressures put on staff, some quite senior, to inhibit the expression of any uncomfortable truths about the defects in the organisation. The last paragraph of my letter reads as follows:

'I believe that there is the need for large-scale economies in LTE and that now is the time to do it. Equally if this is not the view of the Executive, or if it is not prepared to implement this policy, then I think this is the time to say so.'

4. As a result of this letter I had a private discussion with the Chairman and agreed to defer action until the publication of his draft major policy paper which would, amongst other things, deal with the issue of cutting out unnecessary expenditure. The paper was duly presented later in May under the title 'LTE compliance with its statutory duties in the short and medium term'. I took the view that the assessment of the situation made by this paper was generally unduly complacent, and that the virtual dismissal of the possibility of economy measures as a useful factor in our calculations was particularly misconceived. Since the promised discussions on this paper had not taken place, at least as far as part-time Executive members were concerned, by some two months later, I produced my own counter-assessment of the overall position entitled 'London Transport's failure to carry out its functions satisfactorily'.

5. I will not weary you with a blow-by-blow account of events since then especially as for the most part I think it would be more a record of non-events. A good deal is in any case covered by my letter to the Chairman dated 14 November, a copy of which I attach. I do feel it necessary however to fill out in more detail some of the matters covered in that letter since, although the Chairman will have the relevant background information, you may not.

The figures were obtained for me from the appropriate departments by a member of LTE staff made available on a part-time basis for this purpose. While, in consequence, everything is third- or fourth-hand, I believe the facts to be accurately stated, although the conclusions are, of course, mine alone.

6. In para 5 I refer to growing numbers of senior grades. The gross comparison figures produced by LTE staff show that between 1952 and 1979 the number of senior officers and officers had increased from 88 to 169, and the number of principals from 57 to 214. I am told that the staff who produced these figures for me were warned that these comparisons were unfair because they take no account of the reasons for the increases. The 'reasons' are mainly the names of the new activities created or old ones strengthened (a full list is readily available) and I leave it to you to decide whether this really invalidates my criticism. The increases noted above do not, by the way, take account of further increases in senior staff arising from the reorganisation (see also para 7 of my letter of 14 November, on short-term results therefrom). At officer level alone, proposals at present at consultation stage would lift the figure of 169 to something over 200, but this further increase is of course speculative.

In para 7 I say that the reorganisation will not cure our problems, other than in the long term. In fact, it was never intended that reorganisation should contribute to economy. An attempt to prevent *increases* in staff by a group implementing part of the reorganisation proposals brought forth the following directive from the Executive: 'Certainly implementation groups must have due regard to economy but it would be ill-advised to include a cost-cutting and staff-cutting objective. . . .' (John Cameron, Executive member to Angus Greig, then head of O and M, minute dated 25 April 1979 and quoted in my letter to the Chairman of 12 May 1979).

7. In para 8 I refer to 'the disgraceful (as I see it) nature of some of the waste . . .', and I think I should give you some examples from the list (itself by no means comprehensive) of the type of expenditure which comes within this category:

a) There are 26 chauffeur-driven limousines, 15 of them assigned on a personal basis to individual senior officers. At the top of the list are Daimler Sovereigns, Jaguar XJ 3.4 litre and Rover 3.5 litre saloons.

b) The annual basic wage cost of the chauffeurs is £160,000. You will probably know how basic wage bills compare with the full costs of staff including overheads – a 100 per cent addition is not unusual.

c) The chauffeurs work an average of 1500 hours overtime per 4 weeks period.

d) The main areas of work for cars for Executive and Chief Officer are shown as 'Home to Work, out of hours functions, business/personal requirements, requirements from office, assisting pool, i.e. pool of cars, during working day.'

e) The total number of LTE cars used by management on a personally allocated basis is 164 with a further 60 'identified with officers/PEAs'.

Leaving aside, for a moment, the question of costs for an organisation facing acute financial difficulties, it seems that almost everyone in the first five or six levels of management finds our own product unacceptable! As to cost, depending on mileages run, I think £1,000–£2,000 per car is roughly the bracket which is indicated.

8. The catering and hospitality arrangements in force at present are similarly examples of indefensible expenditure. The following figures have been produced at my request. Apparently they have not been available before in this form.

a) Officers' Dining Club 2nd Floor (reserved for senior staff)

| | | |
|---|---|---|
| Direct Labour Costs | £54,860 | |
| Cost of Food & Beverages | 42,272 | |
| Total | £97,132 | |
| Less Total Receipts | 42,818 | |
| Apparent Subsidy | £54,314 | = 56% of cost of all meals |

However, these figures do not take account of the cost of accommodation, heat, light, maintenance, some cleaning, rates, capital depreciation of various kinds and a number of other overheads which are lost in LTE's general accounts. Nor do the labour costs include any allowance for the cost of cooking which is done in the main staff canteen kitchens. No figures are available for these items, but the LTE estimate of the rental value of the club is £42,000 p.a. The average number of meals served daily is 120–140 (say 130 per day or 32,500 per annum, based on a five-day week). This amounts to a subsidy of £2.96 per meal. With the missing costs added in, the subsidy per meal for these highly paid staff is certainly getting on for £4 and may well exceed that figure. Furthermore, the 56 per cent subsidy figure understates the case. Clearly about three-quarters of the costs of all these meals are being paid for by the passengers, the taxpayers and the ratepayers.

b) The financial arrangements for the Executive suite (used by the Executive, Chief Officers and their guests) was even more difficult to analyse. However, the following figures have been provided.

| | |
|---|---:|
| Direct Labour costs | £22,682 |
| Cost of Food & Beverages | 26,067 |
| Total | £48,749 |
| Less Total Receipts | 38,861 |
| Apparent Subsidy | £ 9,888 |

However, further questions elicited the information that the 'receipts' were merely transfers from other LTE accounts, so that the whole cost is borne by LTE. As with the officers' club, only the rental value of the suite is known and this added to £48,749 gives a total of £78,749 without taking account of all the items omitted from the ODC calculations.

The average daily use of the Executive suite is 18–20, say 100 per week, or 5,000 per annum, which gives a cost for every meal served of £15.74. There can be no doubt that with all the overhead and concealed costs added, the full cost of providing free meals to LTE's most senior management and their guests is between £20 and £30 per meal.

c) Though not in a category which I would regard as disgraceful, expenditure on the junior staff of LTE using the ground floor canteen is not inconsiderable. The 'apparent subsidy' based solely on labour, food and drink costs is £125,748 p.a., or 55 per cent of 'costs'.

This, on the basis of 175,000 meals per annum being served, would show a subsidy of 71p per meal. With all the additional hidden costs added, including accommodation, this subsidy would rise to over £1 a meal. This compares with 15p per day allowed for luncheon vouchers for staff outside the public service, after which everything counts as a taxable emolument.

9. Although the figures are less alarming, LTE's ideas on space for themselves are generous for an organisation in financial difficulties. Both the Chairman and the Deputy Chairman have offices bigger than those enjoyed by the Prime Minister, Sir Arnold Weinstock

(Managing Director of the GEC, which makes a profit) or Sir Derek Rayner at the Cabinet Office (where he is helping to reduce the losses).

The average space occupied by all the staff on the 7th floor is about 265 sq.ft. per head, which is about three times the allowance for those parts of the public service with which I am familiar.

10. The last part of para 9 of the 14 November letter refers to the more substantial savings which could be achieved by ending or curtailing in-house activities. Here are some examples, although unfortunately it is not possible to evaluate the potential savings except on an estimated basis.

a) A detailed cost study by LTE staff shows that it would be far cheaper to hire plant than to own and maintain it, even though LT overheads are understated and LT costs used unrealistically long plant life for depreciation calculations (30 years rather than 5 to 7 years).

b) Building and civil engineering maintenance by directly employed labour is badly managed and costs are high. The investigating team concludes: 'There is no effective management control at any level . . . The measure of performance has been judged as the extent to which the budget has been spent with no regard to the economic use of resources or achievement of work.'

c) These are only two of the damning conclusions covered by this report which was made on 13 March 1979. Nothing has been done about any part of it, and the responsibility for this rests with the Executive to whose attention I have repeatedly drawn this report and its implications.

This is not an unsupported view. I attach a letter addressed to me dated 28 September 1979, para 3 of which bears directly on this point.

d) A firm of independent investigators estimated that design and associated work cost 80 per cent more when done in-house compared with the use of consultants.

e) There is evidence of widespread waste of resources, over-manning, diversion of labour to unnecessary tasks, and the use of directly employed labour for activities which could be bought far cheaper outside in all the workshops operated by LTE. This applies most especially to Chiswick, Aldenham and the Permanent Way workshops. No workshop would survive, in a recognisable form, a really thorough investigation, and I doubt if any would survive at all. I suspect the savings would be of the order of 30 per cent – 40 per cent of current expenditure.

f) The planning and development functions, including technical development are very expensive and could without great loss be sharply reduced. I would expect savings of the order of 30 per cent.

g) There is far too much bureaucracy and 'administration' generally, very little of it cost-effective. Quite apart from all the other duplicating and reproduction of documents, the Broadway Headquarters, I am told, produces *1,000,000 photocopies per month*. I would expect a 50 per cent cut in these administration staffs to be possible.

h) Both the Group Supplies Department and the Estates Department should be re-examined. Both perform functions which could in part be reduced in cost, and in part be reduced in scope.

i) All the savings in sub-paras e, f, g and h above would be in the multi-million pound bracket.

11. It may be argued that although the expenditure on, for example, cars and chauffeurs and catering is open to criticism, the amount in total is small and would not take a penny off the price of a ticket. Leaving aside the consequences of this sort of example for the rest of the organisation (see para 12 below) the actual cost cannot be brushed aside. Many passengers complain about dirty trains. The extra cost of keeping a whole train in tip-top condition has been found to be £7,000 p.a. The Railway Board says it cannot afford to do it. But this figure should be compared with, for example, £200–400,000 p.a. for management cars; well over £100,000 for the ODC; probably about the same for the Executive Suite; the £160,000 p.a. basic (? £250,000 p.a. full cost) for chauffeurs; and so on.

12. However, the significance of this type of expenditure goes beyond the hard cash involved. The spacious office suites, the cars and all the rest of the top management's life style reflect in part a social order and a national financial situation which has long since passed away. Such things were in any case the trappings and perquisites of a flourishing, efficient and competitive organisation, and are not therefore something to which LTE is entitled now or has been for some time past.

13. In para 9 I refer to recriminations against staff who report unpalatable facts. The letter dated 28 September, already referred to, bears on this point also.

14. In para 14 (f) (i) I refer to the Railway Management Board's views. I attach a copy of the relevant minute.

15. The lack of effective management action to bring about staff and cost reductions in the past is referred to in several places. One of the questions I had asked was on progress by any earlier cost-saving projects. I was told of only one, which was known as the Clerical Work Improvement Programme. Set up in 1969, at a staff cost of £70,000 p.a., i.e. excluding accommodation, this unit has so far cost over £700,000. The LTE summary is that what it has achieved is 'of little or no value'.

16. The Transport (London) Act 1969, under the terms of which I was appointed by your Council to the Executive, requires (Part II, 5 (i)) that the Executive carry out its duties 'with due regard to . . . economy . . .' I consider that there is abundant evidence that LTE is not, at present, discharging their statutory obligations, and I am not prepared to let matters rest here. Perhaps when you and your colleagues have had an opportunity to digest this letter (for the length of which I am sorry) we could, before either of us does anything further, have an opportunity to discuss it. My own view, however, is that this is public business about which the public should be fully informed as soon as possible.

Yours sincerely
Leslie C. Chapman

At the end of November I spoke at length to Gordon Taylor by telephone. A record was kept of this conversation during which Taylor said that he felt the issues raised in my 22 November letter were too important to be dealt with by anyone other than Cutler. He had sent the papers to him (Cutler) saying that he agreed with every word.

Taylor went on to say that 'although Horace Cutler is making noises he isn't actually doing much'. This was partly because there had been a shortage of hard evidence to justify action but partly because he (Taylor) thought Cutler wanted to wait until nearer the elections 'for a bit of LT–bashing kudos.' I said that I could not accept that.

Taylor said that he was in favour of making public some of the matters I had raised, but no one else at that time had seen the letter, and he asked for 24 hours to allow the position to be digested.

Taylor concluded by saying that the Executive was made up very largely of Conservative Party nominees, and there was concern that they (the Conservatives) could find themselves labelled as part and parcel of the failure.

The Board meeting on 4 December was predictably a prolonged and very unpleasant affair. The principal point at issue was whether I had acted improperly by taking these matters to the GLC. The other members of the Board could not accept that I had the right to do this; I could not accept their view. Neither side moved an inch during these discussions, the sense of which was given in a letter which I sent to Cutler on 7 December.*

I also decided that it would be prudent to seek legal advice on my position, since at one stage legal proceedings against me were being threatened, and in any case I thought it well to resolve any doubts about the propriety of my actions. The advice I was given was clear-cut: as a member of the London Transport Executive appointed by the GLC, I had not only a right but a duty to report to the GLC on matters of policy if I considered them genuinely to be in the interests of the LTE. Furthermore, there being no distinction in the Transport (London) Act 1969 between full-time and part-time members of the LTE, I had an implied right of access to information and staff, and the LTE could not properly deny me such access or regulate it through a full-time member of the Board. In short, it was perfectly legitimate for me to seek to ensure that the duties imposed by statute upon the LTE in general and on myself as an individual member were fulfilled.

The statement at the end of my 7 December letter that if the issues were once again going to be fudged I would resign, was not an empty threat. I felt that I had spent a year getting nowhere, and the London Transport position was getting worse as I watched. Although Cutler was talking in forthright terms to Bennett, as witness his letter of 14 November, he seemed as Taylor had said to be hanging fire as far as action was concerned.

In the week before Christmas I was astonished to find that my letters to Bennett and Taylor had been leaked, at least in part, to the press. Both the London *Evening Standard* and the *Evening News* made front page headlines of those parts of my letters which dealt with meals and other aspects of high living. I spoke to Cutler later that day and asked him point blank if he could trace the responsibility for the leak but he said this was impossible. He thought 'at least a score of

* Appendix 5.

copies' of both letters, and some other documents, were circulating in County Hall amongst both Conservative and Labour members. As far as he was concerned, the matter was out in the open, and a good thing too. He intended to 'require' London Transport to have an independent investigation into the factual matters I had raised, and to report by the end of January.

The investigation was carried out by Deloitte Haskins and Sells, London Transport's own auditors. LT specified in detail the questions which the auditors were required to answer which, whether it was intended or not, did have the effect of limiting severely the ability of the auditors to make the sort of strategic appreciation of the position which was needed. I had said in effect that I 'guessed' or 'estimated' that savings could be made in this or that item, and that we should put in, by way of the Productivity Unit, the staff effort required to investigate. LT's response was to ask Deloitte's what evidence there was to support my statement, deliberately ignoring the fact that if the evidence had been available I would not have needed to ask for investigation! Deloitte's reply that there was no evidence, or insufficient evidence, could then be used by LT.

Nevertheless in this difficult situation the auditors did their best to be fair to everyone including the overriding public interest. Their final report which was made available by the GLC to the press ran to over 100 pages, but they produced a summary which gallantly and very properly tried to get away from detail and deal with the underlying issues which, as they understood, even if LT did not, was what really mattered. This summary is reproduced as Appendix 6. The handling of the Deloitte report by LT will be examined in greater detail in Chapter 9.

Readers can judge for themselves, by studying the summary in Appendix 6, the extent to which I was found to be right on the seven fundamental underlying issues identified by Deloitte. The GLC had no doubt about the implications. They gave London Transport two months in which to provide answers and to put forward proposals to meet the criticisms. Clearly they had not been impressed by LT's Press Release put out at the end of January in response to the issues raised in my letter to the GLC of 22 November. This release, which is reprinted as Appendix 7, needs to be mentioned at this point because, superficially read, it seems to contain a reasoned and reasonable defence against at least some of my allegations. A more careful study will reveal it as a mixture of inaccuracies and possibly misleading statements, and it will be examined in detail in Chapter 9 as a prime example of the ways in which public bodies can, and sometimes do, mislead the outside world accidentally or otherwise.

For the moment, though, Cutler was keeping the pressure on. On 15 February 1980 he told Bennett that he and his colleagues had been 'bitterly disappointed' by LT's responses to GLC directives. LT's 'brave promises and bold words . . . have dissolved into prevarications and delays which have become all too familiar.'

Contention number 6 in the Deloitte analysis of my criticisms dealt with management complacency. The report found that 'We have seen some evidence of LTE management being slow to act but it was not sufficient in itself to support the generalised statements.' It probably wasn't, but that was by no means the only evidence available on this point. I knew that yet another independent and world-famous management consultancy group were looking at LT's management performance and skills and that it would be reporting soon.

# 7

# London Transport: In Politics

The PA International report was submitted in April 1980 and was entitled 'Organisation of the Executive Board'. Two copies were sent in strict confidence to the GLC but otherwise it was seen initially only by members of the Board.

The Board's hope that the report would silence the critics was dashed to an extent which went far beyond their worst fears. So, too, was any hope that at least the full extent of the devastating criticisms could be kept under wraps. An optimistic belief that the report would in time vindicate the Board's policies had caused LTE to make frequent references to it in correspondence with the GLC and in statements which found their way into the press. In consequence, LTE's refusal to publish the report, or to say anything of substance about its contents, immediately and inevitably aroused great suspicion, especially as it was reasonably certain that if the report *had* been favourable it would have been triumphantly published with a great flourish and a minimum of delay. Horace Cutler made no bones about the fact that he wanted it made public, both in conversation with LTE and in his comments to the press. I was the only Executive member who took the same view as Cutler, arguing that if the Board had wanted to maintain its undoubted right to keep the document a secret, it ought never to have been so free with references to it beforehand. Quite apart from this, however, I believed that the report raised matters of considerable importance in relation to the management of a vital public service, which had absorbed every year scores of millions of pounds of ratepayers' and taxpayers' money, and whose functioning affected the daily life of millions of citizens. This was also Cutler's view.

I gave the Chairman of LTE notice that, while I would honour the Board's confidentiality ruling, I was not prepared to remain silent if statements were made by senior London Transport management, including Board members, which directly contradicted the wording of the report (and more especially its main recommendations), or in any other way accidentally misrepresented the position.

During May the Board made one last effort to avoid publication. It produced a memorandum which purported to summarise the report's findings and recommendations and its own response to them. By a dual process of diluting the criticisms and considerably overstating the actions already taken by the Board, an attempt was made (quite a plausible one in the absence of the report) to make it look as if all that had happened was that the Board's fundamental strategy and philosophy had been examined and found to be sound. The impression it gave was that, with a few minor adjustments here and a trifling shift of emphasis there, the path embarked upon two years or so earlier and the management action already in hand would, as the Board had always claimed, lead to the promised land, where buses ran to time, trains were clean, and fares stabilised.

This manoeuvre is used very frequently by public authorities, especially Government departments, and is one that almost always succeeds, given the ability of the authority concerned to keep the facts concealed – an ability which public bodies and large private sector organisations usually do possess. This power derives from two sources. First, the protection offered by the Official Secrets Act or its non-governmental equivalent in the shape of rules for employees and others about disclosure of information. Second, the power of patronage wielded by big spenders, who hardly need to hint that future preferment and opportunities to do business come the way of those who avoid rocking the boat. And for those who do rock it, the consequences are the gradual fading away of opportunities, and the odd word dropped casually in the right ears over lunch. It may not sound much, but it is astonishingly effective.

It is much to the credit of PA International that if such pressure existed in this case, the standard tactics did not work. In a memorandum dated 9 June, the attempt to play down the criticisms and play up the Board's part was effectively torpedoed. PA politely but firmly drew attention to 'a number of differences on interpretation which we detect between our detailed recommendations and those of the memorandum'. It went on: 'there appear to be important differences in emphasis, strength *and in some cases substance**\* between the [LTE] memorandum and the PA Report. . . . From the words used in the memorandum to the GLC it appears to us that the Executive is understating the extent of the change necessary. For example, the memorandum talks of a 'more complete change of management attitudes', which seems to imply that the Executive Board has already

---

\* My added emphasis.

made satisfactory progress in improving its management attitude or that only a marginal additional change is now necessary.' In fact, said PA, what their report had said was needed, and what the situation urgently required in their view, were *dramatic\** changes.

In effect, what PA were saying, in turn by implication, was that it was for the Board to accept or reject the PA findings, but the process of rejection could not legitimately be manipulated to involve a degree of misinterpretation or misrepresentation of their findings. By implication also PA were serving notice that whether such shifts of emphasis and changes of substance were accidental or otherwise, they were not prepared to go along with them by refraining from comment to the Board.

PA's response amounted to a refusal to go along with the Board on a course of action which once again avoided the issues and failed to deal with problems which were both urgent and important. This much-needed second jolt, although delivered in a velvet glove, was even more effective in its way than the original report. For the first time, the Board began to speak and act as if it accepted that there was to be no escape from the need for change. I was astonished, gratified and amused in roughly equal proportions when a Board member, without any prompting (but perhaps sensing new pressures), turned up at the June meeting armed with details for cutting out unnecessary office staffs in one part of the organisation and thereby producing savings of approximately £15 million per annum without any loss to LT activities. A few months earlier a suggestion that savings could be made of even a fifth of that size would have been met by derision and hostility.

Reform and repentance, however, were coming too late. Determined to distance himself and his party from London Transport failures, Cutler was out for blood in the form of public pillorying, and in mid-June (1980) again made it plain in a personal letter to Bennett that the report should be released to the press. He simultaneously made his opinion plain to the press by publishing the letter! With headlines being made every day by its refusal to publish and speculation about the contents becoming closer to the truth, LT finally gave way. On 17 June, the full report was published, accompanied by bigger and blacker headlines than ever before. The London *Evening News*, quite rightly sure that all its readers would know what it was referring to, had a page-wide one-word headline which simply said

---

\* My added emphasis.

'Guilty'. The editorial for the same day began: 'Never has the man-agement of a public service been so coldly exposed and condemned as the Board of London Transport is today. . . .' These were sentiments which were reflected in the reported comments of nearly all the national newspapers, and of TV and radio.

The summary and analysis which the Board had been so reluctant to publish, and on which the media fastened so swiftly, is reproduced as Appendix 8. The analysis lists as the predominant characteristics of the Board:

a) a limited sense of purpose coupled with an element of self-satisfaction;

b) lack of clarity and lack of agreement on objectives;

c) Board's members took narrow individual views of problems and their solutions rather than a corporate approach;

d) strategic policy issues were not discussed and were based on assumptions;

e) initial diagnosis was good but no effective follow-up action was taken;

f) emphasis was on cost not cost-effectiveness;

g) there was a cosy consensus approach to problems;

h) the Board was weak in the skills required to run a big business (this was mainly covered in the body of the report, not in the sum-mary).

The Board had already (in the May memorandum) accepted in broad terms the conclusions and recommendations. What mattered therefore was the action which would be taken by the GLC.

Left to himself, Cutler would, I believe, have been content to make some changes within the Board and to keep Bennett as Chairman, at least until the end of the year, and there is no doubt that this would have paid off. The Board was in no position to refuse co-operation, and I believe that there had been a genuine change of atmosphere. I found for the first time that it was possible to put forward proposals knowing that they would be considered on their merits as potential solutions instead of being dismissed as mischievous, irrelevant, im-practicable or misconceived. For a few weeks it seemed as if the worst was over and everything was within our grasp.

The golden opportunity was thrown away simply because, I sus-pect, the County Hall Conservative leadership was more concerned with taking action which they thought would serve them best politi-cally than with finding solutions to London Transport's problems. A reminder that they could not dissociate themselves too easily from these problems, as Taylor had forecast in his end-of-November conversation with me, was given by the London *Evening Standard* on 23 June 1980. With an accuracy that hit the Conservatives where it hurt, the article* said: 'The impression is that LT is managed to some extent by bumbling idiots. It comes as a shock to recall that most of the idiots were actually appointed by Sir Horace.' The article stopped short of pointing out that at this stage in Cutler's life it was hardly likely that his habit of picking a high proportion of losers was going to change.

In the meanwhile, the uneasy quiet continued. Although the Board went on bravely with the preparation of plans for the months and years to come (and did it with more sense of realism than ever before) it was obviously absurd to do much before the GLC took action. Unfortunately the weeks went by, and no action was taken, although rumours abounded. June became July and it was not until 25 July that the Council agreed to changes on the Board as follows:

1. Bennett was to be given three months' notice and to relinquish his duties forthwith. No replacement was named.
2. Maxwell (Managing Director, Railways) was to be replaced by a T. M. Ridley, hired away from a firm of consulting engineers.
3. The appointments of Masefield and Chapman, part-time members, were to be extended to 31 December 1981 and 31 December 1982 respectively.
4. The appointment of J. Glendinning (member for finance and property) was not to be renewed on expiry in December 1980.
5. The appointment of J. Stansby as Deputy Chairman was not to be renewed, although he was offered a lower-grade post. Although his appointment had only two months to run, it was made clear very pointedly that Stansby was *not* to assume the title of Acting Chairman.
6. The period of appointment of Michael Robbins (part-time) was not to be extended.
7. The salary of J. Cameron (Board member for staff and trade union matters) was not to be increased until the Council was satisfied that more was being done to negotiate higher productivity.
8. D. Quarmby (Managing Director, Buses) was to be reappointed for a further five years.

It would be difficult to find a more disastrous set of decisions relating to the running of a major public service. The treatment of

* 'LT: where does the buck stop?' by Richard Hope, editor of the *Railway Gazette*.

Cameron, which would have been petty and spiteful in any circumstances, was particularly foolish in that, alone amongst the full-time
Executive members, he had tried to do something about overmanning. Similarly Robbins (a part-time member) had contributed more
common sense than most. Quarmby's reappointment was linked
with the proposition that he had been 'the driving force behind the
new bus districts'. There had been no driving force behind this
project or anything else handled at Board level that I had ever seen,
or, I sometimes suspected, since the 1930s.

The worst error was to make the sacking of Bennett 'effective
forthwith' without having a replacement available. This was almost
certainly not of Cutler's choosing. He had told me in June that if and
when Bennett went it would not be earlier than Christmas 1980. He
agreed then that what was wanted was a youngish, thrusting, front-
rank manager from the private sector with the energy and ability
required to take London Transport in hand. What the GLC failed to
understand was that the services of such men can be obtained with
difficulty and not at short notice. If they are hanging around waiting
for a job they are probably has-beens or third-rate or, most likely,
both. Nor was the post of Chief Executive of LT quite the successful
manager's ultimate ambition as the climax to his career that the GLC
imagined. The precipitate sacking of Bennett in which spite, malice
and the Conservative Party view of what was expedient politically all
came together, left the GLC in a hopeless position. Bennett was not
even to be allowed to work out his notice. His sacking was notified to
him on 25 July (the same day as the GLC meeting). He issued an
innocuous LT General Notice (No 2187) on the same day giving
details of this and other changes at Board level and saying that he
would be leaving shortly. The GLC, determined that there should be
no ambiguity about the meaning of the phrase 'terminated forthwith',
and equally determined not to lose any opportunity to humiliate
Bennett, wrote to him on 29 July:

'My attention has been drawn to a statement which you issued within
London Transport on 25 July as General Notice No 2187. You will, I
am sure, understand that I have today authorised Mr John Stansby,
the Deputy Chairman of London Transport, to make it clearly understood that your responsibilities as Chairman have been relinquished
and that accordingly you no longer act as such.'

In the meanwhile, the part-paralysis of planning which had
obtained since the PA Report was published in June, dragged on

through August. Finally, in early September the appointment was announced of Masefield, erstwhile part-time member, as Chairman and Chief Executive.

The most far-reaching and damning criticism of the London Transport Board by PA International had been that it was weak in the skills required to run a large business. The new Board suffered even more from this disabling infirmity. This was confirmed by the attitude which was at once taken up on the issue of cost-cutting which had been central to the disputes of the past year. Cutler had made much of the intention that I should be made responsible for a cost-cutting drive, and had linked this in his public and private announcements with the extension of my period of appointment to the Board.

Whether the need to make this arrangement a part of the package forcibly prescribed for LT was overlooked, or whether the attempt was made and was blocked, is not apparent from the papers, although I suspect it was the former. In any event, when the new Chairman and other Board appointments had been confirmed, Cutler and the GLC Tories were more than ever the prisoners of their own ineptitude. After the unprecedented public inquests and bloodletting, the last thing they wanted was a further round of disagreements with the new LT Executive. Whatever happened, they had not only to keep the peace but constantly to bolster up the proposition that all the problems had been solved due to their decisive action. From a position of total helplessness the Board became overnight the frail vehicle of much of the GLC Conservatives' 1981 electoral hopes and ambitions, and in consequence completely safe from criticism. Although the users of London Transport could have detected no difference in the services they were receiving, not one unkind word was spoken by any Conservative leader in public about Boards, buses or trains before the 1981 election. This sustained public relations exercise was helped by lavish spending on the part of LT through press and TV advertising (and paid for, therefore, by taxpayers and ratepayers) to sell the idea that things were improving, and that the new management was a rip-roaring success.

The cost-cutting project was one of the first casualties of this squalid piece of political jobbery. The commitment had been made too publicly to be dropped completely, and I was therefore offered a job as Chairman of a Productivity Committee, which would have no staff, nor access to staff; no powers; and would consist, apart from myself, entirely of full-time members of the Board. In case this left any

room for useful action whatsoever, the Committee could deal with
nothing but matters normally dealt with by the main Board. The
main Board ('The Executive' remained its official title) was to
become more and more a 'holding' Board, with subsidiary Boards
responsible for most management matters. This shift of powers and
responsibilities away from the Executive meant that the once-a-
month meeting for an hour or two which was all that was envisaged
for the Productivity Committee was, if anything, an over-generous
allowance of time for an exchange of chatty generalities which would
be all that would be practicable. The letter I sent to Masefield
declining the job is reproduced as Appendix 9.

I had no contacts with Cutler at this time, but a journalist asked
him for his comments on my 'non-job' statement. Cutler replied,
apparently quite seriously, that he 'could not interfere in the management of LT'. This statement, in view of the events of the past 18
months, was greeted with profound relief by the Board, and both
inside and outside LT with varying mixtures of derision, astonish-
ment and amusement.

By October 1980, the new style of managment was beginning to
take shape. This included, although it was a consequence of the PA
Report and the aftermath rather than of the change in management, a
greater awareness of the dangers of management complacency –
dangers to management itself, that is! And stemming from the same
source, there was more sense of urgency and realism. But that was
about all, apart from some rather childishly gimmicky tricks.* No
discussion or criticism was to be allowed. It could not be tolerated if
expressed outside LT. On 31 July a notice was issued to full-time
Board members asking them to ensure that no one, however senior,
spoke to the media without a Board member's permission. The
circular went on, rather optimistically: 'it would be a very good thing
if press coverage concerning LT were to be reduced to positive
statements concerning real news events and initiatives directly affecting passengers. . . .' Any statement could be made, any opinion could
be expressed – provided it was favourable to the new management.
Anything else was disloyalty. Within LT, at least at Board level,
differing views could be expressed – in theory. In practice, no secrecy
attached to the rapid progress being made towards the Executive
being deliberately isolated from the running of London Transport.
Such matters as needed to be brought before the Executive, for the

* For example: the monthly financial statement was rechristened *The Howgozit!*

time being, had already been settled by the full-time members, who now had five out of the seven places. It was all very far removed from the intentions of Parliament and the GLC as expressed in the Transport (London) Act 1969.

One swift consequence of the new arrangements was that I was cut off from the flow of papers which over the years it had been agreed should be seen by Board members. As a result I was prevented from seeing the 1981 budget which was designed to sustain and carry forward the joint LT/County Hall Tory confidence trick aimed at persuading the voters that all was well and getting better. Had I done so, I do not think I could have improved on the Labour Party comments* on this document. It was, they said, 'one of the most appalling frauds that the Council had perpetrated on London's public . . . a simple straightforward election fraud'. They went on to ask whether LT had submitted this 'ridiculous document' as a result of political pressure or because LT had learned from the previous year what happened to honest budgets.

Neither was wholly true. What had happened was that LT management and the Conservatives saw advantages to themselves in gulling the public. Cutler offered as his sole reply the profound statement that 'LT was not an easy job'. It does not sound like the same man, or the same party, that such a short time before had been saying that all LT's problems were a matter of management skills, (which was true), and that if the then managers couldn't do the job they must be replaced.

In the meanwhile I had avoided initiating any public statements (or indeed taking any other action in connection with LT). On the other hand I was regularly asked to comment on LT affairs by the media who, in London at least, were faced with the facts of life on buses and trains which looked very different from the propaganda nonsense emitted by LT and the Tories. On these occasions I took the line that no one had the right to tell me I could not talk to the media. I was not prepared to use devices like 'no comment' which, coming from an individual appointed to the Board of a public concern by the elected representatives of the public, seemed to me not so much unhelpful as downright impertinent. I was not prepared to go along with untruthful propaganda. And that left only the answering of questions in a way that was truthful as I saw the facts without gratuitously striving to cause damage.

* At the GLC Joint Policy and Resources and Planning and Communications Policy Committee, 2 Dec 1980.

This was not acceptable to the new régime. A broadcast I made at the beginning of November was taped, and the tape was, to the accompaniment of horrified (and well rehearsed) comments, played at the November Executive meeting. I refused to modify anything I had said, and since it was obvious that this was to be made the occasion for a trial of strength I left the Board meeting, and arranged to see Cutler.

I told Cutler that I thought it would be impossible for me to do a useful job in the prevailing circumstances, and suggested that I revert to the position of retiring when my first term of appointment ended (i.e. 31 December 1980). London Transport was a time-consuming, expensive and disagreeable duty, as far as I was concerned, and I would be glad to see the back of it.

Cutler, very much to my surprise, was anxious that I should stay for the next two years. Surely, he said, I could ride out the dispute with Masefield. The Board had sent him a copy of the broadcast tape and a dossier of press comments over the last two months, as well as copies of some of my letters. There was nothing in them, said Cutler, which could be faulted so far as he was concerned. True, some of my comments were critical but that was what I had been put there for. He proposed to tell Masefield so, and say that he thought the cost-cutting project should be revived in a meaningful way. For a start, he would like to see me tackling the big workshops. Masefield would 'have to consider his position' if he did not like it. In any case his appointment would end, at latest, in September 1981, and desirably well before that. Finally, volunteered Cutler, perhaps detecting rather more than a faint shade of doubt in my expression, he would write to me within a few days making his position clear. I confess that I half expected him to default on this, or at least to write in somewhat ambiguous terms. He didn't do either. His letter of 13 November was both prompt and unequivocal:

Dear Leslie,

## LT BOARD MEMBERSHIP

Following our discussion the other day I am writing personally to let you know that I do not propose to seek the revision or rescission of the Council's decision of 25 July last.

Yours sincerely,

Horace

Masefield (I assume after getting a copy of this letter) telephoned me asking for a meeting. I refused to make a special trip from Wales, but said that I would be attending the next Board meeting. After that meeting I had a private discussion with Masefield, which he attempted to summarise in a letter dated 5 December. His summary was completely inaccurate so far as I was concerned, but I wanted to avoid refuting it at this stage in order to preserve what appeared to be a change of a period, if not of amity, then at least of watchful neutrality. I therefore decided to talk to Masefield again after the January Board meeting.

In the light of Cutler's letter of 13 November I was somewhat puzzled to receive on 3 January 1981 the following letter from Sir James Swaffield, Director-General and Clerk to the GLC:

31 December 1980

Dear Mr Chapman,
You will, no doubt, be aware of discussions between the Leader of the Council and the Chairman of London Transport Executive about the composition of the present Board, future requirements and the need for a period of stability.

In the light of these discussions, the Council has decided that, at least until March 1981, there should be no new appointments or reappointments of Board members to allow time for the new management style to be more fully developed and a careful assessment to be made of the optimum size of the Board and the most beneficial division of responsibilities.

Yours sincerely,
J C Swaffield

The decision not to make 'new appointments' seemed not to be relevant to me, since my reappointment for two years beginning 1 January 1981 had been made back in July. I spoke to Cutler by telephone on 4 January when he arrived home after his Christmas break. He professed to know (and I still believe him) nothing about the letter and took the view that although very ambiguous, it had no bearing whatsoever on my position. The council in full session had approved the extension of my appointment to 31 December 1982. No one but the Council could change that, and such a change had not been and was not going to be proposed, still less approved. Perhaps, he said, the letter was a general one intended for information only. He would look into it and clear things up immediately he returned to work.

I spoke to Cutler again at midday on Tuesday 6 January. He told me that 'nothing has changed. Your appointment for the next two years stands.' He went on to say that he thought it would be useful if he, Masefield and I could meet. I agreed, and it was later arranged that this meeting should take place on 13 January at 4 p.m. at County Hall. I decided that it would be expedient to have my reply to Masefield's 5 December letter on record. This is reproduced as Appendix 10.

Masefield and Swaffield were both present at this meeting. Cutler referred to the 'very ambiguous' letter of 31 December and, without even the briefest mention of his conversations with me, or his letter of 13 November, explained that he had made a 'very confidential and personal agreement' with Andrew Mackintosh, the Labour Opposition leader, in August. The substance of this was that in order to reach speedy agreement at that time on the new Board arrangements and avoid a situation in which the opposition party could have held things up at least for a few weeks (which would have created further difficulties) he had agreed that there should be no new Executive appointments extending beyond March/April 1981. This would leave the field clear for whoever took office after the election in May 1981. He had done this, as had Mackintosh, in the belief that this served best the interests of the public and of London Transport, and he hoped that I would accept the position on that basis. I replied that I could certainly accept it, if it were true. I could understand the circumstances in which such an arrangement could be reached, and the need a few months before to reach speedy settlements.

In the course of the next half-hour or so I asked Cutler three times to confirm that the termination of my appointment was solely due to this private agreement and had nothing to do with my dispute with Masefield which, to the extent that it was mentioned at all, seemed in the light of what Cutler was saying to be an irrelevant coincidence. Each time Cutler looked me straight in the eye and assured me that that was the case. At the end I said I accepted what he said because he had never given me any grounds for doing otherwise but if anyone else had told me the same story, I would have called him a liar. Cutler said more than once that he wanted to have another and private talk with me in the next few days, and I assumed that he would be telling me rather more then. I particularly wanted to know, if only to satisfy my own curiosity, why on earth he had not told me in November that there was a problem; why he had written as he had on 13 November; and why he had said what he had, earlier in January.

I said that I was quite happy to go on this basis, but I insisted on clearing up the charges of disloyalty which Masefield and the Board had constantly made, otherwise I would seek a ruling from the High Court on the point. Cutler said there was no shadow of a dispute over this. He would rule unequivocally, there and then, that I had acted properly and he reminded me, truthfully, that he had already said this several times publicly. Nevertheless, I insisted that he formally disown Masefield's and the Board's statements, and it was left that Cutler should see the Board minutes concerned.

The further private meeting did not take place. After a month in which I had heard no news of Cutler's examination of the papers, I wrote to him again. This letter dated 7 February 1981 and Cutler's reply dated 19 February are reproduced in full as Appendix 11. Cutler, by design or otherwise, continued, by bringing in press leaks, to avoid the real issue. The attacks on me, with Masefield the most vociferous, for taking matters to the GLC were begun, and were at their most vicious, at the Board meeting on 4 December 1979. That was nearly three weeks before any word of the contents of my letters had reached the press.

In March I was able to establish, through contact with Andrew Mackintosh, Leader of the Labour Opposition Party, and Ken Livingstone, then Deputy Leader, and Labour Party spokesman on Transport affairs, that neither had the slightest recollection of the agreement referred to by Sir Horace Cutler, or of any agreement remotely resembling it.

In April, Mr Livingstone was able to provide me with further information. He had said that he had been mildly surprised when he had heard that I was leaving the Board but had seen a document which appeared to explain the position. This document, a confidential paper from the Director-General of the GLC addressed to the Planning and Communications Policy Committee (which I should normally have seen, but did not by some curious chance!) was dated 22 December 1980, but it is noted in manuscript on Mr Livingstone's copy that this paper was not sent to the Opposition until 4.10 p.m. that day. By that time the office was, of course, already in the grip of Christmas break arrangements. I have not been able to trace any Conservative or Labour member who knew of this document until after the beginning of 1981. Those to whom I have spoken then assumed that for some reason I had myself decided not to take up the extended appointment. I reproduce in full the first paragraph of this extraordinary document:

'On 25 July last, the Council authorised a considerable number of changes in the membership of the Board of London Transport Executive. In the four months since then, Sir Peter Masefield has been appointed as the new Chairman and Chief Executive, relinquishing his appointment as a part-time member of the Board, the new Managing Director, Railways has taken up his post and the Vice-Chairman and one part-time member, Mr Robbins, have left the Board as their terms of appointment ended. *During the next month,** Mr Glendinning will leave when his appointment ends and *Mr Chapman's term of office as a part-time member will expire.** Mr Maxwell, who is now acting as Chairman of London Transport International, wishes to retire in March.'

The memorandum ended with a recommendation that no new appointments or reappointments be made until Spring 1981.

The statement that my appointment would expire during the next month can be explained only in two ways, as far as I can see. One is that it was false. The second is that it was technically correct because some piece of procedure in connection with reappointment had been omitted, accidentally or otherwise. Either way it follows that somehow the GLC's decision to extend the appointment, formally recorded, widely publicised, and confirmed by subsequent GLC and LT statements, had been set at nought.

The recommendation looked like an innocent proposal to let matters take their course and old appointments lapse, leaving a few vacancies until the future was clearer. No decisions, except to leave things alone, were required from anyone. This too is how it was understood by those elected members with whom I have had contact.

In a Granada TV programme in the 'World in Action' series, Cutler was asked repeatedly why my appointment had been terminated. I gather that a good deal of film was used up before a clear statement emerged. In this version Cutler made no mention of the arrangement with Mackintosh or of the memorandum. (Indeed I question whether he knew about the latter.) He simply said that it had been necessary in order to 'stop the hassle'.

Readers will no doubt wish to form their own judgments about the truth of these matters.

After the TV programme I received, as is quite usual, a number of

* My added emphasis.

letters from viewers. I reproduce the following one (from a total stranger) for no better reason than that, while expressing views essentially no different from all the other letter-writers, it does so in a way which shows that it is really not possible to fool all the people all the time.

28th April 1981

'Dear Sir,

*World in Action Programme on London Transport 27.4.81*

I was absolutely gripped by this programme, but as I didn't know it was going to be so exciting I did not have a pencil and paper handy to write down the vital facts. Is it possible to have some sort of transcript, if not could I have answers to the following questions?

1. Is London Transport controlled by the GLC, and can it, if it makes a loss, just go to the GLC and ask for more?

2. How many cars do London Transport keep for Executives, and what is the total cost of running these? (If any people ought to travel by London Transport, surely it should be these Executives.)

3. How much does the Directors Dining Room cost? Can I possibly have heard that each Executive meal is subsidized to the effect of £17?

4. Did Sir Horace Cutler sack Mr Chapman? Why should he want to oppose economies? I thought the Conservatives were supposed to want them.

5. Mr Chapman. He sounds a man after my own heart, really ferreting out the crazy waste of money. I would like to know his full name, if poss his address, and also what it was he did before he came to London Transport.

6. What was the name of the super villain of the piece, rather like a fat pink pig, who kept saying "we must work as a team to improve things"? He obviously did not want anything ferreted out.

7. If possible a list of all the expenses that Mr Chapman thought were outrageous. There was one of 15 million.'

I must say that reading this letter, and many others like it, confirmed my feeling that the public is more difficult to hoodwink than is commonly supposed by politicians and their henchmen. I failed to make my colleagues in LT understand the need for drastic remedies for waste. Ratepayers and taxpayers are already rightly suspicious of public sector standards of management and of political motives. I think they will have no difficulty in understanding the implications of the kind of economies which could and should be made in London Transport, and which I shall now examine in greater detail.

# 8

# London Transport Waste

The nature and scale of the opportunities for making economies in London Transport operations provide useful information and pointers about the general problems of public sector waste.

One of the most frequent responses I met in London Transport from Board level downwards amounted to 'Why pick on us? We are no worse than any of the others, and better than many. You should know what *we* know, for example about the GLC.' There was rarely, if ever, a discussion on waste and associated matters where this line of defence did not emerge at some stage, and the shortcomings of the GLC were a never-ending source of complaint.

There was probably a good deal of truth in this, and certainly what little I saw of the workings of the GLC and other London boroughs did nothing to suggest anything but an atrociously low level of management competence – far below the average local authority. Chapter 10 dealing with Camden throws some additional light on this.

From the point of view of the captive consumers of public services, of course, this defence, however true, has a limited relevance. The fact that the ratepayers who willy-nilly pay for the incompetence of the GLC are being robbed is very little comfort to the passengers on LT who are paying more than they need to for their tickets.

The rare opportunity, therefore, to see behind the screen which normally prevents the public from knowing how its money is wasted is too good to be missed. When the size, in percentage terms, of the possible economies is being suggested, it is worth bearing in mind how they are being made, and by whom. They are not wild generalisations, inspired guesses or anything of that nature. They are the products of careful investigation, with the facts and the figures available in detail, and access to the staff concerned. Secondly, the enquiries were not carried out by people with a political or other kind of axe to grind, or motivated by hostility. They were carried out to a considerable extent by LT staff. If there was any lack of objectivity it was a bias in favour of London Transport. If I had a fault to find with the investigations it would be that some of them were far too soft, not too harsh. In some instances, the best that could be said for them was that they were a useful preliminary dose of medicine, perhaps as much as the patient could be expected to take to begin with, which could be followed up later by rather stronger treatment. It is against that background that the following findings need to be considered.

### A.1. *The Cleaning of LT Premises*

A study carried out by the Central LT Productivity Unit in 1980* showed that immediate savings of approximately 15 per cent could be achieved by switching from direct labour to contract cleaning. Further substantial savings would be possible. 'Compared with the cleaning costs of local government offices, LT pays dearly for direct labour cleaning.' Making all possible allowances, 'the annual cost of direct labour cleaning is typically two to five times more expensive than contract cleaning'. Despite the high costs, the report said, the user departments were dissatisfied.

### A.2. *Cleaning of Railway Stations and Bus Premises*

A report† was prepared which in effect covered the cleaning of all areas not included in A.1 above. It was carried out by LT staff who found the familiar evidence of overmanning and waste. On the 1979 budget of £6.26 million savings of £983,000 (i.e. approx. 15 per cent) were identified, with more to come.

### B. *Vegetation Control*

An investigation of the cost of maintaining gardens at a number of works and offices showed that costs could be reduced by 50 per cent.

### C. *Allotments*

The administrative cost of letting allotments was approximately ten times the total rent received.

### D. *Office Accommodation*

A preliminary review of accommodation not involving long-term planning or capital expenditure showed that savings of 13 per cent of the cost of rented accommodation were possible.

### E. *Inspection and Possession of Railway Tunnels and Tracks*

This investigation relates to the methods and costs of making tunnels

---

* 'A report on the cleaning of Head Office, Works, Railway depots, catering establishments and other premises', CPU, April 1980.

† A report on the cleaning of Railway stations and Bus premises, LT, April 1980, carried out by R. M. Wheeler, K. H. Wellman, and I. C. Gledhill, LT Central Productivity Unit.

and tracks available for services of various kinds. It was carried out by
independent consultants,* who reported that 'the evidence clearly
shows that ... substantial losses are occurring and are of such
magnitude as to warrant urgent attention.' The consultants said, of
the potential saving, 'we are convinced ... that it will indeed be
substantial ...'. Unofficial estimates by LT staff put the potential
savings at not less than 25 per cent and quite possibly 35/40 per cent.
The consultants found the position to be '. . . highly disturbing. It can
lead to the impression that costs do not matter.' Much work would be
needed to get things right but '. . . such is the scope for savings that
the effort and cost of doing so will be repaid within the first few weeks
of implementation.'

### F. *Building Departments and Building Maintenance*†

An investigation was carried out, extending over a period of months,
into the way in which LT executed its building maintenance work – a
£15 million per annum activity vital to the passenger-carrying organisation. The investigating team was headed by John Hoban, Assistant Chief Civil Engineer of LT, and included Angus Greig (see
pages 55 and 101) and a representative of a firm of consultants.
Amongst the findings of the team were:

1. *Staff*. An extensive advertising campaign was in progress for staff
of all kinds. There was no management basis for the levels of trades
which existed or for those being recruited.

2. *Budget*. Estimates were prepared without site visits. The bulk of
the year's estimates represent figures for the last year with inflation
added.

The manpower requirements are assessed by taking the budget
produced in this unsatisfactory way and then dividing by a standard
labour rate.

The net effect of these two arrangements was that neither money
nor staff allocated for this work bore any relationship to the physical
work needing to be done. It was merely a system for perpetuating
expenditure at a steadily increasing level.

3. *Use of Contractors*. 'No comparison existed to show the cost of
direct labour work compared with contractors. No real basis there-

* 'LT Railways Pilot Study on Inspection and Possessions, June 1980' Leslie Hayes &
Associates Ltd.
† LT Organisation Review: Building Departments & Building Maintenance, 13
March 1979.

fore exists for management to judge the cost-effectiveness of direct labour.'

In the absence of this management information, the team itelf carried out cost comparisons on a few complete station renovations. They found that 'direct labour costs were 50%–100% more expensive than contractors . . . and work in the joinery shop is normally 50% more expensive . . . and sheet metal ducting work has proved to be twice as expensive as outside contractors.'

*Workshop and Yard Activities*
'No evidence existed for the work content of the money spent.'

'. . . no comparisons were seen of equivalent outside costs. . . . There has been no Works and Building management consideration of the operational requirement or economic viability of the Workshops.'

*Overhead Expenses Generally*
No management control of overhead costs exists within Works and Buildings.

*Plant*
Costs were high; stocks of many items of plant were in excess of requirements.

*Earlier Investigation*
In October 1967, Urwick Orr and Partners Ltd carried out an enquiry and their findings were very similar to those of the 1979 Report (save that by then the situation had noticeably worsened in many instances). The 1979 Report concludes, of the Urwick Orr investigation: 'There is no evidence that due account has been taken [i.e. by LT] of many of the recommendations for improvements.'

*Summary of Findings*
The concluding summary by the team is worth reproducing in full:

'It is considered that Works and Buildings are operating at present without any clear plan or purpose. There is no effective management control at any level and management information has increasingly fallen into disuse. The measure of performance has been judged as the extent to which the budget has been spent, with no regard to the economic use of resources or achievement of work. Unless firm measures are taken the performance of Works and Buildings will continue to decline.

Throughout the investigation the full-time members of the team were struck by the claim, either direct or implied, by staff within

Works and Buildings, as to how they took a commercial approach. In spite of this claim there was at no time any indication that such an approach was ever taken.

## G. *New Construction*
An investigation carried out by independent consultants* found that 'the total number of technical staff engaged on premises schemes in LT was 80 per cent greater than the level we would have expected'.

## H. *Central Office Staffs*
Most of the staff of LT are in either the Bus or the Railway 'businesses'. Some, however, are headquarters and similar staff which it would not be appropriate to include in the two major groups.

In June 1980, in the more realistic climate which followed the PA Report, an Executive member produced proposals for economies in these staffs. They amounted to £15 million per annum on a budget of £62 million, i.e. approximately 25 per cent, with no loss of efficiency.

The savings listed above are not by any means a comprehensive list of those which were found once investigations began. From the end of 1979 I was prevented from seeing a good deal of material, although occasionally snippets reached me unofficially. During 1980 three firms of management consultants,† quite independently of each other, told me that they had been variously shocked, horrified and amazed at what they knew about LT (not necessarily as a result of operating directly for and within LT). They were entitled to do this at the time since I was a member of the Executive. Unfortunately they feel now that there might be some breach of ethics if they give me permission to quote them by name. It will therefore be easy for London Transport to say that I have exaggerated or invented the allegations. If that happens, it will be interesting to see whether this will cause one or more of the consultants to shed their anonymity.

In late December 1981, two months after the typescript of this book had been delivered to the publishers, an end-piece to the story of waste in London Transport was unexpectedly provided by an admirable piece of investigative journalism. Peter Hounam, a reporter with the London *Standard*, accompanied by a photographer, Stuart Nicol,

---

* Report by Atkins Planning on construction management, quoted by Deloitte Haskins & Sells in their published report (paras 177–9 inclusive).
† None of the three was one of those mentioned by name elsewhere in this book.

produced an account (on 22 December) of three days of visits to LT's main transport maintenance works in Acton, London. The following is a summary of their report:

Day 1 '. . . about 200 men are drinking tea, reading books or standing chatting. One machine is being operated. Perhaps another 50 are idle . . . we arrive in the motor shop, where another 100 men are spread among dozens of work-benches and parts awaiting repair. One group . . . is playing cards. Others are listening to radios or reading. We see no one working . . .'

'. . . By now, 3.15 pm, people are busying themselves for going home. Official stopping time is 4.15.'

Day 2 'We go to the canteen at noon. About 100 people are sitting at tables. Many are still there two hours later when we leave to go to the huge motor shop. . . . Perhaps six out of 100 men are working. In the truck shop 150 people are sitting chatting or reading. . . . In a workshop where carriages and engines are stripped and rebuilt 45 out of about 50 men are sitting around chatting. . . . in a [carriage] repair shop five men are slumped in a cabin chatting. In another a man is fast asleep. Thirty others are chatting or reading. No work is being done.'

Day 3 'We return to the carriage shops. . . . only six out of 50 people . . . are working. . . . In the neighbouring paint shop no one is painting. At 2.20 tea is already being served. . . . After tea we visit the motor shop. At 3.05 pm people are already queuing to go home.'

London Transport management declined to answer questions from the media about this report, and on the following day the GLC decided to hold an inquiry.

Many readers, while sympathetic to pleas for reducing waste in the public sector, may feel that its size and the degree of inefficiency it reveals are exaggerated. The *Standard* report is independent, unbiased and backed up to the hilt by photographs and other evidence. What those reporters found in LT Acton is duplicated to my certain first-hand knowledge wherever I went elsewhere in LT, and in the other parts of the public sector to which I have had access.

# 9
# 'Secrecy is a Sickness'

The facts about waste in London Transport are useful as corroborative evidence of management shortcomings in the public sector. Much more valuable are the lessons that can be learned from the way in which LT responded to public criticism, and the light this sheds on the behaviour of public bodies, and the standards of accuracy which can be expected from them.

The process of misleading the public, the media and anyone else likely to be critical is regarded by all public bodies as an essential tactic for survival. It has also become an art form in which its practitioners delight almost for its own sake. The use of *this* word and *that* phrase, which, oh so delicately, nudges the truth a little further into the shadows, is a skill which all first- and second-grade public servants must acquire, polish and practise. It is very likely that if you hear one of these people dismissing Mr X contemptuously as having no political sense, or no loyalty, or no tact (senior professional people such as engineers, doctors, and scientists are particularly liable to err in this way) then the chances are that he has been telling the inconvenient truth. Of course, professional training does tend to discourage those with this different kind of integrity and different values from blurring the facts, or ignoring them if they are unpalatable. This explains why those who are professionally qualified are rare amongst top management in the public sector.

It is not usually possible to dissect, analyse and check against the facts the statements made by public bodies and thereby remove the layers of cosmetics which distort the reality. By a fortunate chance LT has provided one of the rare opportunities for doing so by its detailed response to the publicity which attended the leak of my confidential letter to the GLC of 22 November 1979. I have already referred to this Press Release (see page 71) which is reprinted in Appendix 7. I suggest that you refresh your memory of it now so that, in order to avoid the risk of repetition, I may confine myself in this chapter to quoting only the relevant paragraph numbers and key passages.

Bear in mind that before it was issued this document was seen by most, if not all, the members of the Executive (save myself, of course) and substantial numbers of senior management below Executive level. It was therefore anything but an off-the-cuff statement in which occasional minor lapses, however regrettable, could perhaps be understood and forgiven. It will be for the reader to decide, whether at the end of this analysis, there were 'lapses' which were not occasional, minor, forgivable or understandable.

Anyone reading this document by itself could be forgiven for feeling that this long-suffering organisation had yet again been harshly and unfairly treated by an ill-informed and hostile critic. The organisation courageously and honestly admits that it is not perfect (which group of human beings can claim more?) but generally speaking things are really quite good. Let us now remove the cosmetics and look at the facts behind the statement.

*Paras 1 and 3–6.* These paragraphs read as though LT had bravely suffered in silence while the auditors' report (see page 71 and Appendix 6) was being prepared. They were now free to answer the criticisms but even then were doing so only in an altruistic effort to safeguard the interests of Londoners generally and LT staff morale specifically.

But why at that particular moment? Why make a statement a few hours before the report was due to be published? Londoners generally and LT staff, if they were indeed waiting with bated breath for the report, could obviously have waited another six hours, having already waited six weeks since the first press leaks. The truth is, of course, that it was only possible to make some of the statements in the press release if it purported to have been written in ignorance of the findings of the report. But this was not the case. LT staff had been working with the auditors on the production of the report, and senior management in LT, including the Executive, knew the contents of the report well before the issue of the press statement.

*Para 2.* 'Mr Chapman's detailed allegations. . . . contained a number of inaccuracies', stated the release. The compelling desire to make this assertion was no doubt one of the reasons why the press notice of necessity *had* to precede the publication of the auditors' report, because the latter is quite specific on this issue. The report says (Section II, para 15):

'We have identified the sources of most of the information in Mr Chapman's letters with regard to the level of expenditure on cars, chauffeurs and offices, and have carried out investigations to assess the accuracy of the information given (paragraphs 96 to 150). The information is substantially correct and such differences as do arise do not in our view significantly affect Mr Chapman's argument.'

These are the issues of fact. The question of whether this expenditure on cars, catering, chauffeurs and the like is disgraceful is of course a matter of opinion. The auditors recognise this and say the expenditure is not disgraceful '*if comparison with nationalised industries is relevant** . . .' I did not accept the relevance of such comparison, and neither did many other people including the GLC, the media, or the LT passenger and ratepayers' associations who got in touch with me. The GLC gave the Executive two months in which to submit proposals for dealing with the matters on which there had been criticisms.

*Para 7.* This paragraph suggests that my facts were obtained from 'relatively junior levels' and that they were not checked for accuracy. Again this is best answered by quoting from the source. The following is a minute by Mr Angus Greig to LT's Chief Secretary. This officer was the man whom Bennett himself appointed to provide me with the information I was seeking.

GENERAL NOTICE 2137 (attached to Press Notice 746 dated 31 January 80)

I was dismayed, and indeed upset, when I read Paragraph two on page three of the General Notice 2137 issued to the Press yesterday.

I must point out that the information supplied by me to Mr Chapman in accordance with your memorandum of 6 July, was obtained formally and at a responsible level. The information on Catering Costs was obtained from the Assistant Personnel Services Officer (Catering) after my discussion with the Personnel Services Officer, these two gentlemen being the most senior in Catering in London Transport. On cars the information was obtained from the Distribution Services Manager who cleared it with the Chief Supplies Officer who, I understand, in turn discussed it with his Executive Member, Mr John Cameron. Moreover, Mr Cameron himself supplied me with additional documentation which he said was already known and need not be filed.

In the light of the publicity given to the Chairman's statement and the likelihood of further publicity I am writing to you to put the facts on record.

The theme that I was making allegations without appropriate

* My added emphasis.

consultation recurs in paragraphs 18 and 19. Here is a prime example of another favourite disinformation device – making a totally accurate statement in a way which produces a totally false impression. It is quite correct that there are few records of my having discussions with senior staff, including Executive members. The implication is that therefore no such discussion took place. They did, on numerous occasions, but there had not seemed then any need for records to be kept.

*Paras 8–11.* Cars.(i) 'LT could not operate effectively without the use of cars.' It seems a sad admission from the world's biggest urban transport authority, which spends a good deal of energy and rate-payers' money persuading other people to leave their cars at home because LT is better and cheaper! But accepting that run-about cars are necessary, my objections related to the use of big saloon cars – Jaguars, Daimlers, Granadas, and so on, some air-conditioned, some with chauffeurs. The sort of transport needed for LT's business operational purposes could have been adequately provided by mini vans painted LT red and carrying LT insignia. The only objection to the use of such vehicles was that they were not what LT management wanted for their private use.

(ii) It is not true (para 10) that only twenty people were permitted private use of these vehicles. It is not true that this is on a self-drive basis only. A Granada TV documentary team filmed an LT employee being picked up at his home by a chauffeur-driven car. Presumably it was a regular enough occurrence to enable the TV crews to know when and where to go for their incontestable evidence.

(iii) Although it was claimed by LT in January 1980 that the cars and chauffeurs were necessary for them to function efficiently, by the following April arrangements had been agreed in private to reduce the number of chauffeurs by 50 per cent as a first step towards achieving a defensible number which was later determined to be three. I understand now, with the pressures gone, old life styles may be returning!

*Paras 12–15.* (i) My objections to the catering facilities for senior staff were that separate and increasingly expensive facilities were provided as staff became more senior. It is not true that such a policy is commonplace in the UK among large-scale employers. The Civil Service, for example, provides subsidised catering – and anyone of any grade who wants a subsidised meal can use that one facility.

(ii) 'The dining suite on the 10th floor . . . is used only for business entertainment.' I produced incontrovertible evidence for LT that this statement was false. One item of evidence was the menu for a dinner party for a Scottish football team and some supporters! LT's response was: 'The wording [of the Press Notice] was somewhat truncated and doubtless should have spelt out the full practice. . . . On certain limited occasions it may be made available to Executive Members or top management for private and quasi private guests. . . .'

After this small masterpiece the expression 'somewhat truncated' enjoyed a brief vogue in LT as a euphemism for any statement proved to be blatantly untrue.

(iii) 'Mr Chapman's claim that the cost of meals . . . , including overheads, is £20–£30 is substantially overstated.' Untrue. The auditors' report states (para 137, page 53) that the cost was £17 per head with 'only part overheads included'. The only thing in question, as LT knew, was whether, with all the overheads counted and all the calculations done correctly, the figure could have been kept under £30!

(iv) The need to entertain foreign visitors is stated in paras 14 and 15, and sounds convincing. But meals involving foreign visitors account, according to the auditors, for only 9 per cent of meals served. It was by no means unusual for the visitors to be entertained by anything from 5–10 times as many LT official representatives and hosts, so the overseas flavour was considerably diluted.

*Paras 16 and 17.* Office Space. LT knew that a great deal of waste existed in the use of office space and this was subsequently confirmed by detailed surveys. See p. 89.

*Paras 18–22.* Other Allegations. (1) 'No serious requests for information were made.' False. As already described in relation to para 7, I spent months doing just that, through machinery agreed by Bennett.

(ii) 'Claims that £25 million – £50 million per annum could be saved . . . are not supported by the evidence.' Let the auditors' report answer this. It says (para 32, page 14): 'Mr Chapman's claims that . . . £25 million – £50 million a year could be saved are not proven by the examples given in his letters. *However it is clear from his wording that he does not represent that they are.*'* What the auditors correctly understood me to be saying was that I considered that there was a *prima facie* case for thorough investigations of expenditure extending over a number of years as a result of which I believed economies of that order would be found. Elsewhere in the report the auditors support this statement.

* My added emphasis.

(iii) The statement that '80 per cent of certain building design work could be saved by external contracts' cannot be substantiated. Of course it can't, but I did not make that statement. The auditors confirmed that I had correctly quoted the consultants' findings that staff costs were 80 per cent higher when the work was done in-house (i.e. if costs are 80 per cent higher it is costing 180 per cent of what it should. Reducing that 180 per cent to 100 per cent requires a reduction of about 45 per cent of 180 per cent. The potential saving by using consultants is thus 45 per cent approximately). The auditors also say that the calculations (by the consultants) on which this statement was based are reasonable.

(iv) The statement that '50 per cent of administrative staff are not required' is not substantiated. As with the £25 million – £50 million savings, I had not claimed to have substantiated my allegation. I was arguing for thorough investigations based on my assessment of the position. What LT conceals, however, is that they had already been obliged to concede to the auditors (see para. 17 of Appendix 6) that the organisation had become too bureaucratic.

(v) 'The Central Productivity Unit [was] set up before Mr Chapman's allegations were presented to the GLC' and by implication as a result of the wise policies of the other members of the Executive. The exchanges between Bennett and myself and the dates provide an effective answer to this piece of nonsense. On the same day as the Press notice was published, interviews were being given on radio and TV. The following statement is taken from the official transcript of the BBC's Nationwide programme, 31 January 1980. Similar statements were made on other networks.

Wellings:
(BBC interviewer)

But presumably, Mr Bennett, you're not saying that there aren't areas where savings can and should be made?

Bennett:

Not at all . . . because of that we set up our own Central Productivity Unit to look into all the possibilities of achieving improvements in this direction long before Mr Chapman arrived on the scene.

In fact, I had 'arrived on the scene' on 1 January 1979. The Central Productivity Unit had been set up at the end of October 1979. The setting up of this Unit had been the central point in my dispute with the Executive generally, and the Chairman in particular. It had been that central point for several months and Bennett himself had signed the order setting up the Unit. In those circumstances it was an astonishing slip of the memory on the part of Bennett and the Executive.

Astonishing or not, the effect was to take a good deal of pressure off the Executive. LT's statements, both in the press release and on TV, were given wide publicity and did at first sight appear to give an adequate answer to at least some of my criticisms. By contrast the over-100-foolscap pages of the auditors' report which required careful and prolonged study was read by comparatively few people. My documented reply to the GLC was unpublished.

The wide publicity given to LT's statement was due in part to the activities of its own private propaganda organisation. The possession of large well-paid 'information departments' (well-paid at the rate-payers' and taxpayers' expense, of course) is, however, only one weapon from the armoury available to the public services. The Official Secrets Act is already well known for the effect that it has in central government in keeping a blanket of concealment over things which are far from being 'official secrets' in the genuine sense. As interpreted at present, it provides a cover for every kind of incompetence, malpractice and mismanagement. But while the OSA is the only secrecy-enforcing device which is backed by the law, the non-government public services have their own effective methods of imposing silence and compliance on their staffs. Appendix 12 shows how an attempt was made to close me off from information by requiring me to operate through a bogus rule. This method didn't work. Instead LT staff were told not to give me information, although it is admitted by Bennett in the Press Release already examined that I had a right to it (para 18).

For individuals who had been too honest in reporting accurately what they had found, other methods were used. John Hoban, the senior officer who had been the Chairman of the group investigating building works, was praised for his report when it was first produced. Six months later, in September 1979 (before my disagreement with the Executive became public), he was writing to me as follows:

28th September, 1979
Dear Mr Chapman,
I feel it necessary to write to you before your Budget Meeting on Monday as I and my report are being more discredited as time goes on and Angus Greig is under strong pressure from above due to his unpalatable views and his association with you. He is also suffering in

his attempts to obtain for you the information you require; as I told you once before you are regarded as an outsider and there is great reluctance to supply you with the information which you have every right to receive as a member of the Executive. . . .

The re-organisation is getting nowhere; more posts are being created, more people are being up-graded and more money spent without any improvement in efficiency. In my view it should be halted temporarily at least. . . .

I will not dwell on my report on building maintenance except to say that it was submitted in March and received with acclamation by four members of the Executive including yourself. I was then asked to make recommendations for immediate implementation which I did on 4th April and since then nothing of any consequence has occurred, I have merely become a pariah. . . . A team has been set up to push around my report as a substitute for managerial action and the essential aspects are not being dealt with.

Yours sincerely,
J.B.L. Hoban

Mr Hoban retired prematurely from London Transport in September 1981.

A similar fate overtook Angus Greig, the senior officer seconded by LT to assist me in fact-finding. The following is a letter to me from him dated 12 February 1981. At the time of writing it Greig had been without a job, or even a place to sit, for months.

Mr Chapman
I am writing to you because my position within London Transport has become almost intolerable. . . . I was told that one of [the] difficulties in finding me another job was a consequence of my association with you – hence this letter. It could well be that I am imagining a conspiracy but I doubt it, therefore I enclose a history of events up to the present. . . .

I have been told by my trade union I have a very strong case for constructive dismissal and I must say this is certainly one of the options. One of my most serious objections to going back to the CPU is that the man who worked on the 'Work Study Report' which concluded overmanning was criticised at a promotional interview because he had produced an unpalatable report. The situation really is 'catch 22'.

Yours sincerely,
A. Greig

This was not a new development in LT tactics. I had (quite literally) scores of letters from LT staff and ex-staff complaining of this sort of treatment. I reproduce extracts from a typical one which reached me via Cutler.

*re: Mr Chapman's report on London Transport*
'The *Daily Telegraph*, in its article by John Shaw on Monday 24 December 1979, stated that Mr Leslie Chapman had been told by London Transport to adopt the normal procedure and go through a full-time board member.

This appears to be a clear admission by London Transport that Mr Chapman is getting uncomfortably close to the truth and is clearly designed to obstruct Mr Chapman in his task which you allotted him.

As a former employee of London Transport in its Chief Electrical Engineer's Department, I can vouch for the fact that LT's efficiency leaves considerable room for improvement . . . but LT management would act on a recommendation (only when) the offending employee had been removed from the scene.

For my temerity in daring to suggest that management was not infallible, which I compounded by showing some moral fibre in the face of overt blackmail by my superiors, my previous promotion was not confirmed at the end of my probationary period so that I was demoted and returned to my original section.

Please believe me when I say that this letter is not that of a bitter and twisted ex-employee but is intended to back up Mr Chapman who seems to be fighting a lone battle.

It is my belief that London Transport suffers from its unshaken belief in the divine right of management to be infallible.

LTE's setting up of a productivity unit will be little more than window-dressing; unless Mr Chapman is supported to the hilt, all his efforts to improve efficiency will have been in vain.

I can imagine the frustration which Mr Chapman is feeling at the moment, it is matched by the fist-clenching frustration which I felt many times in the Chief Electrical Engineer's Department.'

I did not receive letters of this kind only from LT staff. They related to many other parts of the public sector. For example in the early 1970s under the Heath Government's policy of getting advice on civil service functions from successful businessmen, Mr Timothy Sainsbury was invited to look at government land holdings and the procedural machinery for managing them. Subsequently there was set up, with a considerable flourish, the Property Review and Development Group. The following letter which I have selected (because I know from first-hand experience that it is wholly truthful and accurate) was sent to me by a Senior Estate Surveyor in the PRDG:

'The PRDG was a newly formed Headquarters' group set up with a degree of urgency in response to political criticism that the Crown was failing to manage its own properties, and that there were many unused and under-used properties throughout the UK, particularly in the Defence Estate.

The Group was unique in reporting direct to the PSA Board. The professional staff were hand-picked, able and dedicated, and no expense was spared in providing support staff, equipment, and accommodation. The Group's function was to examine selected properties which, from background information, had potential development redevelopment rationalisation or sale value. One early discovery was the existence of over ten million square feet of hutted accommodation, some of it dating back to the first world war, a lot of it situated in prime commercial locations.

A series of carefully drafted confidential reports were quickly issued to the PSA Board from the multi-discipline team; but it became obvious within the first year that the in-built resistance to change which permeates the Civil Service, coupled with an unwritten policy by the Commanding Service Officers in charge of the Defence holdings against disposal, would prove to be a substantial hurdle.

In an effort to overcome the inevitable excuse of the lack of public money where capital was required as often happened on rehousing and redevelopment cases, the Group produced a research paper on the Lease and Lease-back system of funding, demonstrating that UK Institutional funds could be used, but this was suppressed by Treasury on the pretext that it could be criticised as back-door public expenditure.

Seeing the increasing futility of the Group's effectiveness which was undermining the morale of the staff, [I] applied for a transfer. PRDG was eventually wound up at a cost of several million pounds to the taxpayer, with great loss of face and without implementing any of the many written recommendations made in the Reports. An opportunity of very substantial saving in public capital investment and optimisation of estate management was lost. One member of the group, a Principal, suffered a heart attack through anxiety, and the remainder of the staff dispersed in a thoroughly disillusioned state of mind.'

In 1980, this surveyor gave up in disgust and took early retirement. Clearly Whitehall has nothing to learn from lesser bodies about the art of blocking the activities and careers of those amongst its staffs who upset the Establishment apple-cart.

Nor have local authorities much to learn about the business of silencing critics and preserving their public façades. The following letter (again one of many involving local councils) is from an architect.

28 April 1981

'Dear Mr Chapman

I watched with interest the TV programme about you in 'World in Action' on Monday. Your experiences seemed very similar to my own.

I was employed as Principal Architect by —— Council, and while there found that overstaffing and the resultant carrying out of unnecessary work, were causing problems in my own section. Having complained about this a number of times, accusations were then made against me. I was accused of "rocking the boat", staff were advised not to speak to me and accusations were made against my wife and family. I was advised to leave, when I did not do so two architects from the Royal Institute of British Architects were brought in to investigate the department.

They reported that the organisation was satisfactory, but that I should be dismissed. As a member of the RIBA myself, I found this very disturbing.

After my dismissal, I found that neither the investigation nor the report were by the RIBA. (If I had not been on one of the RIBA's regional committees it is unlikely that I would have found this out.) The President of the RIBA, at my request, wrote to [my District Council] pointing out the misleading nature of the report. I wrote to [the Council] asking for an explanation.

Despite the intervention of my MP, they have refused to reply and the RIBA will no longer answer my letters. I am now taking legal advice about the situation. Incidentally, three people, out of the eleven in my section, have faced actions for dismissal under similar circumstances. I am amazed at the lengths some authorities will go in order to maintain their systems.'

On 12 May, he wrote again with the following comment:

'It may be of interest to you to know that since being dismissed in

September 1979, I have made 46 job applications. Apart from a preliminary interview in October 1979, no-one will even see me! I appear to be on some form of "blacklist" which operates in both the public and private sectors. In the present economic climate, private firms are increasingly dependent on public authorities both for work and the necessary approvals – which would make such a list easy to operate.'

You may feel this chapter deals with only isolated cases of disinformation, distortion and victimisation, and that occasional lapses by big authorities are to be expected. Here are two further statements which deal not with specific individual instances but with the more general problem:

'Mr Christopher Underwood, president of the Institute of Journalists and Home Affairs Correspondent of the BBC, said at the Institute's annual conference in Bristol that journalists were also being asked more often to suppress news usually because "it would be in the public interest". . . .

There are many areas where there is no apparent reason for official secrecy in which the public are still kept unaware of the facts. The reason would appear to have more to do in many cases with saving the government of the day from embarrassment than with anything relating to national security or public protection. . . .

The other worrying issue was the way the media were being increasingly manipulated . . . by authorities generally. They were finding themselves being fed not just with misinformation but with information that was wrong.'*

Are journalists, in your view, not sufficiently objective on this issue? Here are extracts from a paper by a Conservative MP,† who is now a junior Minister:

'Secrecy is an illness of Society. Since the last war government in Britain has become more and more inefficient. The people have become increasingly unhappy at the way the country is run and they blame the politicians for bad conditions. The real trouble lies hidden behind a wall of secrecy. People are not told the truth because it is a secret and not in the "national interest" to disclose what has gone wrong. . . .

When secrecy hides the work that goes into a job, slovenly irrespon-

*The Times, 29 September 1980.
†Kenneth Warren, MP.

sible workmanship passes undetected. Standards fall and anything goes. The work of our government is traditionally secret. There is a convention of "wisdom" that there shall be secrecy. Secrecy has become a disease spread by bureaucracy. . . .

The deterioration in the efficiency of government in Britain is particularly disastrous because the country is committed to state ownership of industry. The long record of inept management of publicly owned enterprise, which is born of secretive government, creates ready made ammunition for those of use who oppose the nationalisation of industry. . . .

On general principles we are all concerned regarding the success of management by government. Taxpayers pay the piper and should have some say in calling the tune. Secrecy in government deprives them of this elementary democratic right. . . .

There is another aspect to secrecy which transcends all party political considerations. I refer to the most basic of all human rights, the right to know the truth. In Britain we only have a right to know what we are officially permitted to know. It is illegal in Britain to know unless the knowledge has been officially released. Such a state of affairs is incompatible with true democracy.'

Perhaps you feel that misleading the media is the only form of defence which public bodies can adopt when faced by so much hostile criticism. It does not stop there, by any means. Here is the GLC Transport spokesman commenting on the preparation of statistics relating to the use of direct labour, one of the very important ways in which public sector activities and LT in particular needs to be tested:

'In response to a suggestion from Mr Howard that the London Transport paper (i.e. bus maintenance) included a strong argument for the employment of direct labour Mr Mote (chairman) said that 80 per cent of the works through put referred to in para 12 of the LT report had been artificially selected to prove their own views.'*

This is not a PR man talking to a journalist. This relates to the information being supplied by a major public body to the elected assembly who provides much of its money and has the statutory responsibility for the overall direction of its affairs. To adapt a phrase which became well-known in the USA – would *you* buy a second-hand bus from an organisation like that?

* GLC London Transport Committee meeting, 30 June 1980, Item 7.

# 10

# Bad News from Camden

Early in 1981 the slowly growing body of evidence about indefensible public spending was again added to by activities in London.

In 1978 the concern felt by commercial ratepayers in the London borough of Camden about council policies and council spending caused them to commission a report (at their own expense) into what was going on. That report was largely ignored, and at the end of 1980 a further report was commissioned, triggered by the fact that the commercial rate had increased from 92.8p in 1978/79 to 132.8p in 1980/81 (a 43 per cent increase) plus a supplementary rate of 6p making a total increase of 50 per cent. Further heavy increases in 1981/82 were expected.

The investigation was made by Alex Henney who had been a Chief Housing Officer of a London borough, and for a time had worked in the Department of the Environment on a Review of Housing Finance. In that capacity our paths crossed briefly when he visited me at my Southern Region HQ at Reading. After the first edition of *Your Disobedient Servant* was published Henney got in touch with me, and an extract from the subsequent exchanges between us (which have continued ever since) appears in the second (Penguin) edition.

Henney was a good choice for Camden. The report he made to them* was a first-class piece of work and fully deserved the widespread publicity it was given. This chapter is a factual précis of the figures and the main conclusions, taken straight from the report but with added comment and interpretation.

Camden is a relatively small authority compared with other boroughs and metropolitan districts. Its residents are more highly educated and prosperous than in nearly all other London boroughs, and in consequence a lower proportion are in semi-skilled or unskilled jobs.

It has also fewer housing and social problems than many other boroughs and provincial cities. Camden on average ranked thirteenth

* 'The cost of Camden' (1981), a report by Alex Henney made on behalf of the Camden Commercial Ratepayers' Group.

in terms of 'problem indicators' among the 32 London boroughs, and thirty-eighth in England. Accordingly Camden cannot be considered a deprived inner area although there are some poor parts. Camden spends 50 per cent more per head on services than the average of inner boroughs, and its local expenditure (exclusive of rate support grant from the Government) is over twice that of the next door authority, Islington.

Camden employs more people than do neighbouring boroughs:

| | Number | Employees for comparable services per 1,000 population | Multiple of national average |
|---|---|---|---|
| CAMDEN | 7,557 | 40.4 | 2.53 |
| Islington | 5,117 | 30.4 | 1.90 |
| Westminster | 5,967 | 28.4 | 1.78 |
| Haringey | 5,106 | 22.6 | 1.41 |
| Barnet | 4,640 | 15.6 | 0.98 |
| Average England and Wales | | 16.0 | 1.00 |

The report estimates that if all local authorities were staffed at the Camden level there would be another *million and a quarter council employees* in the UK. Domestic ratepayers account for only about 20 per cent of Camden's rate income, but have 100 per cent of the votes. The number of council employees (full- and part-time) increased from 4,260 in April 1965 to 7,897 in September 1980. Camden now employs more staff than most other boroughs; indeed it *employs 2½ times the national average for the services it provides*.

The cost of these employees has increased substantially in real terms over the last two years. Between 1978/79 and 1980/81 Camden's expenditure on salaries and wages increased from £35.5 million to £53.1 million, an increase of 50 per cent during a period when earnings in general increased by about 39 per cent. In part this is due to the very favourable terms of employment, which include a 35-hour week and a wage supplement – 'the Camden supplement' for manual workers which was negotiated in 1979 and ranges up to £10.89 weekly. If Camden's staffing levels were comparable with Westminster's, which is itself generously staffed, Camden's complement of

5,300 people would be reduced by 2,250 (i.e. 30 per cent less) which would save £16 million per annum in employment costs, and about 30 per cent of the cost of accommodation, a further saving of £1.4 million per annum.

The report next examines six council operations in detail, namely:

|  | Net Revenue Expenditure £m |
| --- | --- |
| Housing | 29.8 |
| Building Works | Recharged to Housing |
| Architect's Department | 1.7 |
| Planning Department | 1.7 |
| Developments | 1.1 |
| Leisure Services | 9.1 |
|  | 43.4 |

*Potential areas of reduction totalling £11.55–£16.55 million are identified.*

1. HOUSING

The reason for Camden's crippling debt charge is its big programme of capital spending coupled with the high cost of its new housebuilding programme. The amount of the interest on the housing debt incurred in recent years gives a clear indication of Camden's rate of spending. It is the second highest in London, and is far higher than any provincial city except Birmingham. Over the financial years 1975/76 to 1978/79 the Council's Housing Investment programme cost about £183 million at 1980 prices, and for this provided about 2,750 dwellings. This gives an average cost of about £66,000, a figure well in excess of private sector prices for one-, two- or three-bedroom units in Camden, which range from £25,000 to £50,000.

While some sites have been extremely expensive – Branch Hill £10,000/plot in 1972, Fitzjohns Avenue £25,000/plot in 1975 – the main reason for this expensive housing is not the cost of the land, but the way in which schemes have been designed and executed. The designs have been complex, and have used materials of high and unusual specification. Complexity has resulted in long pre-contractual and construction periods, involving high interest costs at all stages. For example, the Council took four years from site acquisition to the start of construction work on the site called Maiden Lane I; six years to start on West End Sidings; and seven years to fail to start on Speedan Towers. Once on site the average time it took the Council to complete schemes is probably the longest of any authority in the country.

Further costs have been incurred as a result of abortive work on some schemes. For example, since 1973 there have been four abortive designs for major schemes. About £300,000 has been spent on fees, much of which was wasted.

About £295,000 has been spent on design and other fees for a site in Haverstock Hill. The first scheme was cancelled on 15 November 1978 with fees of £250,000 being written off. A second scheme, on which £45,000 has been spent has been suspended and its future is now uncertain.

Another result of the complexity of Camden's schemes has been the high level of professional fees incurred. The fees on a sample of schemes were 12 per cent of building costs compared with a DoE estimate of 9.4 per cent average for London authorities as a whole, and 5–6 per cent for private flats in London. Fees for Branch Hill cost-indexed to 1980 prices are £15,000, £8,000 and £6,000 respectively. This compares with private sector costs of about £500/unit for houses of a comparable size and about £1,200/unit for flats of a comparable size. Eighty-five man years of architectural effort went into Alexandra Road, a scheme of 520 units. (In addition there was substantial input of engineering and quantity surveying.)

Heavy construction costs arose, due both to the extremely high standard of specification of materials – joinery, bricks, concrete work, external works – and to the unusual and complex nature of construction.

The expenditure at 1980 prices is as follows:

|  | Total Cost/Unit £ |
| --- | --- |
| Highgate Newtown I | 71,000 |
| Alexandra Road | 76,000 |
| Branch Hill | 176,000 |
| 48–52 Fitzjohns Avenue | 105,000 |

Despite the high costs there have been a considerable number of complaints about the performance of completed schemes. According to a press report, a recently completed scheme has 'severe water penetration in some flats, drainage problems on parts of the estate, facing bricks falling off, and severe overheating'.

A recent committee report estimates the costs of rectifying leaking windows and dampness on a scheme of 32 flats, completed several years ago, as £77,000.

More money is wasted because the Council has left unused land with a capacity for about 1,000 dwellings. This is a cause of waste of which many local authorities are guilty. Far too many of them maintain land banks for which they have no development resources. In Camden's case the sale of the land would realise about *£6 million* and would save the rates £200,000 per annum.

The District Auditor referred to another cause of wasteful spending in his 1979 report on Camden: 'Some of the acquired properties are not examined by building inspectors of the Housing Department in order for suitability for conversion or improvement to be considered prior to purchase. Since the cost of rehabilitation is usually considerable, it seems prudent the inspections should be made in every case and assessment of the likely cost made prior to purchase.'

The most extravagant renovation scheme was of 1 and 3 Great Ormond Street, to produce flats for 19 people. The cost of works and fees was £300,000, a cost/unit of £37,500 for works in 1976–78, about £60,000/unit in current prices. Adding interest costs makes the total cost/unit about £70,000 in today's prices. There was in fact no need to renovate these properties for housing – they could have been used for offices, a use that would have covered the cost.

If half of the empty units were sold they would realise a sum of the order of £10 million. Selling empty units would save the rates about £0.5 million per year.

In 1977/78 Camden's expenditure on housing maintenance of £5.4 million exceeded the amount spent by all Districts except Birmingham, Manchester, Liverpool, Leeds and Sheffield authorities which had between 2½ and 5 times as many housing units. Despite the high level of spending on maintenance there are frequent complaints about it, just as there were about construction and design. The 1976 Review Panel stated that 'the Council's performance in carrying out repairs has frequently been subject to criticism'. The majority of the 300 letters from councillors that the Housing Department currently receives weekly are about maintenance. The Panel commented on the complex procedures, and noted that the Building Department's costs were high. The reasons for this were analysed, and it was concluded

that the Council's maintenance budget could be cut substantially by:
- reducing the size of the Building Department and using contractors;
- improving productivity in the Building Department and tightening the bonus system;
- reducing the level of internal decorating, which accounts for about 14 per cent of the repairs budget.

Outside London, tenants generally undertake far more of the internal decorations. In 1977/78, while Camden spent £26 per dwelling on decorating, Manchester spent £10, Sheffield £10, and Birmingham £7. It should be possible to halve the cost of decoration, while continuing the same service for elderly people. This would cut the budget from about £1.4 million to about £0.7 million.

Except for a reduction in internal painting, it should be possible to achieve savings of the order of a quarter to a third of the 1980/81 budget of £9.8 million *with no reduction in service to tenants*. Indeed, by streamlining administration, services might well improve.

There are times when phrases such as that used at the beginning of this section '. . . the Council's performance in carrying out repairs has frequently been subject to criticisms . . .' do not adequately express the nature of the problem. I thought that in this case the views of a Camden council tenant might supplement effectively the formal reports. The following is taken from copy letters to Camden council, received by me independently of the Henney Report and the Camden commercial ratepayers:

'It took 13 months and 4 or 5 visits by plumbers – *one* visit should have done the trick – to mend a simple fault in my lavatory cistern. As a matter of fact it *still* would not have been fixed had I not written to the Town Clerk, the Director of Housing, etc. . . . The manner of Camden's discharge of its responsibilities is a paradigm of its other activities, attended by incompetence, philistinism, colossal waste of the public's money, little imagination, less of enterprise, and the oppressive, grey embrace of fraternal love exuded by the tuppenny-ha'penny clerks of Nalgo who, between them couldn't run a charity bazaar and show a profit. . . . [This building] is a stinking cockroach-infested slum. It is also perennially at risk from mice plague. The drains stink, the dustbin site (up against a tenant's flat) stinks, the pipe service channels (a structural defect but it is capable of amelioration) also stink, the hot, dirty, dark, damp basement to the boiler-house also stinks (and now for the good news . . .) the incompetent building dept regularly —'s about with the drains but never masters the problem. . . .

'Recently all casement windows were replaced. Only 33 flats plus staircase. The job took 9 months. It was a balls-up from start to finish. I haven't seen the lying timesheets but I would guess the site was empty (or doing nothing) for nearly half that time.

'It is a tedious, time-and-energy-wasting business sorting out the money-wasting administrative stupidities of Camden Council. . . .

'[We should] dismantle the huge cosy warren of unsackability and inflation-proofed pensions that is Camden Council, complacent, spendthrift, under-productive, over-manned, over-unionised.'

On legal advice, I am very reluctantly and regretfully omitting all the best parts of this gentleman's admirably pithy expressions of opinion on the Council members and staffs. The original letter was sent to the Council, so there should be no problem of checking the validity of the extracts, but if Camden have any difficulty I will gladly give them more detailed references.

*Housing Management*
Camden's general management expenditure per unit is the highest in the country. The costs for 1977/78 were:

| | General Management Expenditure per Unit £ |
|---|---|
| CAMDEN | 145 |
| Kensington & Chelsea | 124 |
| Lambeth | 92 |
| Lewisham | 91 |
| Brent | 89 |
| Haringey | 52 |
| Manchester | 33 |
| Liverpool | 31 |
| Birmingham | 31 |

Despite spending most on management, which includes rent collecting, a DoE survey revealed that rent arrears in 1975/76 amongst London boroughs were on average 5.5 per cent of rents. This was nearly twice the national average. Camden was the highest of all the London boroughs at 14.7 per cent.

A main reason for this considerable management expenditure is the generous staffing levels in the Council. Between January 1971 and December 1978 the staffing of the Housing Department grew from 172 to 429 posts, an increase of 150 per cent. During the same period the number of properties increased from 20,500 to 30,800, an increase of 50 per cent.

Reducing general housing management costs to accord more nearly with those of other authorities would produce annual savings of about £1.6 million.

The cost of other management expenses is also high. Excluding central heating, for which a part charge is made and which is dealt with separately, the cost in 1977/78 was £2.1 million.

The major element of expenditure is caretaking and cleaning, amounting to £1.3 million per annum, followed by the lighting of common parts and lifts. The high costs stem largely from the design of the schemes. The Council's Housing Review Panel suggested in 1976 that 'consideration be given to the possibility of designing future housing schemes with a view to less need for caretaking'.* It seems to be a not unreasonable innovation! In 1979, the Alexandra Road scheme of 520 units was completed. It provides for eight caretakers, one per 65 flats, which is about double the normal requirement. The lay-out has made it necessary to have a nightly security patrol before the Council could get anyone to insure the glass lift. Lights have to be left burning all night in the car park (as they do on other schemes). It should be possible, given an injection of common sense into the arrangements, to make changes leading to a reduction of about 20 per cent in the cost of special services. These services cost £3.5 million in 1980/81 and unless something is done will become progressively higher. The annual saving would therefore be £0.7 million minimum.

The Council is budgeting for a rapid increase in its net contribution (i.e. cost minus amounts paid by tenants) for heating in schemes supplied by district central heating, from £14/unit in 1978/79 to £58/unit in 1980/81, a total of £843,000. Somewhat late in the day a report to the Council in 1979 announced the discovery, long after most other authorities became aware of it, that district central heating was almost twice as expensive to run as individual heating units (and also more prone to failure, which when it happens affects many

* The panel's comparison here was with the Barbican.

more people). The Council ingeniously ensured even greater waste by designing their heating schemes for small developments, where they are even less economic than in larger schemes, thereby getting the worst of all worlds. In the Alexandra Road scheme an extra wasteful twist was added by installing a heating system that cannot be controlled by tenants other than by opening windows and letting the heat out into the open.

Except for cases of special hardship, there is no justification for one part of the community – a certain group of council tenants – having their heating costs subsidised, while other parts do not. Cutting out the heating subsidy for all except those in genuine need (estimated at about one third of those subsidised) would save £550,000 per annum.

*Other Housing Services*
About 91 per cent of Camden's net revenue expenditure on housing is spent on council housing. The other major items of costs are:

|  | £m |
| --- | --- |
| Rent Allowance to Private Sector Tenants | 0.19 |
| Improvement Grants | 0.20 |
| House Purchase Loans | 0.05 |
| Housing Association Support | 0.16 |
| Homeless Families | 0.25 |
| Housing Aid Centre | 0.24 |
| Public Health Inspectors–Housing | 1.29 |
| –Other Work | 0.16 |

Rent allowances and improvement grants are statutory obligations which apply to all authorities. While leaving those untouched, however, there should be scope for reducing the cost of the administration of improvement grants which employed 14 staff in 1977 when 77 full grants were completed and 13 in 1979 when 62 were completed – five grants per member of staff per annum is extremely low. Savings can also be made in connection with home loan subsidies and housing associations.

Camden's Housing Aid Centres cost $3\frac{1}{2}$ times Haringey's (£0.07 million), and there seems to be good reason for believing that these costs could be halved while still maintinaing an adequate level of service. The total savings available in connection with these housing services is about £0.65 million.

## 2. THE BUILDING DEPARTMENT

### A. Maintenance

The Building Department undertakes most of the maintenance, but only 8 per cent of the new building. Its poor performance is a major cause of the high cost of Camden's maintenance work, and a subsidiary reason for the high cost of new building.

In 1976 the Council's Housing Review Panel looked at council house maintenance and obtained quotations for 'broadly comparable decorations'. Taking the lowest cost as the base line the quotations were as follows:

|  | *Index of Costs* |
|---|---|
| Contractor A | 100 |
| Contractor B | 107 |
| London Borough Building Department A | 128 |
| London Borough Building Department B | 111 |
| CAMDEN BUILDING DEPARTMENT | 141 |
| Contractor C | 142 |

The Review Panel found that comparison of costs with the other Building Departments suggested that the basic rate of pay in Camden was 20 per cent higher, the bonus system was more generous, and the Camden operatives worked a $37\frac{1}{2}$ rather than a 40-hour week. The Panel concluded that 'a detailed study is necessary to determine ways in which Camden's services can be made more cost-effective' and recommended that the Building Department 'indicate ways by which its charges can be brought into line with other building departments and contractors'.

### B. Capital Projects

Comparison of the cost of the work carried out by the plumbers and painters showed it to be higher than the cost of similar work carried out by contractors. In the case of plumbing, a comparison based on up-to-date tenders showed that direct labour was about twice as expensive as contractor's work. An important constituent in the high direct labour costs was unjustifiably high bonus levels. The District Auditor stated that the method of calculating bonuses was complicated and unconventional; and that the targets claimed by operatives were rarely checked.

During the 1970s it is estimated that the Building Department have lost £2 million – £2.5 million on capital works; overrun contract times; and must have increased the Council's maintenance costs by between a quarter and a third. The Council has taken no effective notice of the criticisms made in a series of reports and does not appear to have acted with any regard for the interests of ratepayers. It increased its staffs from 895 in April 1979 to 1,162 in October 1980.

## 3. DEPARTMENT OF ARCHITECTURE

This Department's costs are high because:
a) they engage in too much abortive work;
b) the overhead costs are over 120 per cent compared with a comparable figure for large private practices of 80–110 per cent;
c) some of the staff are under-employed.
If this Department were made more cost-effective a saving of about £3 million per annum could be achieved.

## 4 and 5. PLANNING & DEVELOPMENT

The average amount of time spent by development control officers is excessive in view of the minor nature of the majority of cases. Based on comparisons with Westminster City Council, a reduction of costs of about 40 per cent should be possible, leading to a saving of £650,000 per annum.

*Losses on Development Sites*
The Council has wasted ratepayers' money by acquiring commercial and industrial sites, and then taking a very long time to put them to use.

A description of the difficulties and delays with three sites illustrates how money has been wasted. The Swiss Cottage site was originally bought in 1955 for a civic centre by the Hampstead Borough Council for £200,000. Part of the site was reallocated in the 1960s for the baths and library. Since 1968 ten alternative schemes have been proposed. The present situation is that Winchester Road is being rehabilitated for 'community uses', and the remainder of the site is being offered to private sector developers. These delays have cost:

– £534,000 in fees, much of which has been completely wasted;
– the loss of rent and rates amounting to several hundred thousand pounds from the site for many years;
– the loss of jobs for several hundred people.

Elsewhere an 11-acre site known as Elm Village was bought for
development as an industrial site in July 1972 for £1.375 million. In
1977 negotiations were entered into with News International Ltd,
publishers of the *Sun* and *News of the World,* to build premises for
publishing and printing work leading to relocation of several
thousand jobs. The rent and rates would have been of the order of
£400,000 per annum. In July 1978 the Policy and Resources Committee recommended that the Council close with an offer but some
Councillors were concerned by the loss of land for industrial development. A revised proposal was made by News International involving
their premises, using seven acres, with the remaining four acres being
used for a number of small factories which the company would build,
thus preserving the desired industrial-estate character of the development. The Council, however, wanted the same rent for the smaller
site as it had sought for the whole, and News International turned
down the scheme. The first two factory units are now completed *eight
years* after the site was acquired, and some phases will not be completed for another two to three years. The acquisition of the site by the
Council and its handling of the development has *cost* ratepayers about
£150,000 annually in charges; *lost* rent and rates of the order of
£400,000 per annum; *delayed* an increase in the number of jobs in
Camden for two or three thousand people and possibly lost some of
them altogether.

In February 1976 the Council bought the Granary, an old ware-
house, for £1.3 million. Between April and November 1976 there were
four reports by officers setting out a range of options for dealing with
the building. The final recommendations were for the ending of
existing leases and the redevelopment of the building. On two occasions the Committee Members deferred a decision on its use. The
GLC advised the Council on 29 November 1976 that the building
was a 'serious fire hazard', and there was a further report in December. The Committee again deferred a decision in the light of repre-
sentations from the 'Camden Industrial Action Group' that the
building should be converted for industrial and warehousing use. In
1977 there was a series of reports on what had to be done to meet the
GLC and Fire Brigade requirements (the latter called the building 'a
first-class fire hazard'), and on negotiations with developers. Eventually at the end of 1977 quotations were accepted for £129,000 for a
sprinkler system and fire-alarms. In April 1978 agreement was
reached with a company to manage the building. Unfortunately it

burnt down on 1 October 1978. During this two-and-a-half years the Granary was considered by Committees on fourteen different occasions. It took eighteen months to decide what to do with the building, and a further six months to agree how to manage it. In all it took two-and-a-half years to meet the GLC's modest 'immediate requirements' for fire precautions.

The Council also lost £90,000 in abortive fees on a project called Baldwin Gardens and a further £80,000 for abortive fees on examining (and deciding against buying) the ABC Bakery building in Camden. It is, of course, a wise investment to spend a reasonable amount of money and time in checking prospective property purchases in order to avoid buying a 'pig in a poke'. On the other hand £80,000 for a feasibility study for a scheme of this magnitude seems unreasonably high. Camden ratepayers could be forgiven for feeling that their Council seems to operate a choice of two unsatisfactory courses of action: they get involved in a possible project, but withdraw having lost a lot of money; or they don't withdraw, in which case they lose a great deal more.

The report concludes that the experiences the Council had with these two developments, involving spending a lot of money on design and tenders followed by an appreciation that the return it was going to achieve was insufficient, should demonstrate that the Council was not competent to undertake such developments. It is a verdict that can be applied to almost all public authorities.

Over the last six years, as a result of the slowness of its procedures, the Council has wasted nearly £6 million on a portfolio of commercial and industrial sites. It now owns 10,000 square metres of industrial space, much of which is vacant. In addition it has lost rent and rate income, and deferred increasing the employment capacity of the Borough. It is clear that both the ratepayers' pockets and the prospects for jobs in the Borough would benefit if the Council pulled out from a field in which its activities have been so unrewarding. A private sector developer in this position would have no choice. He would have been bankrupt long since. On the assumption that the land and buildings can be disposed of without loss, and that the new owners would be able to put them to use and start paying rates, the retirement of the Council from its development activities would produce long-term savings of about £1.1 million and increased rate income of about £0.5 million per annum in three years.

## 6. LEISURE SERVICES COMMITTEE

### Public Libraries

CIPFA (see p. 159) statistics show Camden at the top of the spending league both in total and in costs per thousand residents. Camden spends 42 per cent more per resident than Westminster.

Camden has more professional posts than any other council except Birmingham (which has a population $5\frac{1}{2}$ times as big) and more staff than any other Borough. A comparison of the number of book issues per head of staff shows that for 1978/79 issues were 7,400/7,700 for Camden, 9,900 for Westminster, 10,100 for Haringey. A very good library service could be provided for £0.75 million per annum less than Camden is spending at present.

### Public Baths, and Parks and Recreation Grounds

A comparison with neighbouring authorities suggests that, while still providing an adequate service, the Council should be able to make economies of £100,000 and £200,000 per annum respectively.

### Play Centres

Spending on play centres has increased by 14 per cent in real money terms. The report gives detailed reasons for doubting if this money is well spent. Based on comparisons with Haringey, a reduction of £400,000 could be achieved while still producing a good service.

### Summary of Leisure Services Reductions

By making the foregoing changes, which include a thorough review of all charges from laundry to putting, the total budget of £9.06 million could be reduced at least as follows:

| | |
|---|---|
| Libraries | 750,000 |
| Baths | 100,000 |
| Parks & Recreation | 200,000 |
| Arts | 200,000 |
| Play Centres | 400,000 |
| | £1,650,000 |

Such a reduction (18 per cent of the budget) would have a negligible effect on the residents of the Borough. It would still leave Camden spending £7.4 million on leisure services compared with Haringey's expenditure of £6 million, for a population that is 20 per cent larger.

When the total possible savings in Camden (between £11.5 million and £16.5 million per annum) are being appraised it is necessary to keep two further considerations in mind, even though it is not possible to put a cash value on them.

First, the report was prepared from outside, and penetrating though it is, access to detailed records and methods of working would undoubtedly have yielded a further harvest of potential economies.

Second, the estimates of potential savings are based on comparisons with other authorities, and mainly with other London boroughs. Many of these, indeed all of them very probably, are themselves wasteful and inefficient. Just how much could be saved if comparisons were made against figures based on moderate efficiency is a matter for conjecture.

The response of the Camden Council to 'The Cost of Camden' was exactly that of all public bodies faced with this sort of criticism. The report, said the Council, was full of inaccuracies. It soon became apparent that this defence could not be sustained, especially as most of such inaccuracies as there were stemmed from errors in the Council's own published figures. The Council then decided that the report would have to be taken seriously. By the end of the summer of 1981 there were some signs of the consequences of this change of attitude, including the defeat of some extravagant proposals in connection with school meals.

In the meanwhile, the stalwarts of the CRA (Camden Ratepayers' Association) were pressing on with their campaign.

In May 1981 the Council sought to impose charges for the removal of refuse from trade premises. This was doubly infuriating for the commercial ratepayers. They were already footing the bill for a large part of the Council's spending, including refuse collection. Secondly, the proposed charges were high. The CRA promptly responded by organising its own refuse collection service, and, despite all the difficulties of starting from scratch, was able to offer a comparable service at 30 per cent lower cost.

Next CRA initiated a high court action brought in the name of three ratepayers, against thirty Camden councillors, for failing to act 'reasonably' on a number of matters; failing to slim its work force; and settling unsatisfactorily the level of council rents. This is obviously an enormously difficult area, a large part of which can quickly become a hopeless mixture of existing law, the reasonable rights of the public, and the reasonable freedom of political parties. Nevertheless even losing such a case would provide a victory in one sense because it would demonstrate the inadequacy of the current system to give the aggrieved citizen any redress through the courts.

Thirdly, CRA are pressing the Secretary of State for the Environment to impose an Extraordinary Audit by the District Auditor on the affairs of Camden.

The future course of activities in Camden will be followed with considerable interest, and some anxiety, by many hard-pressed rate-payers. The implication of the facts already revealed will be examined in Chapter 12.

# Better News from Berkshire

After the account of the bitter battles between ratepayers and the Council at Camden, it is pleasant to be able to record the activities of a local authority in which elected members and officials actively sought to search out unnecessary spending.

In September 1978, four months after the publication of the first edition of *Your Disobedient Servant*, Robert Gash, Chief Executive of the Royal County of Berkshire, wrote to me as follows:

'Senior members and Chief Officers of the County Council have read extracts from your book *Your Disobedient Servant* with great interest. They were impressed at the large savings which your teams of investigators unearthed in the Southern Region of the PSA* and felt that there are some useful lessons for the County Council in your work.

A special group of County Councillors has been set up, known as the "Expenditure Section" to look for ways to reduce expenditure, and I reported to them on ways in which your principles might be applied to the County Council. A copy of that report is enclosed for your information.

The Members were most enthusiastic about setting up teams of investigators.'

The letter went on to propose a meeting at which I could give further information on investigative techniques, and this meeting, held only two weeks later, was attended by a group made up of elected members and senior officials in roughly equal numbers.

The officials were friendly and receptive though I had the impression that one or two had reservations about the practicability and wisdom of embarking on further investigations when the ground had already, in their view, been exhaustively covered several times before. The elected representatives had no such misgivings. The driving force in this group was Lewis Moss, Chairman of the Expenditure

* Property Services Agency, part of the Department of the Environment.

Section, which in turn was an offshoot of the Review and Finance Sub-Committee.

Lewis Moss was a property developer and had already been active in reforming procedures for a more critical use-oriented examination of capital projects. No one with experience of the activities of staff architects let loose in the public sector could doubt the need for that, or for the associated drive to make quantity surveyors responsible to the Chief Executive rather than the Chief Architect.

Robert Gash, the Chief Executive, had himself set up a Research and Intelligence Unit which, it was hoped, would lead to new policies and methods of operation, and produce in years to come significant savings. Two projects on which the Unit had already worked were pupil forecasting and school transport. The latter made use of computer techniques to economise on the running of school bus services. It was estimated, after completion of a pilot study, that this more efficient use could save the authority around £100,000 in a full year.

The two key figures in the investigation were therefore already of a mind to look for new methods and techniques, and no doubt this influenced the course of events.

By the middle of the following month, the decision to go ahead had been approved, and consultations with the staff associations and trade unions began. Not altogether unexpectedly there was a marked lack of enthusiasm on their part for the proposals, and by January 1979 stalemate had been reached. However, the Chief Executive and I met the representatives of NALGO that month, and discussed with them the aims, techniques and possible consequences of the reviews. As always – well, nearly always – I found the attitudes, arguments and questions of these delegates to be very reasonable, and presumably they found our answers equally so, because within a few weeks agreement to go ahead with their co-operation was secured.

The next delays arose from problems about a) who was going to do the investigating, and b) who and what was to be investigated. Acceptance of the inevitability, if not the desirability, of enquiries was all very well while it was couched in general terms. It was a rather different matter when people, including trade unions, found their own interests and departments were threatened by investigations! The first and second choices were eliminated, other possibilities were discussed, and it was not until mid-1979 that it was agreed that there should be a review of property management.

A team of five was appointed: Andrew Allen, BSc, IPFA, came from the Berkshire County Treasurer's Department. Raymond

Chester, ARICS, ARVA, and Malcolm Bowles, ARICS, came from the Property Services Agency. Brian Martin, BSc, M Tech, C Eng, MIEE, was borrowed from Messrs Mars Bars of Slough. Barrie Willcock, PhD, C Eng, MI Struct E, came from the Berkshire County Surveyor's Department.

Although the team was bigger than those I had used, it followed the same broad lines. There was a strong professional flavour which meant that recommendations could not be dismissed as the well-meant but ill-informed vapourings of amateurs who did not know enough to understand the difficulties. Equally there was adequate professional expertise to enable the team to take in their stride attempts to pull the wool over their eyes. Andrew Allen provided the necessary professional skills of a non-property-survey kind, and finally there was adequate capacity on the team from those who owed neither short-term loyalties, future prospects or past experience to the Berkshire County establishment. All these ingredients are, I believe, essential to success, and the Berkshire pattern is one which I would commend to any public authority planning investigations of this kind.

The team did not complete its report until April 1980. It was workmanlike, comprehensive and thorough and – as such reports must – it eschewed generalities and unevidenced opinion. The 150-plus foolscap pages contained the kind of detailed, factual and statistical evidence which was needed to sustain the recommendations, and, perhaps more importantly, to enable any reasonable reader, whether elected representative, official or trade union leader, to judge for himself the validity of what was being proposed.

The main recommendations were as follows:

*Surplus land*

(a) An examination of a sample of properties (which I was assured subsequently was a typical sample) amounting to about 7 per cent of the County's total holdings revealed surplus land valued at £2.6 million. The valuations were cautious, quite rightly, and certainly do not give an over-optimistic estimate of the outcome. Assuming the remainder of the estate followed the same pattern, surplus property of around £36 million could be looked for. The interest which could be earned or saved by the use of this sum would alone make an appreciable impact on the County's needs (about 5 per cent reduction of total annual spend). Even better, it should be possible, or made possible, for authorities to use the proceeds of sales of this kind for schemes such as energy conservation (see below) at present starved of capital.

The team reports that it limited its investigations to land holdings only – no attempt was made to look at the utilization of buildings although it was concluded that this offered potential for a further survey in its own right.

(b) Housing. The team suggested that the county's policy on the disposal of houses be amended. One hundred and ninety two houses valued at £4.8 million (another very conservative estimate) could be declared surplus and sold as and when vacant possession was obtained.

The houses concerned were not local authority housing in the usual sense – they were predominantly houses owned by the Council for accommodation for its own staffs, mainly caretakers, social services staff, fire brigade officers and teachers.

The report makes it clear that the ownership and letting of these houses stemmed from considerations which may at one time have been justified but were no longer so. At one time, for example, firemen were obliged to live close to their station because, apart from their normal duties, they were also on call to provide fire cover in their spare time. This has long since ceased to be true, but the provision of privilege housing has carried on. It is a familiar story. My PSA surveys produced hundreds of cases where this sort of thing had happened.

(c) The team discovered that in 1892 the Agriculture Act had set out to create smallholdings, mainly in order to encourage new people to enter farming and so to give a much needed shot in the arm to the then depressed industry. Like so many forays by government into what was essentially a free enterprise area the scheme was of doubtful value socially, and still less value agriculturally. It dragged on for years but in 1966 it was recognised that smallholdings were not acting as the first rung of a ladder from which tenants moved to bigger and bigger farm units. Tenants tended to stay put. As a result the 1970 Agriculture Act obliged Counties to reorganise their smallholdings where appropriate and permitted them to sell off the remainder.

The team recommended that these powers be used and most of the smallholdings be sold off, realising approximately £950,000.

*Building maintenance section*
Programmed Maintenance.* The Berkshire team found that pro-

* Programmed maintenance consists of carrying out maintenance, repairs and inspections at set intervals, usually based on time or usage. Car servicing at, say, every 5,000 miles is an obvious example.

grammed maintenance can be wasteful if it is not carefully monitored and kept in line with changing circumstances. We found exactly the same thing in PSA. The team's findings were that:

(i) programmed electrical wiring maintenance costs could be reduced by at least 40 per cent from £63,000 to £38,000 in 1981;

(ii) programmed heating maintenance costs could be reduced from £129,400 to £80,000 in 1980/81;

(iii) engineering planned maintenance savings of £20,000 per annum could be achieved on an annual budget of £309,000 (1980/81).

### Heating boiler controls

The correct use of modern time and temperature controls, coupled with maximum load control would, the team said, lead to substantial savings in energy costs without lowering heating standards and without, therefore, anyone being worse off. The total installation costs of new controls were estimated at about £1,000,000 producing total fuel savings (at 1980/81 prices) of about £400,000–£500,000 per annum.

### Lighting controls

It was estimated that 50 per cent of the electrical energy paid for by the county (about £1.5m per annum) was for lighting. The replacement of tungsten lamps by fluorescent lamps would produce a fourfold reduction in energy consumption for the same lighting output. Improved controls could further provide savings of 20–30 per cent of the reduced load. The total savings are of the order of £400,000 per annum (fluorescent lighting £250,000, controls £150,000).

### Energy management systems

More sophisticated computer-based systems are recommended for larger properties. Expected reductions in energy consumption are of the order of 20–30 per cent.

### Water charges

The team conducted limited investigations into water usage. Water and sewerage charges accounted for £439,000 per annum (1980) and the early indications of the effect of better controls were that water consumption could be reduced by 50 per cent. The principal source of saving was the ending of automatic flushing of toilets when buildings were empty.

### Swimming pool heating

It was found that in all the swimming pools visited, recommended water temperatures were being exceeded to the extent that windows were being opened to get rid of surplus heat. The Fuel Efficiency Officer, it was noted, had tried and failed to persuade the Education Department to take action on this. Fuel was being wasted, and a high level of condensation was causing serious deterioration to the fabric of the buildings. In the Reading and Slough districts alone, the cost of heating pools should have been about £55,000 per annum and was in fact, due to the disregard of recommended temperatures about £100,000 per annum.

*Improved insulation of buildings*
A planned programme of insulation and associated work could produce savings, in areas already identified by the team, of about £200,000 per annum, although the team noted that significant savings had already been achieved in this field.

The items listed above are by no means the full measure of potential savings contained in the team's proposals. In some cases, savings could not easily be quantified; in others, more work was required to bring specific proposals to the stage where costs and savings can be measured; in yet others, areas of activity had been identified which the team were confident would produce savings if investigated, but where circumstances (lack of time usually) had prevented any effective detailed investigation.

In the summer of 1981, almost three years after the initial meeting, I had an opportunity to talk again with both elected members and senior officials of Berkshire. By this time, Lewis Moss had become Chairman of the County Council (in May 1980, and re-elected in May 1981).

Berkshire, almost alone amongst the local and other authorities I have had dealings with, has seemed free of neuroses about publicity. They had agreed earlier in the year to publication of the important parts of the report, and now agreed to provide, again for publication, some further information. I asked particularly for the reactions of team members and others to the methods of working; how the team members felt about what had been achieved; and, if possible, details of the action taken to implement the report findings. These were matters which I felt should have some interest both for the public at large and for other authorities contemplating value-for-money studies.

The use of the multi-discipline, mixed-origin team seems to have worked satisfactorily. On this Lewis Moss wrote:

'This brings me to the Chapman-type review of the County Council Property Department on which the Chief Executive tells me that he was very satisfied with the way the Property Review was carried out. The inter-disciplinary Team worked well together and produced a thorough and objective report. Because of the presence of experts on the Team, the recommendations were practical and of potentially great value. Because it was carried out by a combination of outsiders, and internal staff from departments not under review, the report was able to be unbiased and yet related to the particular needs and circumstances of the Berkshire County Council.'

The team members' views on the outcome were rather more equivocal:

'Team members recently contacted say that they felt the experience had been of great value personally. In retrospect, they feel that their recommendations were too detailed, and they would have liked to improve the presentation of the report for the elected Members. They feel somewhat disappointed that for various reasons many of the recommendations referring to building and engineering maintenance were not endorsed by the Panel of Members which considered the report. Nevertheless, they still consider it to have been a worthwhile exercise.'

My own view is that the report was not too detailed. It is necessary to have all the relevant data recorded and available for reference. It does not follow that every recipient, especially the elected members, will need to read every word, still less absorb it all. They should be concentrating on the recommendations, referring back to the detailed supporting data only when necessary because of lack of agreement on action.

Much more important, however, is the team's disappointment that many of the recommendations had not been implemented. I doubt if it will comfort them much, but it is a situation in which they will have the company of nearly all those who try to bring about change in the public services!

Their reaction was understandable. The recommendations were referred to a Members' Panel drawn from the Property and Finance Sub-Committees. In his letter to me Lewis Moss, for convenience, grouped the findings of the Panel into three.

Recommendations relating to building and engineering maintenance were considered unlikely to produce much in the way of cash savings, although there should, it was thought, be other useful by-products.

Although it is true that these sections did not produce the big money savings, the team had drawn attention to a number of potential economies which, if pursued with vigour, would in aggregate have been valuable. Changes in planned maintenance especially can produce worthwhile results if they are carried through by experts in that field. Elected members, accountants and architects are not experts in that field. Generally the team's proposals were referred to the County Architect's Department, but with no instructions or timetable for positive action. My experience does not suggest that this is a recipe for the swift implementation of economies. There is probably both know-how and capacity available within the County organisation to push through the changes needed. If not, I think Berkshire will find that there are private sector consultants who will do the work for a percentage of the savings.

The next group of recommendations were those dealing with energy savings. On this Lewis Moss writes:

'The Team's recommendations on energy savings . . . are of much greater potential value. Restrictions on capital expenditure by local authorities will mean that we cannot proceed as quickly as we would like on the recommended work, but the Team's point was well made and accepted by Members.'

Proceeding 'not as quickly as we would like' in this context had two facets, both of which merit further examination. The Panel decided that schemes for energy conservation with a pay-back period of more than five years should not be pursued, but that *within the constraints imposed by capital expenditure restrictions*\* schemes with a short pay-back (i.e. less than five years) should be considered. In the light of these decisions the Panel presumably thought it unnecessary to deal with the team's recommendation that the county-wide energy conservation programme be shortened from fifteen years to five.

The Berkshire decision is in line with – indeed is ahead of – the rate of progress which I know has been accepted, albeit reluctantly, by other authorities. However sensible the energy-saving schemes may be, they cost money. A very few are so good that the money is saved in the next year. Most require three to seven years. There is an irreducible minimum of high priority schemes of other kinds for which money

---

\* My added emphasis.

just has to be found – so there is a limit to what can be found for fuel economy. It is a familiar Morton's fork dilemma: not enough money to make sensible capital investment to cut back on wasteful current spending which in time would make money available for sensible capital investment!

Yet should we accept the situation merely because it is familiar? We are told constantly through advertising by public authorities (and at great expense to us, the taxpayers and consumers) that fossil fuel-based energy is a scarce resource, which is becoming scarcer and more expensive. A great many public authorities could save substantial sums of money every year by using a variety of forms of energy conservation. They cannot do so, because they are constrained by artificial capital restrictions, which choke off the money supply they need for this purpose. There is no shortage of money for investment. The Secretary of State for Industry recently (1981) asserted that anyone needing investment capital would 'find the country is awash with money'. We are told all day every day about the enormous problem of unemployment, and although telling us does not cost money the fact of unemployment does, and costs cannot be measured in money alone in this case. Yet the firms making the equipment and materials for energy conservation work have reduced their labour forces, are working short time, or in some cases have closed down.

Never mind all the gobbledygook which politicians, economists and the rest keep forcing on us. Is not the situation I have described – and remember it applies all over the United Kingdom – the negation of every kind of sensible government and administration? Is this really the best answer which can emerge from a sophisticated democracy with its wealth of talent available for technology, finance, management, planning and all the rest? Can anyone seriously doubt what would happen if a few representatives of these skills were locked in a room with a handful of political office holders, and told that they would be allowed out to eat only when they had come up with a unanimous, sensible answer to the whole problem? I forecast that they would emerge within an hour or so. Perhaps it really is time that the long-suffering British public began thinking in such terms!

The third group of recommendations related to land and property disposal. On this Lewis Moss says: 'Recommendations ... on property matters have been largely accepted and should pay worthwhile dividends in years to come.'

'Years to come' is right. Accepting that surplus houses should be sold as they become vacant, the Members' Panel noted the NALGO view that staff accommodation should be retained, and the problem of housing for some other groups was referred to yet another sub-committee.

Similarly, while accepting the view that the Smallholders Estate should be disposed of, the Panel decided that these properties should be sold only as and when they became vacant.

Berkshire County Council, like other authorities, has no obligation to wait for vacant possession, nor in most cases any obligation to provide accommodation. It is true that the property will realise more when sold with possession, but it would be possible to make the same argument for local authority housing. In any case, the money realised by the sale could be used for, say, some of those capital-starved fuel economy schemes, and this might well prove to be more rewarding than waiting for possession. Most of all, however, local authorities and other public bodies have no business to hold property or anything else which is not vital to the execution of their duties, merely because they think it is a good investment. Even if they were good at this sort of thing (which generally they are not), it is not their function. There will always be good reasons for delaying action by officials. I fear that as things stand, Berkshire's property holdings will look very much the same in ten years' time.

In his letter to me setting out the advances and economies made by Berkshire in connection with project appraisal and the better use of quantity surveyors (see the beginning of this chapter) Lewis Moss concludes by saying: 'My only regret is that as far as I can see current local government practice in the generality remains unaltered. . . .' He is clearly and rightly puzzled and greatly disappointed by this, but there is no mystery about it.

Most local authorities, indeed most public sector bodies, do not want to listen to other authorities' success stories. One of the most noticeable differences, I find, between private and public sector management is that the private sector cannot wait to pillage everyone's ideas, especially their competitor's, if there is any chance of cutting costs. And a very good thing this is for all of us.

Public bodies as a general rule prefer to do things in their own way, so most of them will not have taken any notice of the very sensible changes made by Berkshire. Those few local authorities who bothered to do anything and have been given clear recommendations for implementation will have referred the proposals to a panel (or a committee, or a working party). A number of minor items will have been accepted immediately. The panel will have accepted a number of others in principle but not for present implementation ('wait for a new quantity surveyor, new architect, the end of the current programme, or the next Inundation'). And the panel will have then referred a number of the main issues to sub-committees and chief officers and other interested parties where the problems can be endlessly chewed over. That is why current public sector practice in this and so many other directions remains largely unaltered. It is also why, I am afraid, current Berkshire property holdings, engineering maintenance and a number of other potential sources of savings will be slow to change.

Clear recommendations for economies are unfortunately not the happy end of the story, in the special circumstances which obtain in the public sector, as many good staff in auditors and management services departments can testify. Before the happy end is achieved they have to be chased, pushed, monitored and progressed every step of the way to final implementation, usually with patience, but sometimes ruthlessly. Take your eye off them for one moment at the eleventh hour and somehow they will be lost in the great official machine.

Despite some disappointments, the Berkshire experience has shown that savings can be made without damage to standards of service, given the right initiatives and methods. A second and similar investigation into a quite different set of activities is now under way. Given enough pressure there is a good chance that this time all the investigation processes can be speeded up and implementation made more effective. In any case, it is movement in the right direction.

# The Need for Investigation

So far this book has had three main aims. The first was to give an impression of public sector spending by presenting a scatter of examples in a variety of sectors, and by considering the trends and patterns over periods of many years; the second, within the framework established by this necessarily broad brush and superficial treatment, to narrow the focus sharply and look in detail at specific demonstrations of the ways in which public money is spent; and the third, to record, wherever possible in detail, the responses of those controlling and directing the organisation concerned, i.e. politicians and officials.

From this diverse assortment of facts it is possible now to draw some reasonably well-evidenced conclusions, which in turn can be used to determine whether change and reform is needed, and if it is what needs to be done.

The first and painfully obvious conclusion is that there is waste in the public sector *and that it is not insignificant*. Historical spending trends can be defended at least in part. The examples of waste and wrong priorities quoted in Chapter 1 could by themselves be airily dismissed as the inconsequential mishaps and freaks inevitable in large-scale operations. But on occasions when it becomes possible to peer beneath the surface and to glean at least some of the facts, it is apparent that similar wasteful spending goes on wherever we look. The examples in Chapter 1 cease to be isolated and untypical. On the contrary, they represent inadequately the insubstantial tip of a massive, well-concealed constituent in the current national economy. Avoidable spending, the investigations reveal, is not marginal: economies proposed are far more often above 20 per cent than below. On the other hand, savings far smaller in percentage terms would be enough to solve all the more pressing problems.

Common patterns emerge also in the nature as well as the size of wasteful expenditure. Nothing in the detailed examples of savings involved any loss of services or lowering of standards. On the contrary some, such as refraining from overheating accommodation to uncomfortable levels, would positively improve the service.

Avoiding overheating, disposing of surplus land, curtailing services in unoccupied buildings – these and measures like them provide the bedrock of the waste-reducing proposals. The investigations which uncover the possibilities, and the proposed solutions, do not involve a high degree of sophistication. The skills needed are readily available from existing resources.

Although occasionally a major capital project catches public attention, this is not the area in which most waste occurs, or occurs without being noticed. The big wastage, dangerous because it is likely to go on for so long without anyone being aware of it (or being aware, able and willing to do something about it), is in day-to-day expenditure. A million-pound capital project which turns out to be a fiasco will normally receive a good deal of attention. Yet 100 unneeded employees will waste this amount of money *every year*. I do not believe that there is a medium or large public body anywhere in this country where that number of staff, or more likely many times that number, could not be saved.

The finding of waste in the public sector does not involve rare skills or highly sophisticated management techniques. The fact that, even so, such waste can be found wherever it is looked for leads unavoidably to the conclusion that, no matter who is responsible, the current systems of control *just do not work*. Evidence of widespread waste in public sector spending, added to all the evidence that costs in that sector for worsening services are rising far more rapidly than inflation, can only mean that control has not been even moderately effective. Furthermore, the failure has occurred across the board. Central government spending, like that of local authorities and nationalised industries, has not merely failed to respond to government policies: it has taken off at an accelerated rate on a diametrically opposed course. M Ps have failed, and many of them admit it publicly. Local authority councillors have failed. Those who purport to control the nationalised industries have not so much failed to be effective as failed even to make an effective start. It follows in turn from this that, unless current levels of waste and growth in the public sector are to be passively accepted, there must be changes in the system of control and direction of spending. It is no use hoping that, given a little more time, somehow the problem will go away of its own accord.

Next, the consequences of waste for individuals need to be considered. The effects on those who pay rates and taxes, and on private sector industry and commerce, have been all too obvious in recent years, and need no further airing here. So too are the consequences of unnecessarily high spending on essential services, and spending of any kind on non-essential services, for the economy as a whole. But what of those who might be expected to benefit from all this outpouring of the community's resources?

At the time when I believed that I would have the opportunity to take effective action on cost-cutting in London Transport (and after it had been publicly announced that I would be doing it), I told Cutler that I would reduce costs by at least £100 million per annum.* I was prepared to state this publicly and, if I failed, to make an equally public recantation. Reductions in cost would be achieved without any reduction in standards of service, or safety, and indeed I was sure that standards would go up, not down. Sloppy management which allows wasteful spending and overmanning does not mean that at least, having spent the money, you get better, albeit expensive, results. The sloppiness spills over. It cannot be compartmentalised and confined to specific areas. Unpunctual buses and dirty trains are symptoms of bad management, not of spending too little money.

As far as LT was concerned, therefore, neither ratepayers nor travellers benefited from high spending. There are those who would argue however that, even accepting that verdict, the staff at LT benefited, in the sense that their numbers were not being decimated by hatchet men.

Nevertheless it is open to question whether in the long run, even in the public sector, staff do benefit from management which is not cost-conscious. LT staff at the operating level come in for a good deal of abuse from their exasperated customers, and frequently hear speculation about the future of the organisation. I believe that a high proportion of them would prefer to work for an efficient and well-managed group, with a well-earned reputation for good service. And, although this can only be a guess, I would confidently expect the employees of Marks and Spencer to be happier in their jobs than their equivalents in LT.

Much the same considerations emerge from the Camden story. The cost of housing units varied from £71,000 (Highgate New Town) through £76,000 (Alexandra Road) to £105,000 (Fitzjohns Avenue) to a staggering £176,000 per unit (Branch Hill). It is hardly necessary to argue that this represents poor value for money for the taxpayers and commercial ratepayers. The same is true for the domestic rate-

---

* My estimate of waste had risen since 1979 in the light of the findings of a succession of reviews and enquiries.

payers, for whom the average price per private-built unit in London was £31,500 (and substantially less elsewhere). It is difficult to follow the twisted perversion of logic, justice and common sense which seeks to justify a system under which owner-occupiers who are working and saving to buy their own homes are bled white to pay for council tenants to live in homes costing $2\frac{1}{2}$–5 times as much; and then, having paid the exorbitant capital costs, go on subsidising for ever more the running costs of these homes.

Supporters of left-wing Labour philosophies may shrug off all this as irrelevant. They claim to be the champions of those in need. But do the Camden figures support their claim, or destroy it? As a result of lavish spending, the poor and the needy have been deprived of homes, not helped in any way. The money wasted in Camden, if spent more wisely, could have provided many more homes – probably between one and two thousand. In perhaps a slightly less blatant form, similar criticisms could be made of many other authorities. And in Camden, as elsewhere, as we have already noted, wasteful spending on maintenance produces a bad service, not a good, albeit expensive, one. Wasteful spending benefits no one, least of all those who most need help.

Nobody benefits. But does anyone care? There are strong indications that ratepayers and taxpayers do, and that they are just beginning to make their concern felt. What of the politicians who have the ultimate responsibility for the overall control of expenditure, and who have had so much to say about the deficiencies in the current situation?

For all the brave talk, the present Government's attempts to reform the Civil Service have proved to be a resounding flop. The GLC Conservatives failed to follow through at London Transport. Mr Heseltine failed to persuade local authorities to cut staffs and spending. Is it that, in the end, Ministers can do very little, or, if they can, are prevented from acting by officials?

The Camden ratepayers cared enough about the problem to commission an enquiry at their own expense. They sent a copy of the report to Mr Heseltine, and his response helps to shed light on the problem.

Approximately 40 per cent of Camden's total spending in 1979/80* was taxpayers' money diverted by the Government to the Council.

---

* The proportion was reduced in later years as a result of the changed arrangements for calculating government financial assistance for local authorities.

Presumably, therefore, what is revealed by this report would be of great concern to any Secretary of State for Environment, and particularly to the present one. No Minister has had more to say about local authority spending. He has been the champion of one Tory conference after another, where to loud applause from the faithful he slew the dragons of overspending, waste, etc., etc. with fine speeches and promises. At more and more frequent intervals he threatens the spendthrifts, promises remedial action, deplores the lack of response by councils to his wise directives and reasonable requests, is 'furious' with others – and notes with hurt surprise that local authority spending goes up and up, faster than ever before. His response to the Camden Report was as follows:

> 2 Marsham Street
> London SW1P 3EB
>
> 4 March 1981
>
> Dear Mr. Wilson,
> Thank you for your letter of 27 February and for the report which you sent to me about spending and rates in Camden. I welcome the sort of initiative you have taken. It is the right of all ratepayers. I am very much in favour of informed and properly researched comment by the ratepayers of a Borough. I particularly welcome the comparative approach which you have adopted – many lessons can be drawn from it. Keep up the good work!
>
> Your sincerely
> Michael Heseltine

It sounds fine at first glance. What does it amount to? He acknowledges receipt; he 'welcomes the initiative' – although since the report has been completed, whether it is welcome or not is irrelevant. He explains that what has been done is the right of all ratepayers. Camden ratepayers know that; that is why they did it. He is in favour of informed comment; is there a politician in the land who would say or has ever said otherwise? He 'welcomes the comparative approach' – which is just as well since this is the standard approach for investigations of this kind, but hardly takes matters forward. And finally, in the half-patronising, half-indulgent tones of a Bishop commending a Boy Scout on his knot-tying efforts, he bids them to keep up the good work. How? By doing another report in five or ten years' time?

The determined onslaught on the Civil Service has ended with few savings, the Prime Minister's own champion defeated on the crucial issues, and civil servants firmly in control. After a similar promising start the GLC Conservatives ended up with the LT Executive more than ever before in the hands of full-time officials, and for all practical purposes insulated from any form of criticism. Moreover, as LT officials confidently predicted, once Labour took control of the GLC the pressure to reduce costs vanished overnight.

The conclusion must be that, for whatever reason or combination of reasons, politicians of both the main parties cannot be relied upon. Labour cannot or do not want to make economies; Conservatives say they want to, but cannot. Any effective investigation of expenditure and disclosures of the facts must be independent of politicians so that short-term expediency ceases to be an overriding consideration. At the same time, full disclosure would make it rather more difficult for politicians and parties to talk so much and do so little. Thus the best hope for first stemming and then reversing the growing misuse of the community's resources lies in effective independent investigations, with the results made available to the public.

To claim that independent investigation is the best hope is not to say, of course, that this is the only reform which is needed. In central government much needs to be changed to make management more accountable and therefore more cost-conscious, and that is only one of many changes which are needed. In the nationalised industries, as the LTE example shows, there needs to be considerable clarification of the role of part-time directors, and the extent to which they can be muzzled, using one method or another, by the full-time officials. In local government the representation of those who pay the bills, especially the commercial ratepayers, urgently needs to be reconsidered. All these and many other proposals, have been, and are being, fully ventilated, and there are reasonable hopes that some changes will be made.

It is, however, vital to distinguish between cause and effect. The Government is currently considering changes in the law which will limit the power of local authorities to raise supplementary rates, or increase the normal rates faster than some limit imposed by Government. If the proposals pass into law, and if they are effective, they may give welcome short-term relief to harassed ratepayers. Nevertheless, such Government action will be treatment of the symptom, not of the disease. It will not, by itself, do anything to cure overmanning and other wasteful practices.

The solution to this remains effective value-for-money audit and the detailed scrutiny of policies and practices involving expenditure. Effective investigations into costs, and the production of a stream of evidence that money has been badly spent, will change far more than the specific activities whose shortcomings are revealed. The case for many of the other and subsidiary reforms, including improved accountability and more cost-conscious management, will be continuously demonstrated. In their own interests, the public services will be obliged to start putting their houses in order.

There are three other characteristics of public spending which emerge from the cases so far studied.

The first is that, no matter how hard the times are, no matter how many school children go without books or how many handicapped people lose services, those in authority look after themselves. Mayors go on getting their Rolls-Royces and Daimlers; delegates of all kinds travel the world in luxury; economies never reach the level of MPs, council chambers, or the boardrooms of the public authorities.

Second, with the survival of their organisations at stake, officialdom fights back hard to defend itself. It is a matter of judgement, with which Chapter 9 may help, whether in this fight the truth is one of the first casualties. It has been suggested that the armed forces of each democracy spend a few years in each century battling against the forces of other countries. The remaining 80–90 per cent of the time is spent fighting their own governments and civil populations in order to hold on to what they believe they need and deserve. Much the same can be said of the civil public sector, and it must be conceded that whatever else they do badly, the defence of their own interests and empires is carrried out very well.

When public sector capital programmes are slashed, it is private sector contractors who lose the work, and whose employees lose their jobs. The numbers of public sector administrators remain much the same – presumably so that they can administer the problems of losing their programmes! The same is true of most other public spending cuts. Job losses in large sectors of private industry have been proportionately ten times greater than in the public sector.

Third, the public authorities make much play with the argument that there is little evidence to suggest that anything is going wrong. Let us leave aside for the moment the possibility that the reason for this may be the measures taken to keep information under wraps. There remains the proposition that, having regard to the enormous demands made by them on the community's resources, it is for the public services to justify their actions and policies, not for the public to find evidence of fault.

Successive governments, the main political parties and an unending stream of committees of all kinds have recognised the need for more effective scrutiny of public spending. Let us now consider the issues involved, and the action that has been taken so far.

The Conservative Government's much-publicised intention of reducing waste and extravagance in the Civil Service petered out within a couple of years. Similar ambitions by the GLC's Conservatives met a similar end. Local authority expenditure, if reduced at all, has been reduced by cutting out desirable services. This in turn has caused unnecessary hardship and has set the stage for the restitution of the spending at the first opportunity. It sometimes seems that no matter what the public wants, or politicians say they will do, there never will be a substantial change, and that this is how things will always be; not, as the defenders of high public spending would like us to believe, because there is nothing much wrong, but simply because the problem is too big to be tackled effectively.

However, I do not accept these gloomy diagnoses. Any proposals for bringing about change must start from the evident fact that the public services are resilient and skilful defenders of their empires. The skills used by these defenders include an ability to manipulate political interests, as well as those of trade unions and other pressure groups. Their weapons include an almost total monopoly of factual information, and the opportunity in consequence to present information in a way of their choosing – to use the most courteous euphemism conceivable! If changes are to be made they will not be achieved by thunderous orations from politicians, or merely by earnest resolve and good intentions. What is needed is a sustained programme of well-directed assaults, based on hard factual evidence, which is almost the exact opposite of the windy generalised verbiage offered by the professional politicians, and the fumbling, if well-meant, efforts of the amateur.

The need for such investigations has been recognised more and more widely in recent years,* although there has been very little action to match the talk. Both Labour and Conservative Govern-

---

* The need has been recognised in other countries also. Appendix 13 gives extracts from a statement by the Premier of South Australia which bears directly on the same problem. South Australians, however, seem to be able to do more than discuss the difficulties and catalogue the obstacles. They are doing something about it, mainly through an effective PAC, currently under the chairmanship of Heini Becker, MP.

ments seem to be content, even if their backbenchers are not, to prepare discussion documents, invite comments, listen to lengthy explanations from officials about how difficult it all is, and then sit back as if the problem has been solved.

Before the change of government in 1979, the Labour administration began a review of the functions of Exchequer and Audit Department which for rather more than 100 years has been the most obvious, if not the most effective, piece of existing machinery for scrutinising central government expenditure.

In March 1980, the Government presented a Green Paper,* basically a consultative document, which stated the current official position, and raised issues on which views were invited. This paper, which will have been drafted almost entirely by officials who are and have been operating the current systems, and are therefore less than completely objective, states in connection with central government audit that Exchequer and Audit have three functions:
(i) the financial and regularity audit, i.e. making reasonably sure that the accounts accurately reflect the way in which public money has been spent;
(ii) value-for-money audit; and
(iii) effectiveness audit, i.e. how successfully things were done to achieve the stated aims.

The first of these is not relevant, except in a very limited and specialised sense, to the problems examined in this book. The second is, and so to a considerable extent is the third. There is no dispute that within common-sense interpretations E and AD have faithfully discharged the first duty. Indeed for anyone who has had occasion to work closely with E and AD staff in the field, the apparently nit-picking approach to minor matters of the propriety of charging a £10 item here rather than there in the accounts was as pointless as it was exasperating.

It comes as something of a surprise, however, to be informed (paras 16/18) that value-for-money, economy and efficiency examinations 'have for many years been a feature of the C and AG's work'. Even more surprising is the discovery that the Government appears to accept this, by talking (para 18) of 'continuing examinations' of this kind – surprising because it was the same Government which only a

---

* 'The Role of the Comptroller and Auditor General', Cmnd 7845, published by the Stationery Office, March 1980.

year before the publication of the Green Paper had rightly made such play with the appalling waste and inefficiency of the Civil Service. If the C and AG really had accepted a value-for-money responsibility and been working on that basis for many years, it follows on the evidence of the Government's own earlier criticisms that it was a function which had been very inadequately discharged.

This was not the only ground on which charges of fundamental inconsistency could be laid against the Conservatives. In the early 1970s, the Heath Government had introduced Programme Analysis and Review (PAR) in order to examine the *effectiveness* of civil service spending. At the end of the 1970s the Thatcher Government had brought in Rayner with the declared purpose of looking at the *efficiency* with which programmes were being tackled. Both PAR and Rayner were represented as being badly needed – yet between them these two covered the same functions as, according to the Green Paper, E and AD had been carrying out for many years. In November 1979, the PAR function was transferred to Rayner, although the effectiveness and the efficiency audits are quite separate and distinct. Well might *The Guardian*, under the wry headline 'Whitehall wins again'*, remind us that 'One of the biggest defects of British government is the capacity for individual departments to protect themselves from scrutiny.' Substitute 'all the public services' for 'individual departments' and that sentence sums up a great many other ills too. *The Guardian* comment was to be massively reinforced less than two years later when Rayner himself virtually departed from the scene.

The same *Guardian* note contained another quotation attributed to a Civil Service Under-Secretary. 'Socrates was the first person to do a PAR. He did it on Athens going round and asking fundamental questions. Athens put him to death. That's why I don't want to do any more PARs. . . .' Once again substitute 'almost any form of critical enquiry into public spending' in place of 'PARs' in that quotation and the statement stands as a neat summary of the experience of individuals described in Chapter 9.

The same Green Paper referred to the possibility that Exchequer and Audit Department could be amalgamated with the District Audit Service, which is largely responsible for audit of local authority accounts. In 1972, the Local Government Act gave the power to Auditors to report on losses due to waste, extravagance and poor value for money. As with E and AD, however, this part of the audit

* *The Guardian*, 14 November 1979.

function was discretionary not obligatory, and, again as with E and
AD, it was made clear later* that this new function was not intended
to apply to matters within the discretion of the council, i.e. the elected
representatives.

In 1976, the Layfield Committee, which had been set up by the
Government to look generally at local authority finances, made its
Report.† The Committee considered that:

(i) the question of value for money rightly attracts much public
attention;

(ii) the performance of the audits in that important field was not very
effective.

To call the standard of performance not very effective was certainly
not an exaggeratedly pessimistic view in 1976, and four or five years
later there was little to show that matters had improved. Working
solely on the basis of facts about costs which are not in dispute, the
case of Camden Borough Council (Chapter 10) revealed glaringly
high figures which one might have thought would very quickly have
attracted the attention of auditors. Yet despite constant pressure the
auditors made only muted and ineffectual comments, did not really
tackle the fundamental problems or issues, and perhaps not surprisingly made very little impact on the Council's activities.

The fault does not lie with the audit staffs. The Layfield Committee
had already diagnosed the trouble. The organisational structure was
wrong, in that the service was fragmented and lacking proper direction and co-ordination. Even more important, however, is the familiar story of not enough auditors and not enough skills. These are
criticisms which apply with some precision to E and AD. Central
government spending, and its range of activities, has soared away in
recent years. E and AD staff numbers have not changed to anything
like the same extent. As to skills,‡ the lack of qualified accountants in
E and AD has been the subject of a never-ending stream of criticism
from committees and enquiry witnesses of all kinds.

* Local Government Audit Code of Practice (Appendix II to DoE Circular 79/93).
† Report of the Committee of Enquiry, under Frank Layfield QC, on Local Government Finance, Cmd 6453, May 1976.
‡ 'Shortage of skills' should, I believe, be taken to refer to formal professional qualifications only in this context. The audit staff are high calibre. Before and just after the war
E and AD had the pick of the open Executive grade examination entrants. I have never
been able to discover whether this was an isolated though welcome recognition of the
importance of their function by some long departed official of the Civil Service
Commissioners, or whether there was some less worthy reason!

If the state of the value-for-money audit services for central and local government leaves much to be desired, the position in the nationalised industries is that, at least as far as outside or independent scrutiny is concerned, there is none whatsoever. With horror the Green Paper records (para 49) that an extension of C and A G's activities into this field would be 'a major new departure'. Considering the record of the public services on one hand and of the audit services on the value-for-money activities on the other, it would seem reasonable to suppose that any improvement would need, as a minimum qualification for success, to be just such a major change.

The Green Paper goes on to say (para 49) that the extension of this type of audit to their activities would be viewed by the nationalised industries as a serious threat to their own commercial freedom of action. I am sure that it is true that this is how it would be viewed, just as it is true that local authorities resent any suggestion of interference in their affairs by central government. And similarly, government departments resent any interference in their affairs from 'the centre' or from Parliamentary Committees, or from anyone else who looks as if they might for a few fleeting moments be effective. Before coming to any conclusion about central audit services, an examination needs to be made of the validity of these claims.

In discussions on value-for-money inspections and audits the point is frequently made – especially by those parts of the public sector which have a commercial flavour – that truly commercial enterprises do not have these indignities forced upon them, nor do they contrive them for themselves. To the extent that this is true, it is irrelevant. The nationalised industries, unlike their private sector counterparts, operate in a sheltered environment. They usually have a monopoly, or near monopoly, of the supply of an essential public requirement in the form of goods or services for consumption in the U K, and this privileged position is frequently protected by statute or other devices. They are thus largely insulated against problems arising from the selling *prices* of their products.

The Government (and as we have seen, it seems to make little difference in practice whether the government concerned is Conservative or Labour) can be relied on, in the end and after varying degrees of protest, to come through with massive injections of further money taken either from private sector industry and commerce or from the taxpayer. The public industries are therefore insulated to a large extent from the *costs* of their activities.

Private sector activities, on the other hand, are subject to the invigorating effects of competition both on prices and costs. If they are remiss on either account they go to the wall no matter how distinguished their name or how successful they were in the past. Like it or not, therefore, the private sector is presented constantly with a rigorous and automatic monitoring service on its activities which is as a rule denied to the publicly owned industries. Where, occasionally, free enterprise market-place pressures do operate to some extent (if overseas competition is involved, for example), it is noticeable that the public undertakings survive only if they make radical changes in their ways, and then only with great difficulty; or by securing, on grounds of the national interest (protection of employment, preservation of a resource vital to the nation, or similar ploys), that some form of discrimination is introduced to blunt the competitive edge of their opponents.

The argument that some form of efficiency-cum-value for-money audit would be inconsistent with, or a threat to, the commercial freedom of the nationalised industries, therefore comes to grief immediately. Commercial pressures do not operate in the very sector where this type of audit is needed. The deficiency must be made up by supplying an imposed and contrived discipline in place of those of the market-place. In present circumstances there is no satisfactory alternative to this, nor is there any need to search further for such an alternative.

Similarly the objection that this type of audit would amount to central government interference in local authority affairs is nonsensical. No one argues more passionately in defence of the independence of local government than the Conservative Party, especially at local level. Conservative Ministers reverently trot out the well-worn clichés about local finance being best left to the local ratepayers who foot the bills and elect the councils. That may have been true once. It is so no longer.

For a start, as we have already seen, 50–60 per cent of local authority spending comes from funds made available by government from taxpayers. Secondly, large rate payments are made by commerce and industry who do not have votes. Thirdly, many voters do not pay rates, or are in some way protected against the consequences of rate increases. The most blatant example of this recently is the decision of the GLC to pay extra money to the 60,000 LT employees to compensate for the increased GLC rate demand, an increase largely occasioned by higher subsidies for LT! The notion that the ratepayer, with his finger on the local council's financial pulse, is an effective financial watchdog belongs with a lot of other Conservative Party traditional mythology, rather than with the realities of today.

In March 1979, despite this deep-rooted concern about inter-ference, the Labour administration set up, without opposition, an Advisory Committee on Local Government Audit. So far, that Com-mittee has found nothing reassuring in the way that the system works at present, but has taken no action to cure this situation.

This is true of the Government's (and its predecessor's) record on the general problem, whether addressed to central or local government or nationalised industry. A great deal of earnest talk, a great deal of concern, much diagnosing of serious problems, offset by prolonged descriptions of the difficulties of dealing with them, has produced committees, reports, and committees to report on reports, but very little in the way of action.

Nevertheless, there does emerge from this welter of paper a number of recurring elements which, if they cannot be said to command unanimous agreement, at least continually crop up without very much ferocious opposition. They include a general feeling that :
(i) there is a great deal wrong;
(ii) the current system for dealing with the situation is inadequate;
(iii) (rather less enthusiastically) something will have to be done, at any rate for central and local government expenditure. A smaller group, including at least some Conservatives,* has the same feeling about the nationalised industries.

Similar common themes emerge from those, including the Layfield Committee, who proffer solutions in respect of local authorities:
(i) The audit effort needs to be stepped up very considerably. E and AD staffs number less than 2,000, very few more than the pre-war numbers despite the increases in their work-load already noted. District Audit numbers are between 500 and 600, which is about one per authority.
(ii) The District Audit services need to be centrally organised as E and AD is at present; and in replacement of the present fragmental District Audit organisation. Nothing exists at the moment for the nationalised industries.
(iii) There is no need to spend a great deal of time on considering whether or not all these services or any two of them need to be brought together under the head of E and AD (the Comptroller and Auditor General). It does not matter for the time being. I would suspect

---

* *Value for Money Audits*, by John Hatch and John Redwood (Centre for Policy Studies).

anyone who makes much of this (the Green Paper refers to it several times) of consciously or unconsciously trying to introduce delaying complications.

(iv) The principal need for the new service or services is that they shall be not only adequately staffed (adequate in numbers *and* skills) but also made independent, as far as is practicable, of political control. I believe that this must be interpreted as meaning independent of party political control, i.e. no one party to direct audit affairs. It would be essential for the audit services to answer to Parliament (as opposed to the Government) and to the Select Committees. There are no great practical difficulties in the way of such an arrangement.

To this list I would want to add one more – namely that each service should have a statutory obligation to report publicly on its activities. Of course, there would have to be safeguards, codes of practice and so on to interpret this requirement but the broad principle of regular publication should be built into the system.

There are several good reasons for doing this. One of the most frightening aspects of public authority operations is, as Chapter 9 details, their practice of screening the facts from the public who are both their employers and their customers, and of stifling any criticism which might threaten them. The best antidote to this practice is the injection of *hard factual evidence made public*, and the new audit services would be the appropriate means for finding the facts, seeking explanations, and publishing the results.

Any suggestion that a new and more powerful system of audit and investigation should be set up produces a number of set responses from those who are to be inspected. Since it would hardly be good tactics for these authorities to tell the truth – namely that they are horrified at the prospect of their activities being examined or made public – they fall back on some other well-tried defences.

The first is that the new set-up will require more staff and more public expenditure. This argument has the advantage that there is some truth in it, and also makes those who put it forward look as if they too are worried about costs.

Again, facts are the antidote. The cost of investigation is trifling compared with the savings. If you look back at the percentage savings put forward in the reports quoted in earlier chapters, you will see that savings of 20 per cent, 30 per cent and 40 per cent or higher are commonplace. It is those below that sort of figure which are the exceptions. These mainly high figures are the results of the first round, quite often carried out by people doing this sort of work for the first time. I have never been involved in any investigation of any sector of public spending which did not produce the evidence for economies to be made, over a period, of between 20 per cent and 30 per cent. And in nearly all cases, the evidence was that a second round would squeeze out further substantial economies.

Suppose, however, that this is wildly exaggerated. The nationalised industries in the late 1970s contributed just under 10 per cent of the total output of the UK and employed nearly two million people. Central government spends about £80 billion a year, and employs over 600,000 staff to do it. Local government spends about £28 billion and employs nearly 3 million staff. Savings much smaller than the evidence suggests are possible, say only 5–10 per cent, would make a profound impact on the national economy, which is of course the sort of promise that won the Conservatives such support in 1979. Can anyone seriously doubt that at the very least these investigations would save their costs? Again, drawing on experience in a large and mixed range of these enquiries, I would put the once-for-all costs at about 2–3 per cent of the *annual* savings. But whether you accept the higher figure, or the most pessimistic ones, cost can be dismissed as a deterrent factor.

This would be particularly true if these new audit services were conducted sensibly. Just one central HQ auditor could be assisted by staff from the authority concerned (it does not take much to stimulate an independent element in the thinking) or by staff borrowed on a loan/exchange basis from other authorities. The central audit department could supplement its own staffs by hiring from consultants, by no means an unusual arrangement, and one with several useful by-products. Indeed, it would be possible for the central group to be largely a directing, organising and reporting organisation with very small permanent staffs, especially in the early years of its existence.

The next line of defence is one which seems to find favour with important elements amongst elected representatives who really ought to know better. It is that value-for-money type audits will interfere with, for example, a Minister's control of his department; or the local council's over its own activities; or the 'commercial freedom' of the nationalised industries. But how can an investigation interfere with management in the way that is implied? The auditors will merely report what they have found. The power of decision will remain where it is at the moment, the only difference being – and it is the difference, of course, which brings the management pains on – that there will be more public knowledge of the consequences of past decisions, and the need for current ones. There is nothing inconsistent about having on the one hand fully delegated responsibility and on the other an effective efficiency and value-for-money audit. On the contrary, such audits greatly strengthen the ability of management to manage.

The last of the strategic defences is a little more difficult to deal with. Like the others it has elements of truth or part-truth within it, and these have been chanted so frequently and winningly that they are in danger of acquiring a bogus respectability. The argument runs like this. Public services are different in important ways from the private sector. As their title suggests the emphasis is on service not on buying and selling, still less on making profits.* To apply the crude pricing and other mechanisms of the private sector to these activities is therefore rather like trying to adjust a butterfly's wing with a spanner and sledgehammer. Anyway, you just *can't* put a price on many of these things – children's education, services for elderly people, the sick, the handicapped and the rest.

There are several specious but fallacious propositions all rolled into one here, but this line of reasoning goes down remarkably well with all sorts of audiences. I have heard it put forward with equal conviction by left-wing teachers, carefully neutral officials, and Conservatives who no doubt believed that they were on these issues somewhere to the right of centre. Anyone who disagrees is immediately in danger of being shouted down, or at best heard in disapproving silence, a response which is brought about by questioning issues on which minds are already closed.

Leaving the emotional phrases on one side for a moment, what are the facts? To begin with, most (though not all) reasonable people accept the idea that no community's resources are infinite. Certainly in this country, for the foreseeable future at least, unnecessary spending, if there is any, is spending at the expense of other services which are necessary. Against this background, who serves best the interests of the sick, the old and others in need? Those who dish out the money in big lumps on the basis that if £1 million is good £2 million is twice as good? Or those who examine the way in which the money is spent, and ensure that every £1 goes as far as possible? Spending more money does not even guarantee a better service, even on a pay-through-the-nose basis. It can sometimes be downright counter-productive, as experience with some parts of the Health Service has

* In an *ad hoc* survey of my own, 17 out of 20 speakers from public service organisations managed to convey, by facial expressions, amusement or distaste at the word 'profit'.

shown. Far too often the main heading of a given category of expenditure throws a protective blanket over all the expenditure which finds its way to that particular part of an authority's budget. To propose a critical look at 'education expenditure' is to invite the rage and bitter opposition of quite reasonable groups and individuals because this is at once equated with depriving children of the opportunity of being properly taught. In practice it can mean, as it meant in Berkshire (see Chapter 11) ensuring that the heating in the swimming pools is not so uncomfortably high that the users have to open windows to get rid of that expensive heat.

Breaking down global titles is also a necessary part of dealing with the defence that a particular service must be performed by the public sector. Using education again as the example, while it is unlikely that the State system will be dismantled, there is no reason whatsoever why some parts of it, e.g. the painting of schools, should not be carried out by private sector contractors – as indeed is already frequently the case. Similarly even if an authority decides that refuse collection shall remain as a direct council labour activity, there is no reason why the dustcarts cannot be maintained by private sector garages.

Not all services need to be carried out by the public authority itself. The refuse collection service referred to above is a good example of the kind of service which can be (and has been, by one authority) transferred wholly to private sector contractors. There is nothing special about this particular service, or about many others, which makes it necessary for the work to be done by council staffs. The responsibilities were assumed by public authorities in the first place for reasons which even if valid then are often no longer so. They are retained because trade unions, management and elected representatives regardless of political flavour frequently form an unholy alliance to keep their empires intact.

This is true not only of local authorities but central government as well. Around 1900 the Army at Aldershot wanted an electricity supply for its barracks, married quarters, stores and offices, and all the other requirements of a population of several thousands. The only practicable choice in those early days of almost non-existent rural electricity supplies was for the Army to have its own generating station, and this was duly built and operated satisfactorily (as far as the users if not the taxpayers were concerned) for nearly three-quarters of a century. By that time the generators were out of date, and so, of course, with the national grid and the CEGB, was the whole concept of private local electricity generation.

The army complexes at Aldershot were no different from those in many other locations in the UK and elsewhere and there was no military justification for a separate supply, but public services do not easily give up their functions. Aldershot power station is still owned by the Ministry of Defence, but now has bigger and better generators.

The switch away from authority-executed services to the use of contractors, wholly or in part, under the direction of public authorities,* is welcome as a first step. It may lead to more fundamental changes in our thinking. Most of us take for granted that at least some important functions at present discharged by government will remain under public control indefinitely. But there is a compelling case for asking whether many of the so-called public services should be provided by public authorities, on *any* basis, whether direct labour or contractor. In his excellent analysis† of the way in which British households are taxed to pay for services subsequently provided by public authorities, Arthur Seldon shows that around half to three-quarters of all taxes raised go back in benefits *to the same households*. The transfer of wealth from those who can pay to help those who cannot affects only those at the top and bottom of income levels. This in turn means that we are paying an enormously high price to have our own money taken from us and returned in the form of spending for us on the services we need, or in some instances, do not need.‡

All these and many more important questions will need to be examined if we are to make the best use of our national resources, which it is in no one's interests to waste, least of all those who most need help. In the meanwhile, returning to the main theme of this chapter, the most urgent need is to cut short the debate and get on with the provision of an effective audit service of the kind we have been discussing. There is no justification for endless delay and debate while an attempt is made to devise the perfect system. It never works out like that anyway, and a good time to start tinkering with the organisation and refining the procedures is after a few years of practical experience.

* One of the commonest objections to a move towards using contractors is that this involves the authority in giving up its responsibilities. This is true in only a limited sense, although it seems to generate a good deal of concern. An authority does not turn its back on its responsibilities when it uses a private sector contractor. It retains them fully, but executes them differently.

† *Charge*, by Arthur Seldon (Maurice Temple Smith Ltd). Arthur Seldon was, until his recent retirement, Director of the Institute of Economic Affairs.

‡ See also *Free to Choose*, by Milton & Rose Friedman (Secker & Warburg and Pelican Books).

Unfortunately these decisions are in the hands of politicians and officials, and there is little we can do as individual citizens except to keep up the pressure on elected representatives as best we can. But while these strategic issues follow their slow course, the councils, the boards and the authorities are going to go their way spending, and often wasting, your money and mine. The next chapter deals with the methods by which individual citizens, local groups, and councillors can make themselves effective as waste warriors.

# 13
# A Citizen's Guide to Cost-cutting

Law-abiding citizens, whether as individuals or groups, who want to conduct a crusade enjoy substantial advantages in this country, and also have to struggle against disadvantages which can be just as big. It is well to have some understanding of these from the outset.

To begin with, lone voices stand very little chance of being heard. So much is happening all day every day, so many burning issues are thrust under the noses of authority and public alike, that the days of the one-man campaigns are gone for ever. It takes a great deal to be heard, and a great deal more to get action taken – which is one reason why people have adopted violent methods as the only way to gain attention. When you have banged your head in vain against a wall of complacency, patronising indifference and sheer stupidity from your local authority or water board, for example, you may well occasionally have to suppress a wistful desire to put a boot behind someone's bottom, or at least heave a brick through the window. Don't do it! You can't win! All that happens is that the ratepayers or the water consumers have to foot the inevitable bill. Instead, be realistic about individual limitations and don't try to go it alone. Join with others of a like mind. There are a great many people who are now very worried – as they should be – about public spending. Join one of the existing groups – ratepayers' associations, your local business or professional bodies, chambers of trade and commerce, or whatever else is available locally.

It may be worthwhile joining one of the local political groups, but be wary of them. Although at first glance they would seem to be the logical choice, they cannot always be trusted to put their weight behind reducing public expenditure. All too often they have their eye on what they see as their best short-term electoral advantage, and that may not be the same as cost-cutting. Persuading them that they are wrong about this may be best done from the outside.

So join forces with others, and if none of the existing groups matches your ideas, form your own. Either way, the next step forward may be to form *ad hoc* federations or alliances of groups who in turn can shout in unison, and be more likely to attract attention. Remember that in the end most of the power is in the hands of officials and politicians. Rational argument and common sense has nothing like as much effect on those groups as the bludgeoning power of a lot of citizens shouting together.

The process of making your case heard will be greatly assisted by the media. Despite all the attempts to muffle and mislead it (see Chapter 9) we still have, thank God, a free press, a courageous one, and by and large a very competent and effective one. This is just as well because, in my experience, the only parts of the machinery of democracy which work effectively in this country are the media. If you can get the facts, the press, whether local or national, will almost always give you a fair hearing.

Getting the facts, and for that matter doing all the other hard work involved in running this sort of campaign, is the next problem. First flushes of enthusiasm to do something constructive about the rates or the charges levied by the public utility authorities tend to evaporate. True, a regular fillip is given every time the latest heavily increased demands for immediate payment come through the letter box, but most of us don't want to use our leisure time for political activities.

And very reasonable that attitude is, too, except that, unfortunately, the money spenders are prepared to do just that. Fortunately, there are numbers of able men and women around, especially with high unemployment in ex-managerial grades, who can give time, energy and skills to an organising secretary's job, just for out-of-pocket expenses, or a nominal honorarium. The amounts of money involved as contributions from members need not therefore be burdensome, and may with any luck be handsomely repaid by holding down rates and other charges.

The next step is to find out where your authority's money is going, and where the waste is. It is quite safe to start with the assumption that there *is* waste to be found. All we have to do is track it down.

All local and public authorities have to produce accounts. These are often published along with pompous 'messages from the Chairman' explaining how the accounts and accompanying report show what care and thought has been devoted to the authority's activities by its talented staffs and able management. It may be true, but these accounts are not usually in a form which enables anyone to form any conclusion about how well or badly affairs are being managed. The account may show that £x millions have been spent on wages and salaries, but there is no way of knowing whether there is gross overmanning so that the figure ought to be only £0.5x million.

For example, every year London Transport produces a glossy brochure in colour with a great many pictures of LT buses, trains and stations, presumably in case there are large numbers of readers who otherwise would not know what they look like. There are masses of figures and explanations of the organisation's problems, and how well they are being overcome. But nowhere will you find statements in a form which will enable you to discover that in thirty years LT's total costs had grown 12-fold and costs per mile 16-fold; or that, after making every allowance for inflation, *costs per mile had tripled.** This is the sort of information which the cost investigator needs to wring out. When you have it, you are on the way to finding out why the costs have gone up.

Faced with these uninformative and largely useless annual statements, how and where do you make a start? The answer is to break down the grand totals into subdivisions which can be critically examined.

Suppose Loamshire County Council spends £100 million a year. This total will be sub-divided under a number of different heads, corresponding with the organisational structure of the authority. Education expenditure is likely to be by far the biggest constituent of the budget, and that brings us to the first of the hurdles which the earnest economiser will have to surmount. *Do not* on any account be put off either by your own misgivings or by the objections of others from subjecting worthy causes to scrutiny. *Do not* let anyone persuade you that economy is all very well in some fields but that education (or welfare, or services for the old or the young or anything else) is too worthy to need looking at.

It may be that some of these services are at a *lower* level than is desirable. All the more reason, then, for making sure that we are getting the best possible value for money. Money spent on education will be used, in part, for essential textbooks for vital subjects for children at important stages in their learning. On the other hand it may be going down the drain. Remember the water wasted in unnecessary flushing in Berkshire. Those costs were charged to education (see page 127), just like textbooks and teachers' salaries. So the searcher for savings must take a robust line in refusing special exemptions for particular forms of expenditure; and in short must refuse to be taken in by the label on the bottle.

Having determined that Loamshire's education budget is not ex-

* Letter from I. Phillips, Group Planning Director LT, dated 6 July 1979, to me.

empt, the next step is to see how the money is spent. The answers may be readily available in some instances; in others you may need the assistance of councillors or the media. Keep reminding everyone that you are talking about *public* services and *public* money, and that you (and a lot of other people) are determined to find out what is going on. It will probably be hard work, but you will usually win in the end. Before that happens you will be faced with some or all of a series of standard objections, which you need to be prepared for.

The first is that it is all very well for busybodies/public-spirited people like you to go around demanding answers to all sorts of questions but the authority's staffs are already under pressure and, with the best will in the world, there just isn't the time and staff capacity to cope with all this extra work. Absolute rubbish. Look in on any electricity board showroom or any council clerical pool, and see how many of the staff are gossiping amiably or chatting on the telephone. Very few public sector employees are under pressure.

Next, what about the cost of all these enquiries, ask the officials, thereby displaying an interest in economy for perhaps the first time in their official careers! Are such enquiries self-defeating in that they themselves need a great deal of money? Like the cost of central audit (see Chapter 12) it is a fair question, and one which deserves to be treated seriously. A number of points have to be considered.

Big organisations do have, for the most part, a fund of data available, although it is often not in the form that is required for cost-investigation purposes. Digging it out, putting it into the form required and analysing it does take time, and therefore needs money although usually not as much as is represented. On the other hand, if the organisation does not have the information, and does not therefore know what costs are, how can it hope to be effective and conduct the public's business economically? How, also, can it possibly be sure that it is right to dismiss attacks on its wasteful spending? The authority cannot have it both ways. If it knows enough to give the lie to its critics, it knows enough to give the answers they need. The people with the answers are right there in the authorities themselves, in the audit departments, the management service groups, and the Treasurers' departments. You will find good staff there, usually in the middle grades and nearly always frustrated by what they know and can do nothing about.

Suppose that very little data is readily available and the expense of getting it in consequence is sizeable, is it still worthwhile pressing home the attack? The answer is that waste, overmanning and poor-value-for-money practices and policies in the public sector are *not* marginal or insignificant, and the costs of investigation *are* justified – a hundredfold or more. Look at Berkshire's figures and the potential savings produced by that one inexpensive survey. Berkshire is cost-conscious and well-managed compared with many local authorities, especially the big city ones. And the worst of the local authorities is roughly comparable in terms of waste, incompetence and general sloppy management with the best (if that is the right word) of the nationalised industries and public utilities. Look back too at the potential savings evidenced by investigations in Camden, and London Transport. Savings of 20, 30, 40 per cent of expenditure are the commonplace findings of the authority's own staffs, based on detailed investigations and hard facts. 'Substantial waste', 'need for urgent action' and similar phrases are in constant use by outside investigators. I have yet to see *one single case* of the cost of investigations of this kind, properly conducted and free to report honestly on the findings, where the savings would not pay the bill within a few months. In fact, on reflection, I cannot remember an instance when this was not true even when the investigation was carried out in a half-baked way, as a number of the LT ones were.

There is therefore no need to be frightened off by expense. Let us suppose for the moment that reasonable arguments prevail and some form of investigation is approved by our Loamshire Council. Where do we go from there?

One of the most effective starting-points for looking at value for money is the technique of cost comparison. There is nothing new in this, nor is it limited, of course, to public services. Housewives know, for the most part, what is or is not good value for money on their grocery list not because they have basic data on the cost of producing and distributing a pound of butter, but because they can compare Sainsbury with Tesco and Fine Fare, and all three with the corner shop. The managements of these organisations in turn know that if they do not stay on top of their jobs, whether in buying, staffing or anything else, the results are soon reflected in their prices. They are supplied with a free-of-charge running check on their efficiency, to the great benefit of their performance and costs, and therefore, to their customers.

What we need to provide for the public services is a similar set of disciplines. This can be done for local authorities, but has a limited application to the nationalised industries.

The reason for this is that, although in theory some at least of the nationalised industries ought to be subjected to the rigours of free competition, they just cannot take it, even though they start with enormous advantages. The Electricity Board is not allowed to buy cheap coal, although it can be shipped here from the USA, Australia or Poland at lower cost than the home product. The Gas Board has its prices artificially boosted so that people will go on using electricity. The Post Office fights like mad to stop anyone else delivering mail or running telephone systems. Because these organisations have monopoly powers and status, the opportunities for the application of free market disciplines, and for meaningful comparisons with others, are sharply reduced.

Let us leave the nationalised industries for the moment, then, and concentrate on cost comparison for local authorities. There are three main constituents in this approach.

First, comparison with other authorities. A great deal of data already exists on this, and by far the most valuable source are the cost-comparison tables produced by the Chartered Institute of Public Finance and Accounting of 1 Buckingham Place, London, SW1E 6HS. The whole *raison d'être* of this body is to provide a Statistical Information Service on local government activities. For our imaginary Loamshire CC, for example, there would have been in the 'Financial General and Rating Statistics' volume a series of figures about levels of income and expenditure, analysed in a variety of ways, with comparisons grouped for similar types of authorities. There would also have been a special volume* (like the General Statistics, a foolscap-sized, approximately 100-page annual publication) relating to Education. This divides expenditure into categories – further education, higher education, nursery schools and so on; and it also provides other information of a non-financial kind, essential to crusading waste-watchers, such as the pupil/teacher ratio, and the number of staff employed in various branches.

You ought to be able to borrow, or at least consult on the premises, your local authority's copies, but if you can't then the £10 approximately a copy is money well spent. There are, however, some small problems about using this sort of statistical comparison which you need to be aware of.

The first is that, although these tables of statistics are clearly set out, they still present a formidable task to the beginner. The inclusion

---

* There is a third publication in this series, which you may find useful if you get heavily involved, entitled 'Local Government Trends'.

of an accountant or someone with a little experience in dealing with figures in your group will greatly enhance the potential value of the statistics, and greatly reduce the effectiveness of the evasive tactics likely to be adopted by your opponents. But in any case if you are prepared to put some time into it, you will manage.

Secondly, these tables necessarily provide only clues and trends and suggestions rather than a complete answer to value-for-money problems. Although they do their best, CIPFA cannot guarantee that all bases for comparison are equal. On the other hand, they do not need to do so. If the comparison tables show that your authority is amongst the most expensive 20 per cent of comparable authorities, that is enough to start with. The pressure and the burden of proof is then shifted to the authority to show why this should be so. Adept as they are at alibis, you should if you persevere find it possible to drive them from one defence to another until eventually you find out what you want.

Thirdly, although being amongst the high spenders is a fairly safe indication that all is not well, being amongst the low spenders is no proof that nothing is wrong. After all, the comparisons are only with other authorities, and none of them, not even the best, is even moderately good, let alone perfect.

Fortunately, the comparison technique does not end there. The second form it can take is comparison with the past. This may not sound very effective, but it is surprisingly revealing and, unlike the first comparison technique, it can be applied to all the public services. Find out what is being spent now, compared with five years or ten years ago (or any other convenient time), and see what the difference is, and why. At London Transport, for example, I argued that we had too many managers and LT disputed it. However, it was possible to show that, over ten years, the number of people in the senior management grades had increased fourfold, although we were managing fewer trains and buses. You can do the same sort of comparison with all sorts of other things; the unit cost of the main product; cost per mile; cost per ton; cost per pupil place and so on. And for the ancillary activities – travel by staff, numbers and cost of telephone calls, space occupied in authority premises, even the number of toilet rolls used! In one authority I know about, the number used had gone up eight-and-a-half times in just over ten years, although the staff had increased by only (only?) 85 per cent. These are the indicators which help to track down the things which have gone wrong.

Do not accept too readily the excuse that inflation provides the explanation for increases of cost. It may in many cases, but there will be others, the cost of clerical staffs for example, where this cannot be accepted automatically. You need to know why inflation on wages and salaries has not been offset at least in part by all the high-priced labour-saving equipment which officials will have been persuading authorities to buy over the years on the grounds that they reduce staffs. Computers, photocopiers, desk-top calculators and a host of other items have been provided for the administrative staffs, and even more has been, quite rightly, provided for other staffs, especially manual workers. The individual wage and salary levels should therefore reflect the upward trends of the last decade or two but the total bills should be at least in part reduced by all the expensive labour-saving devices.

The third form of cost comparison is in some ways the most important and potentially the most productive. This is the comparison between the costs of services provided by directly employed staffs and the cost of buying these services from the private sector. Like the examination of current costs against the past, this technique, too, has a wide application throughout the public services.

The arguments in favour of sharp reductions in the services provided by public authorities have been fully ventilated in recent years, and there is no need to go into them again in detail.* Those searching for economies need to bear in mind two basic propositions. First, the reasons why many services were first assumed by public authorities were frequently far from convincing at the time and have since then become steadily less defensible as a result of social, industrial and other changes. There is therefore every justification for taking a critical look at all the things public authorities do, and asking whether they need now to be done at all, and if so whether the service cannot be bought, wholly or in part, from the private sector. (For further notes on the division between private and public sector see Appendix 14.)

It is quite likely that at least for the time being the greatest opportunities for change will come from the 'in part' approach. If we go back to our Loamshire CC and its education department, for example, we can accept that at least for the foreseeable future the education department will go on employing teachers and running the schools. In theory there are alternatives; in practice they are not at

* The case for less public and more private sector services is set out in *Free to Choose* by Professor Milton Friedman, and *Charge* by Arthur Seldon.

present feasible. But there is more, of course, to the expenditure on education than the teachers' salaries. Why should the council employ directly the maintenance men who look after the school buildings? Or those who cut the grass and maintain the grounds? Or those involved in school meals? Or the cleaners? And of course the same questions arise throughout the council's operations, not just in the education department, as they do in relation to the activities of the other public services. The direct labour works departments of the publicly owned industries are every bit as inefficient as those of local authorities, as witness LT. The only difference is that the facts are known in most cases where local government is involved whereas the others can keep their wickedness under wraps.

The scandal of the direct labour building departments is another issue which has been well-ventilated, and the present Government was eloquent, before it was elected, about what could and would be done. As usual, all the bold words, glowing promises and challenging declarations led to little effective action. True, it is intended that local authorities (but not nationalised industries) will be required to make a limited number of cost comparisons* on certain types of work, but the machinery is too clumsy, and the opportunities for fudging are too great, for these to produce significant results.

Nevertheless, the pressure must be kept up. The savings available if councils and other authorities change their arbitrary and illogical policies must be constantly brought to the attention of those who are suffering cuts in services (usually to produce quite small savings); and of those who are being forced to pay higher and ever higher rates.

As with the other economies we have been discussing, the potential economies are not marginal or insignificant. They could make an appreciable impact on total budgets. The direct labour works organisations are anything from 20–50 per cent more expensive than private sector contractors.

In 1980, Southend-on-Sea Borough Council decided to put all the work carried out by their cleansing department (including refuse collection) to a private contractor.† The saving was over £500,000 per annum, equivalent to 22.7 per cent of the total cost. Following ex-

* A more useful source of information is the Building Maintenance Cost Information Service Ltd, a non-profit-making body which gives a good deal of useful information on this important branch of public expenditure, in the form of an *Annual Price Book*. BMCIS also operate seminars for both public and private sector participants.
† Cleansing can itself be split up if desired. Humberside saved £50,000 per annum by giving school window-cleaning only to private contractors.

perience with this contract, and surveys elsewhere, it is estimated that on a total public sector cleaning bill of about £3 billion per annum at least £500 million per annum could be saved.*

The paper containing these estimates included two further observations which have a familiar ring. The first was that officials up and down the country admit privately that they were overstaffed by anything up to 50 per cent. Both the secrecy of the admissions and the size of the overstaffing correspond with my own experiences. The second gloomy note relates to the response by officialdom. Although it was proved that savings ranging from $17\frac{1}{2}$–30 per cent were available no action was taken.

A separate report, which was made available to the Health Minister, claimed that at least £80 million per annum could be saved on hospital cleaning. Bearing in mind the comparatively trifling sums being saved by the Health Services by devices which are causing real hardship to the public, the response to this, too, is illuminating. Dr Vaughan merely sent a letter to the health authorities (his second) confiding in them his 'disappointment' that so little use is being made of private contractors. The authorities, apparently taking the view that Dr Vaughan can be ignored, have shown every sign of being able to bear up bravely under his disappointment. With a serene disregard for every ascertainable fact and a wide range of experience by central and local government, the chairman of the Oxfordshire Health Authority announced: 'It seems to me that direct labour . . . is more efficient, more flexible and cheaper than contract labour.'

This is a good example for cost-cutters of the kind of reaction they will have to meet and overcome. The cure remains the same: get the facts and publish them – and keep on publishing them. The cost-cutter must then be ready for the next series of defences and counter-attacks.

One public sector management† defence against cuts which has become very popular in the last two decades is to announce that 'the unions will never stand for it'. It is usually a good sign when this stage is reached because it suggests that there are no rational and factual arguments left. It is quite true that at national level most trade union

---

* Local Government Programme Management (Anglian Group) Seminar. Paper presented by Richard Barlow, Group Marketing Director, Exclusive Cleaning Group Ltd.
† The private sector was for a brief period also guilty of this ploy, but it seems to be going out of fashion again there.

leaders are more concerned in their public statements with political posturing than their members' interests. Most of them will also feel that, whatever the logic of the situation, their position would be untenable if they did not put up spirited protests against any reduction in job numbers. This is a particularly easy line to follow in the public sector where, after all, a bit of overmanning here and there merely means keeping up income tax and rates. This philosophy is shared to some extent at lower full-time-official levels, and the following extract shows trade-union officialdom at its most unhelpful, but also devoid of pretence that there is any concern about anything other than keeping staff numbers up at all costs. It is more usual to find this self-interest disguised as concern about maintaining standards of service for the public.

'Dear Mr. ——
*"Chapman-style" Investigation*
I have again sought advice from the men's representatives and they are still adamant that their original decision stands. They feel that men of the calibre of Mr. . . . closely controlled by the various County Council Committees cannot be successfully advised by junior investigators. These Officials, some of different departments, surely cannot have the experience and expertise of senior surveyors.

All I have stated in recent letters is reiterated to the full. The men have received enough reviews, manpower or otherwise, in recent years. They refuse to co-operate in a future enquiry that could possibly endanger their livelihood and standard of living.

I regret that on this occasion I cannot be more helpful.'

The biggest danger to be expected from the trade unions and staff associations is that, without taking any initiative, they provide a standing army for those who, whatever their reasons, do not want reductions in public sector staffs, spending, or powers. Given Labour councillors who assert openly that they are not prepared to agree to the reduction of their authority's spending or staffs for any reason, the unions' role is made very easy. Conservative councillors who are somewhat half-hearted about reductions (and there are many of them, once they are out of opposition and in office) are similarly easy to threaten or cajole. In the nationalised industries the task is easier still. There are no councillors to ask awkward questions, and cosy agreements between officials and unions, usually preceded by the obligatory threatening words on both sides, are the order of the day.

Negotiations are made doubly easy by the fact that these officials, like those in local authorities, are themselves usually members of the association they are dealing with.

These officials are conscious too that the unions have a powerful voice both in the sense of public comment and in the choice of appointments to management. Those officials who contrive to conduct their affairs in a way calculated to win the approval of organised labour and its political extensions are therefore assured of powerful support. It is a form of symbiosis which is not good for the public services, but it is hardly logical to blame the unions. As they see their function, in this country at least, it is to look after the jobs and employment conditions of their members, and leave others to look after themselves.

On the other hand, my own direct experience with trade-union representatives has been that, while they are not enthusiastic about cost-cutting proposals of this kind, they are never in the end wilfully obstructive and have frequently been constructive and co-operative. This is equally true of the white-collar staff associations, whose local unpaid representatives seem to adopt a very sensible approach to enquiries of this kind. No doubt they are helped by the fact that many authorities have no-compulsory-redundancy agreements or understandings, so that the worst contingency to be faced is a gradual run-down of staff numbers through natural wastage. Generally, I believe that, after a few ritual displays of unconvincing indignation, public sector cost-investigations can go ahead if not with the co-operation of trade unions then at least without active opposition. The following extracts from a NALGO branch circular (not Berkshire), while appearing to take a somewhat aggressive line is, I think, representative of the reaction to be expected, is not unreasonable, and provides a basis for proceeding in consultation:

## —— BRANCH – NALGO

'The Council has called in Mr Leslie Chapman to advise on a "war against waste". . . .

The Leader of the Council admits that the politicians have gone as far as they can in cutting services and that's why they are turning their attention to "waste". . . .

Nobody can deny that there are areas of waste in any organisation but we should be wary of what is meant by waste. A lot of people have already suggested areas of waste in *other* people's jobs and there do not seem to be many who admit that their job is a waste. In addition we must appreciate that one man's waste can be another man's service. . . .

What we must also emphatically reject is the widely held view that the public sector is somehow responsible for the country's economic ills. It is the failure of the private sector to invest which has held back economic growth but there do not seem to be any Leslie Chapmans investigating private firms. A continuation of cuts in the public sector will speed the country to the two million unemployed which is forecast for the near future. On Mr Chapman's own admission three-quarters of the savings which he achieved in the civil service were by lost jobs. . . .

The first effect of the Chapman exercise is on the morale of our members in the Management Services Division. . . .

The second effect is on the members whose work will be under investigation. . . .

It is clear that the intention is to do away with posts and some members' jobs will therefore disappear. The Council has reaffirmed the policy which we negotiated some time ago against no forced redundancies but the deletion of a post will result in redeployment and all the problems that will entail. Widespread deletion of posts will make it increasingly difficult to maintain the policy against forced redundancies and will also put extra pressure on remaining staff. . . .

*What should the Union do?*

The immediate reaction of many union representatives is to tell the Council to get lost as we are not prepared to be attacked again and again for alleged waste and inefficiency. Others feel that we have nothing to hide and an investigation will demonstrate that the officers in local government are not responsible for vast areas of waste. *Telling the Council to get lost will get us bad publicity and some of our members might be prepared to ignore the policy anyway.** . . .

The middle course is supported by some who think that we should go along with the investigations but scale the exercise down to a few pilot schemes or topics on which we agree. This would allow investigations into the politicians' waste, but could, of course, still end up with loss of jobs. . . .'

I do not know which prevailed – the threat of bad publicity, the possibility that some members might refuse to be unhelpful to the investigators or, as I believe, the sense of public duty of many of those

* My added emphasis.

in local authorities and the Civil Service. Whatever the reason, the final outcome was not affected by union opposition.

And what if the unlikely happens, and there is active opposition, even after proper and adequate consultation? Then I believe that the authority should go ahead anyway, since the alternative is to accept the proposition that public sector staffs are never reduced whatever the justification. It is unlikely that a union unwise enough to adopt such a line would find much support except from the professional wreckers.

Closely linked with the Trade Union argument is the proposition that the public services ought not to go around reducing staffs since the only result is to increase unemployment – the cost of which merely falls on a different part of the same public purse. It was a case made to me by a variety of sponsors including a conservative MP fifteen years ago, and the recent rapid increase in unemployment has naturally given it a considerable boost. High unemployment notwithstanding, it is not a valid argument. If it were, the logical extension of it would be to find jobs somewhere in the public sector for all the currently unemployed and our troubles would be over. The truth is – in an admittedly somewhat over-simplified form – that the community as a whole spends all its wealth. Whatever it stops using on unnecessary public expenditure will be spent elsewhere, on something more of its own choosing. The jobs lost to the public sector will be gained by the private sector.

Another recent addition to officialdom's defence mechanism is concern about the morale of the organisation. Perhaps there is some waste and overmanning here and there, it is conceded, with a brave show of determination to be frank at all costs, but people get upset by the thought of being investigated, and the prospect of being publicly criticised. The result could be counterproductive. Would it not be much better to work along quietly, using the existing procedures with a gentle boost, and achieve the required savings quietly and tactfully?

The short answer to this is 'no'. It would not be better to use the existing procedures. They are the ones which have brought about the present thoroughly unsatisfactory situation and all the evidence shows that they do not and cannot work. In any case all the talk of morale is so much claptrap. The only reason why it persists is that since there is no way in which it can be measured, all sorts of fearsome references to services suffering because 'morale is at rock bottom' can be bandied about without fear of being disproved by hard statistics.

When the dispute at London Transport was at its height there were

constant references to the damage being done to morale, largely
because that was all there was left by way of defence. Yet I talked to
bus crews by the score; and to a reasonable cross-section of other
staffs from secretaries to middle management; and received a considerable number of letters from staff. Far from morale suffering, all of
them seemed to think it was high time that there was a shake-up in the
organisation and that in the end nothing but good could come of it.

In the interests of strictly accurate reporting, I must also record
that a very large proportion of those I spoke to displayed unseemly
glee at the spectacle of the top echelons being done over! Do not worry
therefore about damaged morale. The only vulnerable morale involved belongs to the managers and those to whom they are responsible, whether councillors, boards, authorities, or the like, who fear
that when the facts become known their perks, their comfortable
grooves, and even their well-paid jobs may be at risk.

A variation on the morale defence which you are likely to meet is
that investigations into costs and efficiency amount to a vote of no
confidence in current management by implying that they have not
done their jobs properly. There are substantial numbers of well-
qualified judges of these matters who, I suspect, would not be in the
least unhappy to justify investigations on precisely those grounds!

However it is not necessary to exacerbate sensitive feelings. Cash
and financial audits are an invariable rule where public and most
private monies are concerned, and no one takes this to imply that the
treasurers have been stealing the petty cash or misappropriating the
stamps. It is merely a prudent safeguard against the outside chance
of failure. Value-for-money audits should be regarded in the same
light – an automatic and invariable adjunct to the normal machinery
of public administration.

There are two more defensive screens that you are almost certain to
meet at some stage.

The first offers an apparently sensible, down-to-earth answer to
those who persist in producing evidence of waste. It is especially
popular as a defence against charges of extravagant spending on the
part of those who have the authority to treat themselves generously. It
is likely to be used when it is no longer possible to deny that the
expense has been incurred. It is true, runs this argument, that this
spending was not absolutely essential – perhaps, even, as its critics
claim, it was positively not necessary by any stretch of the imagination – but does it matter? If those concerned had not had a jaunt to
the Caribbean at the ratepayers' expense, or the mayor had not had a

second Rolls-Royce, or no smoked salmon had been served at that last jamboree, no one would have noticed the difference. The amount saved would not have taken a halfpenny off the rates (or off the price of a bus ticket, or a unit of electricity, or a gallon of water depending on the authority concerned).

Like all good disinformation material, there is some truth in this, but it is truth which is misleading. Although not enough to affect basic charges for services, economies in this field can certainly be better spent in the public interest. If LT had ceased to use chauffeurs to drive senior staff, the £250,000-plus-a-year which would have been saved would not have been anywhere near enough to reduce the price of a ticket. It would however have been quite enough to produce a marked improvement in the standards of cleanliness on the under-ground trains, and thereby improved the daily lot of millions of travellers. The doesn't-really-matter defence is only made to appear sound by using a misleading financial starting-point.

The next stage in this defence is to question whether the money would have been better spent if the extravagance had been avoided. Those who fight so manfully in the public interest are surely entitled to some rewards, in return for which the public can look for even greater displays of selfless, untiring, efficient management. It is an argument which, with slight variations, is advanced to justify massive salary increases for MPs, chairmen of public concerns and similar deserving causes. They deserve the extra money, and it is right that they should have it.

Is it? The cuts in the supply of textbooks for schools, and in services for the sick and disabled, were not made on the basis of merit or just deserts. No one was claiming that the need was not there. The cuts were being made simply because the money was not available, and were regretfully accepted by many on that account alone. Even if generous assessments of the value of the services provided are accepted, therefore (which must be in doubt in many cases) high living cannot be justified by meritorious service.* If the expense cannot be justified because it is essential (and I have not known a case where it could be) then it is not acceptable.

We come now to the very last smokescreen you are likely to meet at this stage. It purports to appeal to the nicer, kinder side of potential

---

* One rule for those in authority, and another for the rest is not a purely civilian phenomenon. In his book *The War between the Generals*, David Irving records how in the darkest days of the last war one UK commander had 3 tons of scarce and rationed commodities flown to England from the Middle East in a special aircraft.

critics (and the listening public) rather than to the (by implication) not-so-nice and not-at-all-kind instincts which cause us all to worry about value for money. People, it is claimed, cannot be treated like objects, or counted like units; human needs and emotions cannot be measured; we may not be able to prove that what we are doing is cost-effective (or even effective in any other way) but at least we are *trying* to help.

These are arguments which have had an almost undisputed run for the last thirty years. They are constantly used in connection with expenditure on welfare and its associated activities, and since some 25 per cent of public expenditure is consumed in these activities, it is essential that we look at the way it is spent, and satisfy ourselves as far as possible that we are as a community getting value for money.

Despite the smokescreen, there is no reason why this should not be done. Many of the constituents of spending on health, welfare and education *can* be analysed, measured and compared with similar activities by other bodies and with past records (see Chapter 12). Still more to the point, even if the methods, beliefs and theories of these organisations are made of stuff too delicate for the rude handling of those interested in costs, at least the results they achieve can be looked at. After all, if those who are spending the money cannot, for whatever reason, justify what they are doing, how can they know they are right? And if they can justify it, why cannot the rest of us, including those concerned about costs, share in, and have an opportunity of evaluating, the justifications.

This is a vitally important subject, and one which fortunately is now being tackled as it should be. A series of brilliant studies* of the nonsense talked about these matters was published last year, and if you have any interest in this field of public spending I strongly urge you to read it. This book is being followed by a series on similar lines commissioned and published by the Social Affairs Unit of the Institute of Economic Affairs, and I commend them to you also. The first was entitled *Breaking the Spell of the Welfare State*, a title which goes a long way towards explaining the content and purpose of the book. The following passage is taken from the introduction: 'For today's critic of the welfare state is not debating in ideal circumstances. He is dealing with a complex of ideas, official reports, half-hidden practices, undisclosed assumptions, alliances of vested interests . . . sentiment-laden appeals and ideology.'

Today's critic of public waste, and the crusader for better value for

* *The Ignorance of Social Intervention*, edited by Digby Anderson (Croom Helm).

money will soon find that what was said of welfare applies with equal force throughout public sector spending.

If the Loamshire County Council is persuaded by your arguments and your persistence (both are necessary) and agrees that some form of value-for-money investigations should take place, there are further obstacles to surmount.

To begin with, accept your own and your helpers' limitations, whether you are councillor or member of the public. You can create the climate which causes enquiries to be put in hand. You can help to ensure that they are done in the right way. And you can put a lot of weight behind the push that will be needed to see that action is taken on the findings. What you cannot do is to make effective enquiries yourself. There is no place there for amateurs and part-timers. Getting the facts means hard slogging away at masses of very dull records week after week, full-time. Even if you were allowed access to the records (and there might be perfectly valid reasons for permission being refused, if you are not in a recognised position of trust) you are unlikely to be able to find that sort of spare capacity. Anyone willing to let the job be done in a couple of hours a week after normal office closing time should be regarded with deep suspicion. So, rule no. 1: no amateurs.

Rule no. 2 for good investigation is, no one-man bands. Single individuals, unless they are geniuses, do not have the breadth of experience and professional knowledge to enable them to cope with all the devious wriggling and evasions which can be expected from officials defending their empires. Interrogations of really hardened, experienced and clever criminals are, I believe, usually conducted by two police investigators. For efficiency and value-for-money audits, and the investigations that go with them I found three to be the minimum desirable in the Civil Service. Berkshire CC used five; London Transport used more. I would not suggest for one moment that there is any significance in those figures, save that posses rather than lone rangers seem to work best!

Next, try to ensure that at least one of the team comes from outside the authority being investigated. I do not suggest that the poor chaps on the team will otherwise be pressured into telling less than the whole truth, but the poor chaps in question seem to have a curious and persistent conviction that they will be! So just to keep them happy, have an outsider in. Any failure to suppress embarrassing bits of evidence here and there, or refusal to soften the findings in some convenient way, can then be explained by reference to the intrusion of the disobliging foreign body into the otherwise loyal and cosy domestic scene.

The outside element can be provided in a number of ways. Hiring from a management consultant is one way, but loans from other organisations (see Berkshire again) can also work quite well.

The team should desirably have a range of talents and qualifications, and I am strongly in favour of having at least one qualified or experienced auditor/accountant member. Do not, however, make the mistake of leaving it entirely to these admirable characters. If you are looking at the functions of water authorities, for example, as was done recently at the behest of that same Mr Heseltine mentioned in Chapter 12 you must have qualified engineers amongst your investigators. They will be able to obtain the sort of revealing answers which are needed almost without stopping to think. Accountants, however good, would not know the questions to ask, let alone be able to evaluate the answers. That is why the investigation of the water boards produced so little in the way of savings. But you do also need more than the strictly professional approach of the discipline most involved – so have both, and be safe.

For example, if an authority's transport services were selected for investigation I would suggest a team made up as follows:

– A transport expert certainly from a separate authority and desirably from a private sector group operating a fleet.
– An auditor/accountant from the appropriate department in the authority – County Treasurer, Finance Division, etc.
– A non-professional who could be hired from a consultant, borrowed from another authority, or if neither of these were practicable, one drawn from the administration of the authority – Chief Executive's staff, County Secretary, etc.

Once appointed, the team's terms of reference can be quite simple:

i) look at all the money being spent on the activity under review;
ii) decide whether it needs to be done at all;
iii) if it really must be, can an acceptable (i.e. not necessarily the best) service or product be provided at lower cost by changing methods or standards or in some other way.

The team will usually settle their own methods of working between themselves, but I prepared some notes for guidance for a new team which at one time looked as if it might start operating at short notice, and I have included these as Appendix 15.

When the team has finished its investigations, recorded the facts, and proposed its recommendations, it should put these together in the form of a comprehensive report which should go not only to the senior officials concerned but also to the elected representatives, or the members of the authority's Board, or whoever is the controlling body. The team should not prepare draft reports for discussion with Heads of Departments, or with anyone else. Whether action is taken on what they have found is not for the team to decide, but what they say in the report should be their decision alone. No compromises; no deals; no softening the sharp edges.

This requirement, for reasons which need no elaboration, often causes a good deal of consternation and opposition. Those opposing it will almost certainly be able to point to long-standing customs and practices where several drafts are produced before the final one is agreed. Don't give way. Look where the compromises have got us.

So far, this chapter has dealt with the action required when Loamshire responds and agrees to tackle its financial problems. You must be prepared, however, for the more likely contingency, which is that it will:

1. Tell you to mind your own business and leave the organisation to be run by the democratically elected representatives, the properly appointed members of the authority, or whatever.
2. Thank you effusively for your kind assistance, but explain either that all is well or that plans are in hand to make it so.

The answer is that it *is* your business – you are paying for it. For the commercial, business and industrial ratepayer the democratically elected angle won't wash – they suffer taxation without representation in a far worse form than that which lost us the USA as a captive market for teabags. And finally, the evidence that all is *not* well is everywhere to be seen.

None of this will get you far, and what you now have to do is to concentrate on the last part of that sentence, and start producing the evidence in relation to your selected authority. This is difficult to do from the outside, but far from impossible. You do it by reversing the process described in the first section. Instead of working through the activities and examining the costs and weeding out what is not essential, you begin by fastening on examples of non-essential or wasteful expenditure, putting price tags on them, and use these as justification for demanding a more orderly and scientific approach.

You will need all the help you can get, and this is where groups like the National Federation of Self-Employed, the Chambers of

Commerce, other dissident ratepayers and councillors can contribute. Put together a dossier of waste – it abounds in all authorities. Let it be known that you are doing so, through the local press, and information will start to flow in. Make a fuss, and then make another one. Do officials and councillors (and their wives) go off to a conference? Get the costs, and explain to angry parents how many textbooks could have been bought with the same money. Does the mayor get a new car? Ask the friends and relatives of people no longer receiving meals on wheels to make sure that everyone knows how much it costs the ratepayer for the mayor to use his wheels. Are the rates going up again, partly because the costs of, say, refuse collection are increasing? Ask why competitive quotes cannot be sought from the private sector, and how many dustmen finish work at midday or earlier. Are the rates going up because building costs are higher? Ask the local branch of the N F B T E to consult its members about the direct labour organisation. Are the rates going up because fuel charges are going up, a circumstance over which the authority has no control? See how many lights are burning in empty rooms; how much heat is being wasted (look at Berkshire again); how many miles of private car travelling the authority is paying for compared with ten or twenty years ago. Are the rates going up because telephone charges are increasing? How much does telephoning cost now compared with a few years ago, and how does the increase compare with charge increases? And what about the council letting a few organisations of the kind we have mentioned club together to find the money (it doesn't need much) to have all the calls monitored for a week or two!

You will be able to get help with at least some of the comparative cost studies which are so effective both in pinpointing wasteful practices and in suggesting better alternatives. A number of organisations will make surveys and cost investigations without charge or any other obligation. Of course they are doing it with an eye to business, but it can serve you too. If you can find out, or get your councillors to find out, some of the basic facts on costs, these firms will give quotations for an alternative service. You should be able to get such help with cleaning services, energy controls, use of telephones, building services of various kinds, electricity tariffs, many forms of engineering and vehicle maintenance, and probably others besides. You are in a good tactical position on this: if an alternative quote doesn't cost anything, the burden of proof to show why it should not be sought must fall fairly and squarely on the authority. And, whatever you do, tell the press.

In short, make so much noise that doing something effective about expenditure becomes less unpalatable to those in power than continuing to refuse to do it. You will become very unpopular in the process, and you will find few friends in the two main political parties largely because both have been closely associated with past failures. You will also find that some groups, like the C B I for example, are full of talk but surprisingly short on action; surprising, that is, until you discover that a significant part of their revenue comes from the nationalised industries. They are therefore very happy to see local authorities' expenditure criticised but will have no part in tackling the far greater waste in the nationalised industries and publicly owned authorities. It is not only politicians who, as potential allies, need to be treated with reserve.

Get your own local groups to join with you, get the facts, and tell the media. It will seem an uphill and largely unrewarding task but the climate is changing slowly. Anything and everything you can do to shine more light into the dark corners will help to speed up that process of desirable change.

# Appendix 1

## Local Authority Manpower and Expenditure, GB, 1952–1979[1]

| Year | Total[2] manpower[5] (000s) | Expenditure (billions) |
|---|---|---|
| 1952 | 1,448 | 1.60 |
| 3 | 1,470 | 1.76 |
| 4 | 1,487 | 1.89 |
| 5 | 1,515 | 1.98 |
| 6 | 1,556 | 2.12 |
| 7 | 1,594 | 2.32 |
| 8 | 1,625 | 2.43 |
| 9 | 1,671 | 2.53 |
| 1960 | 1,709 | 2.73 |
| 1 | 1,755 | 2.96 |
| 2 | 1,821 | 3.33 |
| 3 | 1,887 | 3.64 |
| 4 | 1,964 | 4.08 |
| 5 | 2,025 | 4.61 |
| 6 | 2,123 | 5.12 |
| 7 | 2,212 | 5.63 |
| 8 | 2,287 | 6.22 |
| 9[3] | 2,344 | 6.67 |
| 1970 | 2,387 | 7.92 |
| 1 | 2,466 | 9.13 |
| 2 | 2,584 | 10.30 |
| 3 | 2,699 | 11.95 |
| 4[4] | 2,697 | 14.87 |
| 5 | 2,814 | 17.64 |
| 6 | 2,862 | 21.23 |
| 7 | 2,827 | 23.96 |
| 8 | 2,840 | 25.43 |
| 9 | 2,898 | 28.64 |

NOTES
1. Expenditure figures are taken on March 31 at the end of the financial year. Manpower figures are taken at the following June and so the two sets of information are not strictly comparable.
2. Totals include police forces but exclude police civilians, cadets, traffic wardens and agency, magistrates' courts and probation service staff.
3. About 20,000 employees were transferred to Passenger Transport Executives between 1969 and 1970.
4. An estimated net total of 90,000 employees were transferred to Regional Water Authorities, to the National Health Services and to Passenger Transport Executives on 1 April 1974.
5. Excluding Special Temporary Employment Programme/Job Creation Programme.

SOURCES
*Manpower*
(England and Wales) – DE to 1974; DOE/Local Authority Associations Joint Manpower Watch from 1975. (Scotland) – DE to 1975; Scottish Joint Manpower Watch from 1976.
*Expenditure*
*Annual Abstract of Statistics*: ch. 16 – Home Finance. Central Statistical Office.
Statistical abstract for the United Kingdom from *Ten Billion Pounds: Whitehall's Takeover of the Town Halls* by Tyrrell Burgess and Tony Travers (Grant McIntyre).

# Appendix 2

# Non-Industrial Staffs of Government Departments, UK, 1902–1979

'Non-industrial civil servants' is the official title of the white-collar workers in government departments. They include the staffs with whom the public normally have contact, and range from junior clerks to the head of departments. (See also the notes below.)

Industrial staff are skilled and unskilled manual workers, the majority of whom are employed in defence and associated departments.

| Year | 000s | Year | 000s |
|------|------|------|------|
| 1902 | 50 | 1939 | 163 |
| 1910 | 55 | 1944 | 505 |
| 1914 | 70 | 1945 | 499 |
| 1918 | 221 | 1946 | 452 |
| 1919 | 194 | 1947 | 457 |
| 1920 | 161 | 1948 | 445 |
| 1921 | 158 | 1949 | 458 |
| 1922 | 133 | 1950 | 433 |
| 1923 | 124 | 1951 | 425 |
| 1924 | 115 | 1952 | 429 |
| 1925 | 114 | 1953 | 414 |
| 1926 | 110 | 1954 | 405 |
| 1927 | 108 | 1955 | 386[3] |
| 1928 | 106 | 1956 | 384 |
| 1929 | 109 | 1957 | 381 |
| 1930 | 111 | 1958 | 375 |
| 1931 | 118 | 1959 | 375 |
| 1932 | 119 | 1960 | 380 |
| 1933 | 118 | 1961 | 387 |
| 1934 | 117 | 1962 | 394 |
| 1935 | 128 | 1963 | 410 |
| 1936 | 133 | 1964 | 414 |
| 1937 | 142 | 1965 | 420 |
| 1938 | 152 | 1966 | 430 |

| | | | |
|---|---|---|---|
| 1967 | 451 | 1974 | 511 |
| 1968 | 471 | 1975 | 524 |
| 1969 | 470 | 1976 | 568 |
| 1970 | 493 | 1977 | 571 |
| 1971 | 498 | 1978 | 567 |
| 1972 | 496 | 1979 | 566 |
| 1973 | 511 | | |

NOTES

1. Numbers taken at 1 April; to the nearest thousand; in full-time equivalents; established and unestablished.

2. All figures exclude Post Office staffs, who were counted as civil servants for differing purposes at different periods. Up to 1939 Post Office staffs were bigger than the whole of the remainder of the Civil Service.

3. In 1954 7,000 non-industrial staff were transferred to UK Atomic Energy Authority.

SOURCES: *British Labour Statistics, Historical Abstract 1886–1968;* (figures from the Civil Service Department).

*Civil Service Statistics* (figures from Departmental Quarterly Staff returns).

*Annual Abstract of Statistics.*

# *Appendix 3*
# Four Letters from Sir Keith Joseph

CONFIDENTIAL                                        House of Commons
                                                        5 April 1977

Dear Mr Chapman,
I read with fascinated interest your two articles in the Sunday Times.
As one of those responsible for Conservative policy I plainly have
much to learn from you. Perhaps the key issue is how to motivate
leading civil servants to do that which needs to be done.

   Would you be willing to spare me time for a talk? If so, would you
perhaps telephone my secretary, [—] and she will consult your
convenience and mine to arrange the chance of a talk. If you are too
busy I shall reluctantly understand.

                                                    Yours sincerely,
                                                    Keith Joseph


                                                    House of Commons
                                                        28 June 1977

Dear Mr Chapman,
I kept a note of the talk we had when you kindly came to see me. I see
from the note that you were kindly going to prepare a paper and then
meet my colleagues, David Howell and Kenneth Baker, for a talk.

   I am very ready to fix a date to meet. I assume that there will be a
paper which all of us can then discuss. We put great importance on
the subject on which you have given such insights and been so
effective – and that is why I am following up.

                                                    Yours sincerely,
                                                    Keith Joseph

15 May 1978

Dear Mr Chapman,
Thank you for sending me a copy of your book. I had already bought one which I have now finished reading and marking – in practically every case with an enthusiastic tick.

The book is admirable. It constitutes a background against which my colleagues and I must now sharpen our own thinking.

I am sending the copy you sent me to David Howell, who has experience of the relevant work in government and whom you met. I shall be consulting him and Kenneth Baker – and have already asked Edward Du Cann to talk to me when he has read the book.

I am, to-day, writing to Mrs Thatcher who heard you on the radio and spoke to me enthusiastically about what you were saying. She was pleased to know that we had already been in touch.

I would very much welcome a talk with you when I have had the consultations mentioned above. Would you, perhaps, let me know when you are likely to be in London so that a mutually convenient time and day can be arranged?

Please speak to me or Sue Clarke, reversing the call, or send me a note of any day or days you know you are going to be available.

Yours sincerely,
Keith Joseph

3 August 1978

Dear Mr Chapman,
This note is to let you know that David Howell, Kenneth Baker and I have recently met again to confirm our interest in following up. We intend that when we have the chance, we should strengthen the C. and A.G. as you have proposed, and by using cash limits together with the techniques described in your book, we shall seek to reduce public spending as is necessary if we are to reduce borrowing and to reduce direct taxation.

I hope that we may keep in touch. Do please write to me at any time.

Yours sincerely,
Keith Joseph

# Appendix 4
# An Exchange of Letters with Sir Derek Rayner

Cabinet Office
29 June 1979

Dear Mr Chapman,

When we met last month, I undertook to write to you when I had carried further forward my consultations on and my thinking about my assignment from the Prime Minister. Considerable progress has now been made towards establishing in each of the major departments a study of an activity or function which might be unnecessary, or wasteful or too costly. Each of these studies will be carried out by an official of the department, working to a Minister and in consultation with me.

As Clive Priestley told you on the 'phone last week, I would have been very pleased if you had addressed these officials at my first meeting with them on 28 June, when I briefed them on the right approach to their work. I, and I am sure they, would have enjoyed and greatly benefited from having an account from your own lips of your success in promoting efficiency and eliminating waste.

As I understand it, you have such a strong reservation about my assignment and about the Government's approach to the questions of efficiency and waste that you felt that if you came to my meeting it would give a false impression to the wider audience which you are trying to help inform. I believe that the Government's initiatives will produce substantial benefits for the taxpayer in due time. Even so, I quite appreciate your desire for an unimpaired freedom of action.

Looking to the next stage of my work, I think that we can see ourselves as seeking the same ends and that you have elected to do so from a position of complete independence. If I have interpreted it correctly, perhaps we should agree to leave things on that footing for the time being?

All good wishes.

Yours sincerely,
Derek Rayner

20 July 1979

Dear Sir Derek,

Thank you for your letter of the 29th June. My feeling that I could
not, after all, help you with your assignment did not stem primarily
from my desire to retain freedom of action. It is quite simply that I do
not believe that the scale of effort, the techniques, or the organisation
which you intend to use begin to match either the size or the nature of
the problems you are tackling. Equally, I do not think that by any
test, your suggestion that my contribution to all this should consist of
one address to the individuals in the Departments who would be
carrying out the investigations, bears any relationship to the 'sharp
edged job' which was the phrase you used more than once in this
connection during our discussion.

I hope, as every taxpayer must, that I am completely wrong about
this, and that you and your colleagues will have a resounding success.
If this happens I shall hope to know about it early enough to be
among the first to congratulate you.

All good wishes,
L. C. Chapman

2 August, 1979

Dear Mr Chapman
Thank you so much for your letter of the 20th July and your good
wishes for the task which I have in hand.

The initial work that I have arranged is, as you know, to examine in
depth with individuals working full-time to me but within the departments, some key aspects about how Government goes about its work,
including accountability and promotional prospects for experienced
'Managers'. From the work already done it is likely that there will
emerge some major tasks to be undertaken in the Autumn.

Yours sincerely,
Derek Rayner

P.S. You will of course not be surprised to hear that the story you
unfolded in your book is likely to be found elsewhere in Whitehall.

# My Letter of 7 December 1979
# to Sir Horace Cutler

Dear Sir Horace

We have discussed by telephone my letter to the Chairman of LTE dated November, 14, a copy of which was sent to you by him with a covering letter dated November 20. You have also had a copy of my letter dated November 22 addressed to Dr Gordon Taylor as Chairman of the GLC's London Transport Committee.

My letter to the LTE Chairman described the serious policy differences between the remainder of the Executive and myself which began to emerge in March 1979 and which have become steadily worse since then. I believe that the conduct of affairs in LTE at present shows evidence of extravagance and waste in a variety of ways. While much of the waste is by no means new, some of it is particularly difficult to excuse in the current financial climate. I recognise that there is an element of opinion and conjecture in some of the criticisms I have made because the facts have not yet been established. However, it follows that the same degree of guesswork is to be found in the opinions of those who defend present practices. In some other areas I think I have, despite obstacles, provided in my two earlier letters a fair amount of evidential support for my claims.

At a prolonged meeting of the Executive on December 4, I went over the ground once again. By the end of the discussion I think the differing views had crystallised as follows:

a) The Executive generally rejected my belief that there was substantial wasteful expenditure. They believed that if there was any it did not amount to much either in absolute or percentage terms. This was particularly true of the expenditure on chauffeurs, cars, catering and hospitality and allied matters, and in any case such benefits for senior staff were similar to those enjoyed by private sector staffs.

I do not think I can add anything about the nature and scale of waste to the statements I made in my letters of November 14 and 22. As to the analogy with the private sector in relation to benefits for senior staff, I think it is open to question on two counts. The first is that in my experience I have not seen expenditure for these purposes on a similar scale. Second, private sector companies are subject to the constraints of the market place and the views of shareholders. These are usually replaced in the public sector by rules which are scrutinised by elected representatives of ratepayers and tax payers. In these matters L T E seem to operate with all the benefits of both private and public groups and the discipline of neither.

The Chairman said in his letter to you dated November 20 that he would, if my criticisms were publicised, insist on an independent enquiry. Since, if the policy differences cannot be resolved they are bound to become public sooner or later, I suggested that all our problems would be solved quickly and simply by holding such an enquiry forthwith. The Chairman's worries about the diversion of time and resources which this would involve are, I think, groundless. Some of the allegations about extravagance (paragraphs 8 and 9 of my November 22 letter, for example) could be checked in a day or two by an audit type examination of records. Others, such as those relating to failures to implement reports and surveys already completed would involve looking at a handful of existing documents and a few staff interviews. This would also be true of the charges that staff associated with criticisms of the organisation have been unfairly rebuked.

All in all I believe that the whole enquiry need not be spread over more than two or three weeks. The objective would not, of course, be to establish whether there is (my paragraph 10) "waste of resources, over manning, diversion of labour to unnecessary tasks, and the use of directly employed labour for activities which could be bought far cheaper outside". All I think we should ask the enquiry to do is first to decide whether there is prima facie evidence of such waste, as I believe. Or whether it can all be dismissed as "wild generalisations" as the Chairman believes. Second, to indicate whether a central group directed and partly staffed by people who have not been responsible for planning or executing the policies and practices to be questioned (as I believe) would be more effective than the self-examination which the Executive proposes.

With the exception of one other part-time member the Executive rejected the proposal for an enquiry.

All the members of the Executive objected strongly to my initiative to take the dispute outside L T E. They believe the doctrine of corporate responsibility requires that however much I may argue my view within the Executive the majority verdict must not only prevail, but must not be questioned outside. Once again private sector company practice was quoted.

I do not accept that there is for this purpose a very close analogy between a body like LTE and a private company for the reasons given in paragraph three above. In any case, directors are frequently nominated to boards, and such nominees report back to their principals. I therefore see no reason why I should not (and many reasons why I should) turn to you in a matter of this kind. Nor do I see any reason why I should not ask your agreement to making at least some of the facts public. The Executive view is that I can do this only if I resign.

While still disagreeing with this view I feel that the urgency of the situation is such that a lengthy debate on the ethics of resignation from public bodies is not practicable. At the end of the meeting the Executive decided to consider once again whether it will:

a) adjust its policies and proposals, including the structure and operation of the cost-cutting unit to arrive at something on which a substantial measure of agreement is possible, or

b) agree to the holding of an independent enquiry, or

c) hold firmly to their existing policies and proposals.

I have been considering this situation very carefully since the Executive meeting, and I thought that I should tell you that if c) above is selected, or if no action one way or another is taken, I shall tender my resignation to you.

Yours sincerely,
Leslie Chapman

# *Appendix 6*
# Report by Deloitte Haskins and Sells

## SECTION II – SUMMARY OF FINDINGS

13. In this section we summarise the underlying contentions contained in the two letters and our comments thereon. . . .

14. We consider that there are seven underlying contentions which lead Mr. Chapman to the conclusion that L T E is in breach of its statutory duty under S. 5(1) of the Transport (London) Act 1969, '. . . . it shall be the general duty of the Executive to exercise and perform their functions . . . . with due regard to . . . . economy'.

15. The first contention is that the level of expenditure on non-salary benefits (i.e. cars, chauffeurs, offices and catering) for top management is disgraceful. L T E dispute this. We have identified the sources of most of the information in Mr. Chapman's letters with regard to the level of expenditure on cars, chauffeurs and offices, and have carried out investigations to assess the accuracy of the information given (paragraphs 96 to 150). The information is substantially correct and such differences as do arise do not in our view significantly affect Mr. Chapman's argument. We have made comparisons of expenditure on catering, cars and office space for certain nationalised industries and companies in the private sector with the level of that in L T E. Except that the number of chauffeurs is probably higher proportionately in L T E, the comparisons indicated that the levels of expenditure and facilities provided are similar to those of nationalised industries. If such a comparison with nationalised industries is relevant, we do not consider that the level of expenditure by L T E is disgraceful (paragraphs 116/7, 143/7 and 150).

16. The second contention is that reorganisation will, only in the long-term, ease L T E's financial difficulties and that therefore there is an urgent need for a cost-cutting unit. We have examined memoranda and minutes and have had discussions with L T E officials in connection with the setting up of and progress made on the reorganisation scheme (paragraphs 89 to 95) and the Central Productivity unit ('C P U') (paragraphs 58 to 63). It is evident, and the Executive

have confirmed this to us, that the main aim of the reorganisation was
to seek to improve the transport services to the public by setting up a
management structure which would give rise to clearer accountability thus giving managers the opportunity to manage better. The
reorganisation was not intended simultaneously to seek out economies but, by clarifying accountability, to enable areas for economy to
be identified. We consider that the reorganisation, of itself, is unlikely
to ease materially LTE's financial difficulties in the short-term.
LTE set up the CPU in October 1979 and therefore Mr. Chapman's
contention that a cost-cutting unit is required is accepted by LTE.
We comment in paragraph 21 on the CPU.

17. The third contention is that LTE is too bureaucratic and the
number of managers has been allowed to grow unreasonably. Mr.
Chapman's statement on bureaucracy is based on his own judgment
and on discussions with LTE staff and not on direct evidence. LTE
agrees that, for historical reasons, it is too bureaucratic and this is a
reason for instituting the reorganisation. The Executive dispute that
the number of managers is excessive and believe management in
certain areas needs strengthening. We have undertaken a review of
the increase in the number of managers (paragraphs 81 to 83). We
find that Mr. Chapman is correct on the growth in numbers, but the
contention that there are too many managers cannot be established
without a detailed study of all significant parts of LTE.

18. The fourth contention is that potentially large cost-cutting savings could be made while maintaining current service levels. Mr.
Chapman is relying in part on his own judgment and experience and
in part on reports prepared for LTE. It is not possible to quantify the
potential cost savings in any of the areas cited by Mr. Chapman
without further investigation. We find that the reports referred to do
suggest that costs could be reduced in the two areas examined (Building Maintenance, paragraphs 151 to 169, and Construction Management, paragraphs 177 to 179), but the potential reduction in costs is
not quantified. In our view the report on Building Maintenance
suggests the need for further investigation of the use of direct labour
and other matters to determine the scope of economies. LTE accept
that there is scope in this and other areas and they also accept the
need for further study.

19. The fifth contention is that LTE concerns itself with activities
some of which are not necessary to the provision of efficient road and

rail operations in the Greater London area and others which could
more economically be provided externally. We have considered the
areas mentioned by Mr. Chapman. His contention is not based on
quantified evidence (paragraphs 180 to 185). LTE considers that
London Transport International and the Estates function for example are necessary; however, they accepted that some support
functions performed by LTE could be given to outside contractors.
We consider that specific areas can be identified for detailed study
with a view to establishing the economics of contracting out certain
work.

20. The sixth contention is that most LTE managers are of moderate
competence, and are complacent, as shown by their failure to take
action on certain specific reports which show scope for cost-saving
and by attempting to stifle criticism arising therefrom. LTE disputes
this. We have seen some evidence (paragraphs 170 to 176) of LTE
management being slow to act but it was not sufficient in itself to
support the generalised statements. It is probable that in a large
bureaucratic organisation there will be some managers of moderate
competence and some will be complacent. We have examined the
evidence with regard to the allegations of attempts to stifle criticisms
and have interviewed a number of officials on this matter (paragraphs
46 to 54). We consider that there have been some personal recriminations made against certain individuals.

21. The seventh contention is that the new productivity unit will
prove inadequate. The main aim of the CPU is 'value for money'
rather than pure cost-cutting. It is too early to judge what effect the
unit will have. The contention that the unit would prove inadequate
is based on Mr. Chapman's view that insufficient time would be
devoted to it by its top management and that in any case they were
not sufficiently independent to be effective. Judgment on their independence will need to wait until reports have been completed on some
current projects, although it appears to us that the top managers are
behaving in an independent way. A number of projects are already
being examined by the CPU and it appears to have made a purpose-
ful start. It intends to operate by the use of existing LTE staff,
supplemented by external assistance where required. This method of
operation appears to be accepted by both Mr. Chapman and LTE,
although Mr. Chapman appears to consider that, because of the
urgent need for cost-cutting, a greater weight of outside assistance
will be required. The present head and deputy head of the CPU have

largely devoted their time to the unit but will shortly move to their designated posts of Personnel Directors of Road and Rail. It appears to us that the impetus of the CPU may be lost when these Officers move and if the proposal that the CPU will be merged with the Management Services Department is adopted.

22. A judgment on whether or not the Executive is in breach of its statutory duty can only be made after a thorough examination of all the evidence on all aspects of LTE's statutory duty, that is 'with due regard to efficiency, economy and safety of operations, to provide or secure the provision of such public passenger transport service as best meet the needs for the time being of Greater London'.

## *Appendix 7*
# Press Release from London Transport

LONDON TRANSPORT COMMENTS ON
"WASTE" ALLEGATIONS
STATEMENT BY CHAIRMAN, MR. RALPH
BENNETT

[1] London Transport Chairman, Mr Ralph Bennett, said today that he firmly rejected allegations by part-time Executive Member, Mr Leslie Chapman, that London Transport was guilty of 'disgraceful waste' and inefficiency.

[2] Mr Bennett said that Mr Chapman's detailed allegations about cars, catering and office space – which had led to extensive and emotive publicity – contained a number of inaccuracies. His more sweeping allegations – including suggestions that £25m. to £50m. a year could be saved without affecting services, and that white-collar staff could be cut by half – were not supported by his evidence.

[3] Mr Bennett said: 'During the six weeks that an independent enquiry into the strength of Mr Chapman's allegations has been carried out by the auditors of London Transport appointed by the Greater London Council, I have felt it right not to comment. That enquiry has now been completed and the auditors' full report will be delivered to me later today.

[4] 'I shall be sending a copy of the auditors' report to the Director-General of the Greater London Council as soon as I receive it, but the auditors have already told me that it will be a very long document needing a great deal of study. It is therefore clearly impossible for London Transport to comment on its contents at this stage. However, we shall be providing the GLC with comments on the allegations in general terms, and I feel that I can now break my silence by voicing some of these comments publicly, knowing that this will in no way influence the course of the enquiry.

[5] 'I owe this to Londoners generally but most of all to London Transport's 60,000 staff, many of whom have a detailed knowledge of the true facts and who resent the allegations which they feel reflect

unfairly on themselves as well as on the organisation they serve. When the auditors' preliminary report on certain factual aspects was made early in January some Press reports claimed – quite wrongly – that it largely substantiated the allegations. We denied this at the time, and now I am free to expand on some of the reasons behind that denial in the hope that by doing so I shall help restore the morale of our staff.

[6] 'By any standards London Transport is a large industrial organisation producing a product – urban passenger transport – for sale. As such it differs fundamentally from an administrative Civil Service or Local Government department. With capital employed of about £1000m. it ranks in the top ten in the public sector among some 20 nationalised and directly-owned enterprises. Compared with the private sector in this respect it ranks alongside the top 20 enterprises. These are the standards against which its policies and expenditure should be judged.

[7] 'Mr Chapman's detailed allegations about cars, catering and office space contained a number of inaccuracies, and his accusations of 'disgraceful waste' are not accepted. It appears that whatever information he had at his disposal was obtained at a relatively junior level and was not checked for accuracy or context at a level where the whole picture was known. In fact he states some of it was 'third or fourth hand'. Perhaps I can put some of the allegations into proper context.

## CARS

[8] 'London Transport could not operate effectively without the use of cars. Its network of stations, bus garages, depots, workshops, power generating and distribution facilities, offices – more than 600 locations spread throughout and beyond the Greater London area – have to be visited with varying rates of frequency to keep the business running round the clock.

[9] 'This work cannot always be done effectively by public transport alone, so in addition to buses and trains, London Transport uses some 160 motor cars for business purposes (not 224 as stated by Mr Chapman) of which 21 have drivers allocated to them. This is not a large number for the work that has to be done, and any suggestion that senior people are not prepared to use LT's services is wrong.

[10] 'Only some 20 of the most senior people, including the six

full-time Executive Members, are permitted any private use, which is on a self-drive basis and only outside business hours.

[11] 'This private use benefit is much more restricted than the level prevalent for a wide range of managers in public and private industrial organisations in the United Kingdom from which London Transport frequently has to recruit managers, technical and professional staff. We believe that it is because London Transport's benefits in this field are so restricted that we have sometimes found it difficult to retain staff.

## CATERING

[12] 'Mr Chapman criticises the catering facilities provided for senior staff at 55 Broadway because the prices charged (now £1 for a two-course lunch with coffee) only recover about half of the assessed cost, including overheads. This is a reasonably accurate assessment but cannot rank as 'disgraceful waste'.

[13] 'London Transport's catering pricing policy, which applies to all staff whether in garages, workshops, railway depots or offices, is to recover the cost of the food, and a proportion of overheads. The aim is to have a common level of subsidy for staff catering of about 50 per cent of gross cost. This policy is commonplace among large-scale employers in the UK, including the GLC.

[14] 'The dining suite on the 10th floor of 55 Broadway is used only for business entertainment hosted by an Executive Member or the top grade senior management. Mr Chapman's claim that the cost of meals served here, including overheads, is £20–30 is substantially overstated. In any case, as part of its business, London Transport has to receive and in some cases entertain countless official visitors from home and overseas, including ministers and senior management of public transport enterprises.

[15] 'Many of these visits are encouraged by Government departments and are linked with the drive to sell British exports of transport equipment and the "know how" in which London Transport is still acknowledged to be a world leader. Corresponding entertainment would cost much more in hotels and restaurants, without the same benefit of confidentiality.

## OFFICE SPACE

[16] 'Mr. Chapman's estimate of the office space occupied by full-

time Executive Members is of the right order. The areas are not out of
line with recommended standards in the public and private sectors.
In any case, 55 Broadway is a grade one listed building which inhibits
change in layout or structure, and the offices are also used for board
and management committee meetings.

[17] 'My own office occupies 900 sq. ft. because it was built that way
50 years ago and is considered to be of special architectural merit, as
well as fulfilling a regular role as a board room. Partitioning or
reconstruction would, I suspect, lead to allegations of architectural
vandalism, and listed building consent would be certain to be withheld.

## OTHER ALLEGATIONS
[18] 'On Mr Chapman's more general allegations, which appear to
be matters more of opinion than of fact, the record indicates most
limited consultation. No serious requests for information at senior
levels were made, although Mr Chapman, as an Executive Member,
is entitled to such information.

[19] 'Apart from meeting Executive Members and some senior management at large formal meetings, there is no record that Mr Chapman had consultations with the Managing Directors or Heads of
Departments on what the business was all about.

[20] 'London Transport has never contended that it is perfect and
has always accepted the need for change. But Mr Chapman's more
sweeping allegations, which include claims that, generally, managers
are only of moderate competence, that £25m. to £50m. a year could be
saved without affecting services, that 80 per cent of certain building
design work could be saved by external contracts, that 50 per cent of
administrative staff are not required, that track and vehicle maintenance cost could be cut by 40 per cent by contracting out, and so on,
are not supported by the evidence he has produced.

[21] 'The fundamental difference between Mr Chapman and the
other Members of the Executive is on methods for achieving change.
The other nine Executive Members, five of whom have had successful
careers in large, profitable private sector organisations and four of
whom are career professional public transport executives, are all
appointed by the GLC. The unanimous view of these nine men is
that effective management and improved services to the public on the
most economical basis can best be achieved on the foundation of the

fundamental restructuring of management which has been carried out over the last two years, and which is now beginning to bear fruit, coupled with the Central Productivity Unit appointed and set up before Mr Chapman's allegations were presented to the GLC over the heads of the Executive.

[22] 'Unlike Mr Chapman's concept of an external cost-cutting team, the Central Productivity Unit has the characteristics necessary for ensuring the co-operation of staff and Trade Unions without whose confidence constructive change and improved productivity and service to the passenger will not be achieved.

'This we believe is the positive way forward.'

# *Appendix 8* LT's Shortcomings: Extrac

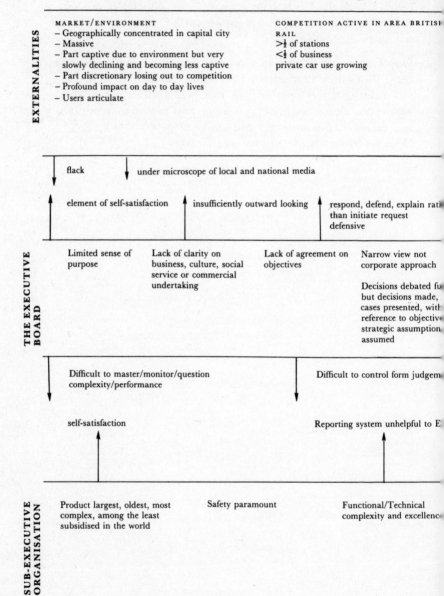

**EXTERNALITIES**

MARKET/ENVIRONMENT
- Geographically concentrated in capital city
- Massive
- Part captive due to environment but very slowly declining and becoming less captive
- Part discretionary losing out to competition
- Profound impact on day to day lives
- Users articulate

COMPETITION ACTIVE IN AREA BRITISH RAIL
$>\frac{1}{2}$ of stations
$<\frac{1}{2}$ of business
private car use growing

flack    under microscope of local and national media

element of self-satisfaction    insufficiently outward looking    respond, defend, explain rat than initiate request defensive

**THE EXECUTIVE BOARD**

Limited sense of purpose

Lack of clarity on business, culture, social service or commercial undertaking

Lack of agreement on objectives

Narrow view not corporate approach

Decisions debated fu but decisions made, cases presented, with reference to objective strategic assumption assumed

Difficult to master/monitor/question complexity/performance

Difficult to control form judgem

self-satisfaction

Reporting system unhelpful to E

**SUB-EXECUTIVE ORGANISATION**

Product largest, oldest, most complex, among the least subsidised in the world

Safety paramount

Functional/Technical complexity and excellenc

# from PA International's Diagnosis

GLC – 1969 ACT
- transportation/highways
- budget approval
- fare policy
- appointment of Exec

CENTRAL GOVT
- Public expenditure
- Constraints
- TPP

INCREASED INVOLVEMENT DUE TO
- TPP
- Fare relief grant
- No fare increases mid 1970s
- Contractual services

- exposure to constituents' moans
- LT falls down on budget
- Service deteriorating
- Impression of inefficiency

flack, criticisms, questions, directions, increased involvement

Execs are personal appointments

confusion of roles

shell-shocked criticisms low morale

inevitability of

don't shout success from roof tops

Preoccupied with day-to-day problems

Strategic issues not discussed

Initial diagnoses good but no action no follow-up

Emphasis on cost, not cost-effectiveness nor revenue nor business

cosy consensus approach

Sigh of relief

Limited contribution of part-timers

Administer/authorise rather than manage

Respond rather than instruct/direct

Decisions which shown to be mistaken not reversed

Union resistance to most obvious productivity gains and to trimming of schedules

costly solutions of isolated problems may not solve corporate problems

Incapable of change?

Easy to thwart change

Large organised labour force working in large groups

Departmental responsibilities

Functional approach

Chief officer syndrome

Pinnacle of ambition

Varied response to challenge of accountability

Some improvement in bus performance

*Appendix 9*
# My Letter of 1 September 1980
# to Sir Peter Masefield

The Chairman
London Transport Executive

1 September 1980

Dear Chairman,

Thank you for your letter of the 14th August, which was written so promptly after our telephone conversation. Unfortunately it was sent to my Cotswolds home, which nowadays I visit only infrequently.

Thank you also for what you say about your being misquoted by the Press – but I had not thought for a moment that you had been discourteous to me, especially as I do not equate disagreement with discourtesy.

What had taken me rather by surprise was the fact that you had disagreed so publicly with the conclusions of the PA Report, in view of the fact also widely publicised, that the Executive had accepted them and had so informed the GLC.

I shall be interested to hear sometime, for my own enlightenment if for no other reason, exactly how you reconcile this with your vigorous opposition to my action in expressing, in confidence to the GLC, my disagreement with the Executive last November.

However, all this can wait until we have the opportunity for a talk.

The proposal that I should take over the Chairmanship of a Productivity Committee, on the lines you suggest, is unacceptable to me. It is completely different from what I had understood was in mind by the GLC, but it doesn't matter now where the misunderstandings arose.

I could not possibly accept any responsibility for progress on productivity or waste reduction (or rather, as I would see it, an inevitable lack of progress) by taking that sort of role. The papers we would see and the arguments and reports which would be presented to us would, I fear, be the kind which have made the Executive so ineffectual in the past. The facts are selected, rearranged and presented in a form which is frequently different from the whole truth.

You may feel that this is a somewhat jaundiced view of things, but I notice that Mr Mote, talking about bus maintenance problems at the GLC/LT Committee on 30th June 1980 said: '. . . 80% of the Works throughput referred to in paragraph 12 of the LT Report had been artificially selected to prove their (i.e. LT's) own views.'

So far as I know, I have never spoken to Mr Mote on this, or any other subject, but his analysis on bus maintenance accords exactly with my experience of LT submissions generally.

I cannot think that you seriously suppose that a couple of hours a month on a committee will so transform the position of a part-time Member as to dispose of this kind of problem. After all in this same position during the seven years you were a part-time Member of the Executive, (years which have certainly seen the biggest part of LTE's decline to its present appalling state) you were not able to voice effective criticisms on policy, still less to stem the decline.

I would see your proposals as (quite inadvertently I am sure) tending to allay public concern about our affairs while constituting in practice only one more of our many talking, debating, no-action committees.

Incidentally, I see that you refer still to a Central Productivity Unit. Are you sure that there is going to be one? As I understand it, proposals have been made for most of the functions and staff of even our current tiny unit to be dispersed.

I spoke to Sir Horace Cutler on the morning of the day he was leaving London – August 12th I think – and agreed that I would not reach firm decisions or make them public before he returned. I am, however, being pressed daily by the media to make a statement and have staved off enquiries only by saying that I hope to give them something definite around mid-September. I shall want to adhere to this timetable.

I am sending a copy of this letter to Sir Horace Cutler.

> Yours sincerely,
> Leslie Chapman

## *Appendix 10*

# My Letter of 13 January 1981
# to Sir Peter Masefield

13 January 1981

Dear Sir Peter,

Thank you for your letter of 5 December 1980. It contains so much that is misleading from my point of view that I had thought that, rather than engage in what might become an exchange of lengthy letters, we could discuss matters again at the time of this month's board meeting. However, since events seem to have overtaken us to some extent, I think it best to have my views on record too before the meeting with the Leader of the GLC on 13 January.

There is between us, and has been for well over a year, a fundamental difference of opinion about the functions and obligations of part-time LTE board members. You have consistently attacked me personally for taking my criticisms of LTE outside the boardroom (after prolonged and unproductive discussions with the Board and after adequate notice) to the GLC. Your views are recorded fully on several occasions in the Board minutes and most particularly after the reference to the GLC. While you insist on linking my actions with words and expressions like 'disloyalty' and 'back-stabbing' and 'rocking the boat' my task of doing the best for the public service – which is every bit as important to me as it is to you – is made more difficult. My interpretation of my position is that I had not only a right but a positive obligation to act as I did, and as I have told you more than once I have taken both legal and other forms of advice on this point.

So far as I am aware no authority or individual outside LTE has raised even a shadow of a question about the legality, propriety or the necessity for what I did.

I am well aware of your fixed ideas about corporate responsibility and I dare say that there are circumstances in which they are relevant. I do not believe they are appropriate to the special circumstances of LTE but on the other hand I do not criticise you for this. I am quite sure that according to your lights you were doing the right, the loyal and the honourable thing by sitting on the Executive for year after year and either making no criticisms of policies or confining to board meetings such comparatively minor matters as you chose to

APPENDIX 10 201

raise. After the best part of a decade of this, the standing of LTE was at an all time low – and deservedly so. The Leader of the GLC had publicly criticised LTE management in terms which I have never seen equalled – and every word was fully justified. And finally the PA report accurately and properly made an assessment of the Board's performance and capabilities which seems likely to remain for a very long time the most scathing report ever written about a public body.

As I say, I do not criticise you for your passive role over the years or even for the way in which you positively tried to prevent remedial action being taken at the end of 1979. But please do not attempt to impose upon me your philosophy of the pre-eminence of corporate loyalty above all else in the LTE board members' duties. I have never, as your paragraph 3 states, suggested that the ends justified the means I used. As far as I am concerned, the means have never required justification.

It is quite true that I said that the last few months have seen the beginning of a change for the better in a number of ways, primarily in the reduction of management complacency. I do not think that nearly enough attention is being paid to reductions in waste and overmanning but hopefully this will improve. In the meantime, should the occasion arise, I would not seek to take away from the new Board any credit anyone is disposed to give for those changes although my private opinion is that more is owed to the way in which the GLC, fully backed by outraged public opinion, decided last summer that enough was enough and took the action needed to begin the process of reform.

There is one other statement in your letter which I must refute. You talk about the way I have in the past stood apart and criticised. In October 1979 and again in July 1980 (that time at the invitation of the Leader of the GLC) I agreed to take on the responsibility for a major drive on cost-cutting and increasing productivity. It would have been virtually a full-time job for several months and fairly onerous thereafter. And I said I would do it without pay or even out-of-pocket expenses. Both offers were blocked by the Executive. I have not the slightest doubt about the reasons for this. I believe there were widespread and very well founded fears about what would be revealed! But whatever the reason for the decision to keep me out of an effective role it was the Executive's and not mine.

And just in passing, the only member of the Board who has publicly stood apart from Board decisions is yourself when, within hours of your appointment, you said that you did not accept the PA report in direct contradiction to the Board's own publicly expressed unanimous view.

I am sending a copy of this letter to Sir Horace Cutler and I look forward to our meeting next week.

All good wishes for 1981.

Leslie Chapman

## *Appendix 11*
# An Exchange of Letters with Sir Horace Cutler

7 February 1981

Dear Sir Horace,

When we met, together with Sir James Swaffield and Sir Peter Masefield, four weeks ago, you explained how it had come about that my appointment to the L T Board would not be extended beyond the end of March 1981. Although you said I was free to use this information if I felt this was unavoidable, you would prefer me not to do so; I understand your motives.

However I also said that, more especially as a result of remaining silent on that matter, my departure in these circumstances at a time not expected by most people (including me) would add credibility to the view already the subject of gossip and speculation inside L T that I was being got rid of because I had acted wrongly by taking to the G L C the policy differences between the Board and myself. Sir Peter Masefield had been one of the leaders of a series of personal attacks on me on this question.

Sir Peter Masefield said that the Board had not taken such a view. He had said that three courses were open to me:– a) to accept the corporate board view, b) to go the G L C, or c) to resign. I insisted that he and the Board had spoken only of the first and last of these.

Your view was that this issue, which I regard as serious, could be resolved only if you saw the Board minutes. Your office was not sure yesterday whether you had seen them and so I enclose copies and have marked some of the more pertinent passages.

Like most formal documents these minutes considerably understate the force and venom of the criticisms of my action. Nevertheless I do not think it can any longer be disputed that I was being attacked for going outside the Board room to the G L C and this is more obviously true of 4 December meeting before my letter was leaked to the press.

I was glad that at our meeting you gave immediate and unequivocal support to the view that I had not acted improperly, disloyally or destructively. I told you this was fully confirmed by legal and other advice which I took at that time and since. I am afraid however that support and reassurance given in private is not enough as far as I am concerned, to dispose of misinformed public gossip. My feelings about this are reinforced by the fact that Sir Peter Masefield's recollections of these fundamental issues in dispute (see above) as he described them at our meeting are so inaccurate. I find this lapse of memory surprising and disturbing in view of the leading role he played.

In the circumstances I must ask what action, if any, you now propose to take to clear the air. I had understood perhaps wrongly that you had in mind to write to me and to have a further meeting, but yesterday your office could give me no information on either point.

Yours sincerely,
Leslie Chapman


The County Hall
19 February 1981

Dear Leslie,

I refer to your letter of 7 February and accompanying copies of Minutes of meetings of the LT Board. You will appreciate that I do not normally see such documents and that I have regarded them (and continue to do so) as internal records of LT.

There is, I consider, little value in my attempting to place on record an interpretation of the meaning or implication of certain of the expressions recorded and I am sure that you are right in saying that the written word cannot reproduce the tone employed in its delivery. It seems to me that in some of the discussions in the Board, communication of views to the press was treated as being synonymous with communication of views to the GLC and this may well have led to some confusion. I suggest that it should suffice for me to say, as I said to you when you saw me in January, that I do not regard your behaviour in communicating your views to the GLC as having been improper or disloyal to your colleagues.

I trust that this will serve to clear the air.

With best wishes.

Yours sincerely,
Horace

# Appendix 12
# An Exchange of Letters with the Chief Secretary of London Transport

*Extracts from my letter dated 31 December 1979:*

'In a letter to me dated 14 December 1979 the Chairman has asked that in future I "conform to the normal procedure adopted by part time members of the Executive by discussing any information [I] may require with the appropriate full time member". I do not accept this ruling. . . . I need to know where the procedure is laid down. . . .'

*Chief Secretary LTE to Leslie Chapman, 7 January 1980:*

'. . . the procedure referred to is not laid down formally in any document. . . .'

*Leslie Chapman to Chief Secretary, 8 January 1980:*

'. . . will you please let me have a copy of any LT document which without laying down the procedure formally makes it clear that this procedure exists. . . .'

*Chief Secretary LTE to Leslie Chapman, 9 January 1980:*

'. . . So far as I am aware there is no London Transport document formal or otherwise, referring to the normal procedure. . . .'

## Appendix 13
# Extracts from a Speech by the Premier of South Australia, August 1980*

'. . . there is a need for Parliament and the public to be much better informed as to what is done by the Administration. . . .

'First, a very significant portion of public expenditure is not in fact included in the budget at all. This is because a wide range of Government functions are undertaken by Statutory Authorities which are not accountable on a day-to-day basis to Parliament. . . .

'The other main deficiency with the way budget estimates are presented is that they do not tell Parliamentarians very much about what the Government does. Information is presented in terms of salaries and wages, office expenses, maintenance and so on for each department, but very little indication is given of what the Government achieves or seeks to achieve with these resources.

'It is not possible, for example, to determine with any precision what activities a department may have spent its money on, or with what success the money was spent.

'It is not possible even to determine the relevance of departmental activities to the policies of the Government of the day. No information is supplied on the number of staff involved, or the value of resources employed, or on the benefits which may have resulted from the investment of public funds.

'Instead, the same single-line estimates usually recur in every annual budget, the normal change from one year to the next being an increase in the amount of money allocated to each line.

'Implicitly, therefore, the existing budget documents reinforce the unsatisfactory notion that government progress can be defined solely in terms of more money spent.

'For these reasons, some of the changes currently underway are designed to improve the accountability of the Government to Parliament – to ensure that members of Parliament really do understand what is involved in expenditure proposals and that they are able to scrutinise the widest possible range of government activities.

'The second consideration which has led the Government to intro-

* The speech, by the Hon. David Tonkin MP, was made to the Royal Australian Institute of Public Administration.

duce changes in public sector management is the very size and complexity of the Government's activities in modern times.

'Long past are the days when governments levied taxes solely to maintain an army or navy, or to finance just one or two public works departments. These days government activities are so multifarious that to acquire a detailed knowledge of the government's total financial involvements is almost beyond the capacity of any one person.

'There is an urgent need, therefore, for elucidating in straightforward and comprehensible terms, the activities of all departments in terms of objectives, finance, manpower and performance.

'The third consideration is the need for the public sector to achieve as much as it is achieving now, perhaps even more, without necessarily increasing in size. The reason for this, both simple and compelling, is that the community will no longer tolerate a constant expansion of the public service at ever-increasing costs to the taxpayer, and certainly not where examples of government wastage and imprudence have already been clearly demonstrated.

'The fundamental obligation upon governments is to ensure that revenues from taxpayers are effectively used, and further, to refrain from seeking greater revenues until that basic requirement has been achieved.

'The key steps in this process are to identify the purposes to which taxpayers' money is being put, to identify the relative importance of those purposes in the government's overall priorities, to set objectives for the purposes which are worth pursuing, and to decide whether they are being fulfilled in the most effective way. . . .'

## *Appendix 14*
# The Business of the Public Sector

The frontier between public and private sector activities has been referred to in passing in a number of places in this book. It is something which is likely to crop up regularly in all examinations of public expenditure, and especially in connection with the use of private sector contractors in place of direct labour. There is room for many opinions and never-ending argument, but Lord Harris, until recently Director of the Institute of Economic Affairs, has produced a useful basic summary:*

'To reverse the almost indiscriminate growth of spending and taxation calls for a rigorous distinction between what Bentham called the agenda and non-agenda of government. For economists the role of government is first an issue of technical analysis rather than of ideological bias. Keynes, after all, agreed with Adam Smith that the primary function of the state was to provide those services which could not by their nature be supplied by competing producers in markets catering for consumer choice.

'Modern economists have usefully refined this distinction by specifying the characteristics of what the textbooks call "public goods". The most familiar examples are national defence and law enforcement. Their qualification is not that they may be judged essential services, since clothing, shelter, food and, dare I say, drink are no less essential without calling for government supply. Not even Wilson or Whitlam thought of enforcing a national diet, uniform wardrobes, equal accommodation – not to whisper state beer parlours.

'The special feature of "public goods" is that their benefits cannot be confined to those who would choose to pay. Thus since national defence yields an indiscriminate service for all citizens, its cost must be financed through compulsory taxation: if government relied on voluntary donations, non-payers would get away with a "free ride".

* 'The High Cost of Big Government', by Lord Harris. Reprinted in *The End of Government* and reproduced by permission of the Australian Institute of Political Science.

In short-hand, "public goods" are consumed collectively and must therefore be provided – or at least financed – on a straightforward collectivist basis.

'The catalogue of "public goods" includes the framework and enforcement of law on property, contracts, competition, to prevent the rule of force and fraud. It has customarily been assumed to include a stable monetary unit and extends to specifying minimum standards of public health, weights and measures, purity, and environmental standards, for example, against polluting the public domain of "clean air". Minor examples of "public goods" include local roads, street lighting, drains, sewers and open spaces that could not be financed by charging individual beneficiaries, or where the cost of collection would exceed the revenue.

'The list might arguably be extended, but it would still exclude many major services which are now commonly provided by government and financed through taxation but which are not "public goods". Most health services, education, housing, refuse removal, swimming pools, libraries, broadcasting, sports facilities, even beaches, like marinas, are personal consumer goods for which individual preferences differ widely and which can be provided by the market in return for prices that cover costs.'

# *Appendix 15*
# Draft Notes for the Guidance of Investigative Teams

1. The —— Council has given approval in principle to a detailed review of how it spends its money, what it gets in return and the extent to which, if at all, it could change policies and practices to secure better value for money or other acceptable reductions in expenditure.

2. This decision . . . has been taken in the context that the Council has already done all that is possible by way of cuts in services of the kind that is possible from examining the data normally placed before elected representatives. Quick solutions and soft options are therefore no longer available.

3. The Council have therefore decided that the next step should be a detailed and comprehensive study of every aspect of their activities and functions which involve spending money. Nothing is exempted.

4. For this purpose a number (probably six) of multi-discipline fact-finding teams will be appointed. The make up of the teams will vary with the tasks assigned to them but will normally be one or two specialists and one or two others. It is likely that every team will include one member with audit/accounting experience. An essential feature of the inspection work will be that teams will contain a leavening of staff drawn from sources outside the Council – primarily other public bodies but possibly also staff hired from consultants. I have agreed to act as an honorary adviser to the Council and to assist in any way possible, particularly in making proposals for overall strategy and methods of working at the beginning of the operation. The day-to-day direction of the teams will, however, require a full-time or nearly full-time senior individual with experience in this and related fields and at the beginning it is likely that this individual will be hired from a consultancy.

5. The functions of the teams will be limited to ascertaining facts and making recommendations. The former function is the more important. Teams will, as a matter of course, consult at all levels as part of the fact-finding process but they will be solely responsible for their reports which will not attempt to reach views based on an agreed

consensus. No draft reports will, therefore, be prepared. Reports will go simultaneously to the Leader of the Council, the Chief Executive and the Chief Officer(s) concerned and to such other recipients as the Council may designate. Reports will be numbered.

6. Decisions on action to be taken on the reports will be made only through and by the normal decision-making machinery of the Council, i.e. Chief Officers, Chief Executive and the Council as is appropriate in each case, and the normal consultative machinery will also be used.

7. The teams will have three main objectives:
  (a) To ascertain whether any money is being spent for purposes which, in their opinion, could be discontinued altogether.
  (b) To ascertain whether some activities could be carried out in a way or to a standard which, though still acceptable, would cost less.
  (c) To identify activities which, in their view, could be regarded as falling short of being essential, or otherwise are perhaps open to question on a 'value for money' basis having regard for the overall national and local financial situation. Details of methods of working are given in paragraph — below. Potential savings should be evaluated both in terms of money saved and of consequences so that a range of options is presented to those taking decisions.

8. Teams should be prepared to offer opinions where this seems to be appropriate. Nevertheless they should be conscious that much of the value derived from exhaustive and expensive fact-finding is the continual narrowing of the area open to conjecture and argument. A report which creates a situation which will enable action to dissolve into open-ended debate will have failed in its primary purpose.

9. In theory, and to a considerable extent in practice, the teams should not regard anything as sacrosanct or above question. However there are some constraints which, in practice, will need to be observed – for example, when looking at alternative methods of doing work, teams would be expected in some cases to consider the possibility of buying the services from an outside source – building design and building maintenance are two obvious examples of this. On the other hand, a study based on abandoning the present State system of education in favour of buying places at private schools would not be likely to provide a useful or meaningful range of practicable options

but again it could possibly be useful to record as an item of fact the cost per place in the two types of school. Much more likely though is that expenditure can be analysed and compared on a functional basis, i.e. one type or group of schools compared with others; one school compared with another; and the cost of items within the totals, e.g. telephones, energy, grounds maintenance, building costs, etc., similarly established and compared.

10. Instructions on methods of working and sources of information, especially for comparison purposes, will be given to the teams before they begin work. A list of proposed projects will also be discussed. The current target date for starting is —. With the agreement of the Council I would propose to spend the whole of the ensuing week with the teams on preparation work of various kinds, including a number of briefing sessions for both elected representatives and senior officials.

However it may be helpful for it to be more generally understood that I would expect that the fact-finding process would usually include at least the following:

(a) a detailed examination of actual functions and costs and the justification for each as opposed to the accepted or official views. It is probable that there would be no difference between the two at least on issues of importance, but questions could arise on subsidiary activities. Because of this, teams will need to begin their work by seeking a discussion with the appropriate chief officer(s) not only as a matter of ordinary courtesy but in order to get an authoritative brief on functions. Equally, however, teams will need to have access to source documents of all kinds, to talk to staff at all levels and to make full use of suggestions which any member of the staff may wish to put forward.

(b) Analyses of the need for functions or parts of functions would include comparisons with other authorities and also comparisons between present and past levels of expenditure by the Council. Such comparisons may be inconclusive because of the difficulty of being sure that like is being compared with like. And although marked differences usually provide at least prima facie justification for questions the absence of difference does not, unfortunately, prove conclusively that there are no questions to be answered.

(c) Functions may be wholly or largely necessary yet still be

capable of being performed satisfactorily at lower cost either
by using different methods or adopting different (but acceptable) standards or different timing. Different methods will
certainly include the obvious possibilities of using contractors instead of direct labour – or vice versa. Teams will also
consider using technological advances of various kinds – e.g.
extended use of automatic instead of manual controls, and at
the other end of the spectrum should also note the possibilities of making more use of voluntary workers.

(d) Changes of standards which produce results no less acceptable than those being replaced will present no difficulty.
Teams must bear in mind however that the Council may be
faced with the necessity for frequently choosing between
options none of which is particularly palatable, and factual
reports on consequences in this situation will help the decision-making processes. Teams may therefore need to report
possibly without making recommendations on further practicable choices in this field.

(e) Teams will need similarly to consider time factors. Quick
responses are apt to be expensive but may yet be justified. As
with standards, therefore, it may only be possible to produce
a range of evaluated options rather than firm recommendations. It is not likely that any of the techniques outlined above
will lead to dazzling new insights into the way in which local
authorities discharge their functions, welcome though these
would be! It is much more probable that savings will accrue
from the aggregation of many comparatively small economies spread over the whole field of the Council's operations,
many of which may otherwise continue much as they do at
present.

11. The Council has, from the outset, been conscious of the necessity
for full consultations with trade unions and staff associations and the
desirability of working with their co-operation and help. . . .
Whether we work with their co-operation or otherwise, however,
teams must ensure that any discussions and negotiations are conducted by someone from the Council's personnel staff, although it will
often be necessary for team members to sit in at such discussions.

L. C. Chapman

# Index

straints present economies 130; reduction prevented 139–43; failure of
machinery of control in UK 135, 137,
146–7; in S. Australia 203–4; need for
new investigation machinery 142–52;
on local authority staffs 1952–79 176;
*see also* Public Accounts Committee;
*see also* Waste in public expenditure

Freeman, Nicholas 29
Friedman, Professor Milton 41

Garrett, John (MP) 39
Gas Board *see* British Gas
Gash, Robert (Chief Executive, Berk-
shire County Council) 123, 124
Glasgow 8
Glendinning, J. (LTE Board member)
77, 86
Graef, Roger (LTE Board member) 53
81
Greater London Council (GLC): direct
labour department 9; planning
applications 12; statement by Leader
on spending restrictions 16; compar-
ison with LCC 20; and London
Transport 45, 46, 48
Greenway, Henry (MP) 10
Greig, Angus (LTE Management ser-
vices) 55, 64, 90, 96, 100–1
Guest Keen and Nettlefold Ltd 28

Haldane, Eric (Luton) 12
Hampshire County Council 4, 18
Haringey Borough Council 8, 9
Harris, Lord 205–6
Harrogate District Council 6, 8
Hayes, Leslie, & Associates 90
Hayhoe, Barney (MP) 43
Heath, Edward (MP) 37
Health & Social Security, Department
of: PAC criticism, 1981 19
Henney, Alex 107 & fn
Heseltine, Michael (MP) 27, 28, 40,
63, 137–8, 172
Hoban, John (Civil Engineer LTE) 50,
90, 100, 101
Hounam, Peter (*Evening Standard*) 92
Howell, David (MP) 36, 180, 181
Humberside, Council 7

Income Tax: black economy 15, 16;
numbers of taxpayers 27
Institute of Economic Affairs 170

Irving, David 169

Joseph, Sir Keith (MP) 36, 40, 131,
180–1

Kellner, P. 39
Kensington and Chelsea Borough
Council 29

Labour party and government 3, 34–5,
61, 84, 137, 139, 142, 147
Lambeth Borough Council 2, 6, 7, 8,
9
Layfield, Frank (QC) 144
Lincolnshire County Council 6
Liverpool County Council 2, 6, 8
Livingstone, Kenneth 85
Local Authority expenditure: growth
18; increases in staff 1952–79 176;
and staff costs 176; rate increases
under Conservative government 28–
9; effect of government cuts 31–2;
consequences of secrecy 104; in Camden Borough Council 108–23; in
Berkshire County Council 123–33;
need for effective audit 142-53; *see also*
Public expenditure
London Transport: Chapman appointment to Board 45; policy disagreement (July 1979) 49–53; comparison
of costs 54; report to GLC (November 1979) 58–69; investigation by
Deloitte Haskins and Sells (January
1980) 70–2, 187–90; Report by P. A.
International (April 1980) 73–5, 195;
Board reorganisation (July 1980) 76–
9; termination of Chapman appointment 82–6; cost investigations and
waste 85–93; inaccuracies in published and other statements 94–100,
106; treatment of staff 100–2; report
in the London *Evening Standard* on
Acton workshops 92–3
Lothian Council 7
Luton Council 12

Mackintosh, Andrew 84, 85, 86
Maldon District Council 7
Manchester City Council 4, 6, 8, 12
Manpower Services Commission 11
Margolis, Cecil vii
Marks & Spencer 37, 38, 43, 136
Martin, Brian 125
Masefield, Sir Peter 77, 79, 80, 82, 83,
84, 85, 86, 198–9, 200–202

Merseyside 12
Moss, Lewis (Chairman, Berkshire County Council) 123, 124, 128–33
Mote, H. T. (GLC) 106, 199

National Association for Local Government Officers (NALGO) 165–6; and gas boards 13
National Federation of Self-Employed 173
National Health Service: empty hospitals 6; delays 7; staff problems 7; staffing structure 11; staff numbers (CBI Report) 12; staffing and costs (PAC Report) 18–19
Nationalised Industries: standards of service 20; prices 21, 27; cost to taxpayers 29, 30; need for effective audit 145–9
Nicklaus, Jack 13
Nicol, Stuart (*Evening Standard*) 92

Official Secrets Act 74, 100
Oxfordshire Health Authority 163

PAC (*see* Public Accounts Committee)
PA International 72–6, 196–7; *see also* London Transport
Postal charges increases 121
Prentice, Reginald MP 3
Printing and Publishing Training Board 10
Programme Analysis and Review (PAR) 143
Property Service and Agency: cost of remedial work 3; and Property Research and Development Group 102–4; economy surveys 126–7; government grant to depressed areas 13
Public Accounts Committee: cost of tax evasion 16; National Health Service 30; NHS staffing and costs 1981 Report 18–19

Quarmby, D. 77, 78

Racial Equality, Commission for 9
Rayner, Sir Derek 37–41, 43–4, 67, 139, 143, 182–3
Ridley, T. M. 77
Robbins, Michael (LTE board member) 53, 77, 78, 86
Rochford District Council 7

Royal Institute of British Architects 104

Sainsbury, Timothy (MP) 102
Seldon, Arthur 152
Shanks, Michael 27
Smith, Douglas 9
Southend-on-Sea 162
Southwark Borough Council 9
Stansby, J. 77, 78
Strathclyde 4
Swaffield, Sir James 83, 84, 203

Taylor, Dr Gordon 51, 62–9, 184
Telecommunications charges 21
Thames Water Board 5
Thatcher, Margaret (Prime Minister) as a spending minister 40; and Rayner, Sir Derek 37, 40, 42, 43; size of office 67; response to *Your Disobedient Servant* 181
Tonkin, Hon. David (MP) (Premier of South Australia) 203–4

Underwood, Christopher 105
Urwick Orr & Partners 91

Vaughan, Dr Gerard (MP) 163

Warren, Kenneth (MP) 105
Waste in public expenditure: extracts from press reports 1–14; generally 15; on NHS 18–19; Conservative Party promises 24–5; escapes government cuts 31–2; Sir Derek Rayner appointed 36; defeated 38–43; achievements 43–4; in London Transport 46–7, 50–3, 58–61, 62–9, 85–93; effect of secrecy 94, 100–6; results of Camden investigation 109–20; results of Berkshire investigation 125–8; effects of spending constraints 130–1; impotence of ministers, MPs and local councillors 135, 138; ineffectuality of current audit arrangements (C & AG, District Audit) 141–5; proposals for effective audit 146–53; role for private citizens 154–5; methods of investigation 156–75, 207–10
Water Boards 5, 7
Welsh Office 9
Weinstock, Sir Arnold (now Lord) 66–7
Willcock, Barrie 125
Wolverhampton Council 11